MW00878362

ONE LONG ROAD

FROM MISSILES TO MEDICINE

ONE LONG ROAD

FROM MISSILES TO MEDICINE

An Autobiography

KENNETH L. CARR

"A Tree in the Meadow" Words and Music by Billy Reid
Copyright © 1947 by Campbell Connelly & Co. Ltd. International Copyright Secured. All Rights Reserved. Reprinted by Permission of Hal Leonard LLC.

"Traveler, Your Footprints"
The Landscape of Castile, Antonio Machado, translated by Dennis Maloney and Mary Berg, White Pine Press, 2005. Reprinted by permission of White Pine Press.

Cover Image:
The End of the Road, watercolor (21" x 28") by John Gable, Woolwich, Maine. Copyright 2023. Reprinted with permission by the artist. www. johngablefineart.com

Disclaimer:
This book is autobiographical and reflects the author's present recollections of past experiences, events, and conversations over time. It endeavors to present an accurate timeline and depiction of the people and events involved. This is not intended as a text book, but as a personal narrative. Any errors or omissions are unintentional.

ISBN: 979-8-8672833-9-1 *(paperback)*
ISBN: 979-8-8672839-3-3 *(hardback)*

I dedicate this book to my friends and colleagues and to the people who have thanked me for doing my best to make this earth a better place. I did the best I could.

–Ken Carr

"I hope that my achievements in life are these:
That I fought for what was right,
That I took risks for things that mattered,
That I helped those in need,
And that I left this earth a better place
Because of what I did."[1]

CONTENTS

FOREWORD

Abstracted from the 2022 MTT-S Microwave
Career Award nomination form

Kenneth Carr's professional career included meritorious achievements and outstanding technical contributions in the field of microwave theory and techniques. Ken's technical contributions include his state-of-the-art ferrite work in the 1950s, and the co-founding of the Ferrite Division of Airtron (1956–58) and Ferrotec (1958–70). In 1960, shortly after the invention of the stripline in the 1950s, Carr integrated suspended substrates incorporating low-loss transmission lines into ferrite devices, which were used in F-14, F-15, and F-18 fighter planes' radars. His most outstanding historical contribution at Ferrotec was during the 1962 Cuban Missile Crisis, namely, the eight-day development of the 150kW millimeter-wave waveguide switch. This novel device enabled high resolution radar images from US planes surveilling the Cuban missile fields. He has eight patents in the ferrite and component technology area.

Ken's passion was then devoted to microwave devices in medicine to help humanity. He was selected to be the IEEE MTT-S Distinguished Microwave Lecturer and delivered his speech on "The Use of Microwaves for Medical Applications" to the US, Europe, and Asia from 1985 to 1986.

Ken was president of Microwave Medical Systems (MMS) from 1985 to present and applied his knowledge of Microwave Theory and Techniques to address challenging medical problems beyond the prevailing state-of-the-art medical methods and treatments, with the objective of improving patient outcomes. This work was in concert and synergistic with the Army's Small Business Innovative Research and NASA's goal of developing commercial applications of its space-related techniques.

Ken hit a roadblock with the medical community and FDA in the use of microwaves in the medical field but finally convinced them that the numerous devices he innovated were safe. He has forty-six published patents in the medical field (see Appendix). Some examples of Ken Carr's medical innovative microwave devices include:

In-line Fluid and Blood Warmer

Monolithic Microwave Integrated Circuit-Based Microwave Ablation System

Early Detection of Neonatal and Pediatric Extravasations

Air Emboli Detection

Newborn Brain Temperature Monitors

OncoScan—Early Detection of Breast Cancer

Sterile Docking

Detection of Vulnerable Plaque

Viral Inactivation in Blood Using Microwave Heating

Intra-Vascular Blood Warmer

Measurement of Flow Rate and Volume Infused

Ken solved challenging medical problems with the innovative application of microwaves in medical devices with an effective safe and affordable device that improves the patient's outcome. He took every opportunity in life and throughout his professional career to do the best he could.[2]

Edward C. Niehenke (nominator), former Senior Advisory Engineer for Westinghouse Electric Corporation

Alejandro Chu (endorser), principal lead engineer for MITRE

Harlan Howe Jr. (endorser), former publisher and editor, *Microwave Journal*

Richard Sparks, (endorser), past president and Honorary Life Member of IEEE

Richard Snyder (endorser), president of RS Microwave

INTRODUCTION

As a boy, mapping the advance of Allied troops with checker pieces on my bedroom floor, little did I know that in a clandestine laboratory just one mile from my family's house, a team of the country's most elite engineers were developing a high-powered vacuum tube—the cavity magnetron—to help our soldiers win the Second World War. Just how this groundbreaking technology came to be built in my hometown of Cambridge, Massachusetts, was the result of a top-secret scientific mission.

In February 1940, the year I turned eight, British physicists Henry A. Boot and John T. Randall drilled a copper tube with special holes, or "cavities," that efficiently produced microwaves, long-ranging waves of invisible energy on the upper end of the electromagnetic spectrum. Considered by many to be the most important technological contribution of the war, the cavity magnetron enabled the development of high-powered radar systems small enough to install on planes and powerful enough to detect German aircraft, ships, and submarines at a distance, even through clouds. Although radar itself had been invented roughly a decade before, the magnetron produced power at microwave frequencies, allowing for much higher resolution and accuracy.

However, that summer after the fall of France and with the beginning of the Battle of Britain, the British secretly packed their prized invention in a tin trunk stowed aboard a ship headed across the Atlantic.[3] Accompanied by six scientists, the expedition became known as the "Tizard Mission," after the London chemist and mathematician Sir Henry Tizard who directed the team. After a series of top-level meetings in Washington, D.C., the Massachusetts Institute of Technology (MIT) formed its now-famous Radiation Laboratory to research and develop this new technology. Called the "the greatest cooperative research establishment in the history of the world," the "Rad Lab" employed more than four thousand scientists who developed more than one hundred radar systems.[4] Eighty percent of the magnetrons for these systems were built by Raytheon, a former Cambridge refrigerator company.[5] Credited with helping turn the tide of the war, the cavity magnetron helped bring about an Allied victory and launched a new industry: microwave engineering.[6]

At the time, however, microwave products had few nonmilitary uses, so after the war, the Rad Lab closed. But many scientists who worked for the lab launched local businesses designing microwave circuits, components, and systems, kick-starting the microwave industry and making Boston the unofficial microwave capital of the world. To preserve the research and techniques pioneered by Rad Lab scientists, MIT produced the first and finest textbooks on microwave theory, the twenty-eight-volume *MIT Radiation Laboratory Series*.

In 1949 when I enrolled at nearby Tufts University to study electrical engineering, there were no courses on microwave theory. You did not go to school to build missiles or become a microwave engineer. You went to school to get a basic education. However, during and after the war, Cambridge was an extraordinary place to grow up. Everything I learned after graduation was based on curiosity. I never considered myself as being all that bright, but I would really pursue something to its end. That is what most people remember about me.

So many technical advancements occurred after the Second World War, it made what we were doing exciting. We went from tri-motor planes to jets. The transistor, which increased the flow of electricity through a circuit, had just been invented. Today, the Americans who stormed the beaches of Normandy and liberated Europe are known as "the Greatest Generation." I believe that the engineers who made these achievements possible—and those who followed them—were the Greatest Generation of Engineers. When I look at the people I have worked with and the friends I have made along the way, I truly believe it.

Over my seven-decade career as a microwave engineer, I co-founded a microwave component company developing ferrite devices and microwave integrated circuits, led a technical team at one of the world's largest microwave technology companies, designed components for aircraft fire control systems and radar-guided missile systems, consulted for NASA, gathered intelligence for the CIA, lectured around the world, served as a staff researcher for several leading medical centers, was awarded fifty-six U.S. patents, and am credited with introducing microwave technology to the field of medicine. I have also played a little hockey, pitched some fast-pitch softball, and experienced my share of heartache, disappointment, and loss—including a shocking betrayal that cost me much of my life's work.

The road I traveled has not been easy, but in 2022, I was honored to receive the Microwave Pioneer Award from the Institute of Electrical and Electronics Engineers' Microwave Theory and Techniques Society, recognizing my achievements and contributions to the field of microwave theory and techniques. I am very proud of what I did, both for the military and introducing that technology to medicine.

My journey began on the streets of Cambridge, where I learned how to fight. It wound up country roads, past the farms and fields along the Maine–New Hampshire border to my grandmother's farm, where I discovered the value of hard work. It wove around the suburbs of Boston, where I married the first girl I ever dated, rebuilt a house to make room for our growing family, and suffered a devastating loss. And it wandered from continent to continent, crisscrossing the globe with a team of friends and colleagues who have joined me on what has truly been a most remarkable ride.

CHAPTER 1

AN UNHAPPY CHILDHOOD

I was born in Cambridge, Massachusetts, on February 15, 1932, a time of impending calamity. Americans were struggling to survive the economic devastation of the Great Depression. Dust storms were pummeling the Great Plains, driving farmers from their fields. The Japanese Imperial Army had recently invaded Manchuria, leading the world one step closer to war. And my mother, Doris Carr, had to walk through the cold and snow to the Cambridge City Hospital while she was in labor with me because my father, Lorenzo, was off on a job.

My father was an easy-going guy, but he worked hard. His Carr ancestors arrived from England in the early 1700s, buying land in Andover, an early manufacturing center in what is now Massachusetts. His mother's family were French and Scottish. They settled in Berlin, a small farming community west of Boston.

My mother, whose maiden name was Libbey, grew up in Brighton, a Boston neighborhood of Irish and Italian immigrants known for its stockyards and slaughterhouses. Doris had two sisters, Althea, who was so pretty she was selected as Miss Brighton, and Irma, who married a Coast Guard officer and moved to California. Their father, Eugene Libbey, who went by "Gene," worked as chief mechanic for Broadway Chevrolet in nearby Somerville. He traced his family tree to John Alden, a Mayflower crewmember whose descendants helped establish Lyndonville, a picturesque village in the Northeast Kingdom of Vermont. We used to ski up there, and it seemed every other person we met was a Libbey. Eugene's wife, Catherine O'Neil, was Irish. In the mid-1800s, her grandparents escaped the Great Irish Potato Famine, quarantining on an island in Canada's St. Lawrence Seaway before making their way through Montreal to Hudson, Massachusetts, just east of Berlin.

My father spent most his life in Cambridge, just across the Charles River from Boston. Home to Harvard, the country's oldest university, and the Massachusetts Institute of Technology, by the 1920s Cambridge had become a leading industrial center, manufacturing everything from Lever Brothers' popular soap flakes to the New England Confectionary Company's colorful NECCO wafers. My father opened the city's first store selling and repairing radios. He also worked as a projectionist for the Olympia Theater in Central Square, where I believe he met my mother. At the time, he was twenty-one and single. She was nineteen, intelligent, good looking, and spoke fluent French. They married on October 22, 1929, without telling his mother, Grace, who was not shy about sharing her opinions.

"Well, you made your bed," she told my father after learning of the marriage. "Now you can lie in it."

My grandmother did not have a good influence on marriages. She did not like any of her boys' wives. Nobody seemed good enough to marry her sons.

One week after my parents began their life together, the stock market crashed, launching the country into the Great Depression. Since few people could afford to buy or repair a radio, my father's store went out of business. To guarantee that he would always have a job, he earned a journeyman's license and became a master electrician. My mother worked as a secretary for the United Fruit Company, now Chiquita Brands International, and later waited tables. Together they rented a house at 16 Fairwood Circle, Cambridge, a nice neighborhood of modest homes.

One month before my parents' first anniversary, they welcomed my brother, Curtis. I arrived sixteen months later, and my parents bought a house on nearby Prospect Street, which was closer to the theaters and the center of town. My sister, Doris Shirley, who went by "Shirley," was born two years after me. I do not remember much of my childhood, but in summer we played baseball on a nearby vacant lot; and in winter, we walked a mile up Broadway to skate on the Cambridge Common, where George

Washington once organized the Continental Army under the famous Washington Elm.

On September 21, 1938, when I was six, one of the biggest hurricanes in recorded history struck southern New England. I stood at the front window, awestruck as winds of up to 186 miles per hour knocked out the power and driving rain and tree branches hit our house. The storm killed 700 people and left another 63,000 people homeless.[7] Although our house survived, my family had its own kind of trouble.

There was not much happiness in our house. My father was a meat-and-potatoes guy who never owned a pair of pressed pants, and my mother wanted more in life. When people don't get along, they find so many unimportant things to argue about. If my father came home and set a couple of tools on the table, my mother would yell at him to "Get those goddamn things off the table." After a long day's work, he'd walk in with clumps of dirt on his shoes, and all of a sudden, every little clump became a mountain. My father was an awfully nice guy. It was not intentional. He was just not aware. After my mother screamed at him, my father would take his tools off the table. He was very quiet and never raised his voice. I am more like my father that way. I rarely get angry, but if there is anything I learned from him, it is that you have to pay attention to your wife.

Because my father knew the marriage was not going anywhere, he often took jobs at construction sites in Maine and stayed in boarding houses. When jobs came up out of town, those were the jobs he took. He was away much of the time.

I was an unhappy child. My mother wanted all of us kids out of the house. When I turned five, she made me take a test to start first grade one year early. That way, I would be out of the house as soon as possible. But my father enjoyed spending time with us. One of my earliest memories is of sitting at the kitchen table with my father and brother, building a crystal radio set. We used a crystal to act as a semiconductor and a coil of metal wire. Then we put everything in a big glass or metal bowl and played with the wires until we picked up a little sound. To a kid, this was magic, sparking my interest in the invisible waves of energy that would become my future.

About the time I turned eight, our parents bought a large two-story house, just around the corner on Gardner Road. The property included a half-acre lot, a couple of pear trees, and a big barn that my parents used as a garage. Our family lived in one half of the house, number 8. The other half, number 10, contained two apartments. Curtis and I shared one room. My folks had a room, and Shirley had her own room. Downstairs we had a parlor, a dining room, and a kitchen—the only room with heat. My mother often griped about how cold the rest of the house was. In fact, my parents did not put in a furnace for central heat until after I started college.

Our family doctor, Harry Levine, rented the downstairs apartment attached to our house. Along with the other men in my family, Doc Levine and my father were Masons who attended the Cambridge Masonic Temple a few minutes away on Massachusetts Avenue. My father was so involved, the lodge later dedicated an auditorium to him. In 1953, I became a Mason too.

Doc Levine and my father were close friends. After graduating from medical school, Doc Levine had suddenly gone blind while looking out a window. Although he never recovered his sight, he continued practicing medicine and lived next door with his nurse, Viola Amende, who helped care for him. When a patient came into his office with a problem such as a wound, Viola described what she saw, along with any symptoms the patient was having.

"Seeing the wound doesn't help solve the problem," Doc Levine often said. "Most problems you can't see."

To keep up his studies, Doc Levine listened to audio tapes and brought home books in braille from Harvard Medical School. "I'm probably a better doctor than most," he would say, "because I take all of the medical courses I can."

Although Doc Levine never married, he was married to medicine. Both he and Viola became like part of our family. When he grew older, Doc Levine moved in with my father, who took care of him.

Because my mother often worked late, she relied on us kids to do chores. After walking home from school, I frequently peeled potatoes to start dinner. I also regularly pulled my red Radio Flyer wagon up Hampshire Street to the Boston Ice Company in Somerville to buy two metal jugs of range oil for the kitchen stove, which ran on kerosene. "When I was thirteen, I arrived home from school one day while my father was out, and my mother sat me down at the kitchen table."

"I want to talk to you," she said, sitting across from me. "When you turn sixteen, I want you out of this house." Just as blunt as that.

Did it bother me? Yes. But I accepted it. So did my father, who did not like to get involved. That is when I began planning my life in five-year increments. You should not make a decision for your whole life because your situation often changes, as did mine. So, with just three years to make something of myself, I decided to go to trade school like my father to become an electrician.

Rindge Tech

One mile from my house, Rindge Technical School taught boys practical skills such as woodworking and drafting. Founded in 1888 as the Cambridge Manual Training School for Boys, Rindge Tech is one of the oldest trade schools in the state and became a model for schools around the country. Engraved in granite above the front door of the three-story building I attended on Broadway are the words of the school's founder, Frederick H. Rindge: "Work Is One of Our Greatest Blessings," they say. "Everyone Should Have an Honest Occupation."

My father graduated from Rindge in 1927. All four of his brothers and my brother, Curtis, also graduated from Rindge. And if my family still lived in Cambridge, my kids would have graduated from there as well.

Because Harvard and the Massachusetts Institute of Technology were both within a mile, Rindge had good faculty. I believe my English teacher was an associate professor at Harvard, and I had a math teacher from MIT.

Rindge Tech was also one of the first schools in the Boston area to participate in formal athletic competitions. I really enjoyed sports, especially baseball and hockey, but that did not make anybody in my family happy. In those days, sports figures did not make big money. People were in a sport because they loved the game, like me. But my family called sports "games for the idle rich." They thought I should be preparing to work, so my family never came to my sporting events, including track. The year the state finals took place at the Boston University field, I ran the quarter mile. I don't remember the exact time, but I think I finished in fifty-four seconds. Pretty fast. When the race ended, parents were hugging and congratulating their kids, but my parents were not there. I jogged to the locker room and left.

One year ahead of me in school, Curtis was a good student, but he tired easily and did not enjoy playing contact sports the way I did. Because Curtis could never do much physical work, I thought our parents took it easy on him, but despite our differences, we were very close growing up. In college, Curtis suffered from a spontaneous pneumothorax—a collapsed lung—which caused some health problems. Decades later, he had a stroke. A doctor noticed his disproportionately long arms and legs and suggested my brother had Marfan syndrome, a rare disorder that affects connective tissue and can damage the heart.

In high school, other guys picked on Curtis. They looked for the guys who would take a punch. Curtis would not fight back, but I was not cut out that way. Rindge Tech had a school newspaper, *The Rindge Register*. One time, another guy took Curtis's paper. "It's not important," my brother said.

The size of a bean pole, I looked like an easy target, but I was scrappy and did not tolerate people pushing me around. Nobody was going to take my paper. Instead of caving in, I would fight back. I got Curtis's paper back for him. Even if you lose and have to take a beating, the other kids will respect and leave you alone if you stand up to them.

Strictly for boys, Rindge Tech adjoined Cambridge High and Latin School, which admitted both boys and girls, so we called it the "girls' school." The Cambridge Public Library separated the two schools. Because our teachers feared we would say something out of line, trade school students were not allowed outside at the same time as the high school students. As a result, I had zero experience interacting with girls. I always opened doors for them and was very formal and careful. I thought that was the way you were supposed to act, but the guys who ran off with the pretty girls were more aggressive.

Going to an all-boys school was probably my downfall. I got along great with the guys, but when it came to romancing, I was hopeless. Once a week I pulled on a shirt, tie, and sports jacket and walked down Massachusetts Avenue for the weekly dances at the YMCA, a big brick building across from City Hall. I loved dancing and was pretty good at the jitterbug. Later, I even learned to waltz on roller skates. To celebrate the end of the school year, Rindge Tech held a dance and invited students from Cambridge High and Latin to attend. Since the girls did not know us, they lined up on one side of the gymnasium, looking across the floor at us boys like we were a bunch of gorillas.

"Who's going to walk across the gym?" one of the boys standing by me asked. "Who's going to break the ice?"

Well, a terrible thing happened. Somebody said, "Ken, you go. You're good with people."

In those days, dances were brightly lit, so you could not hide while walking across the floor. So I walked underneath the bright lights and asked some young lady, "Would you like to dance?"

"No, I would not," she said.

It would have gone down easier if there had been some discussion, but I was embarrassed.

"Atta-boy, tiger!" the other guys clapped and whooped while I walked back across the gym with my tail between my legs.

At sixteen, my sister, Shirley, married Frank Clapp, a guy from Cambridge she met at a YMCA dance. Like our father, Frank was an electrician, but my sister was ill prepared for marriage. Growing up, we had one of those counter-top electric ovens, and she would turn it on without checking to see what was inside. If a cake was stored in the oven, the frosting would melt off. Or if she used scissors to remove the label from a suit jacket, she would cut a hole in the jacket instead of cutting the thread holding on the label. By the time Shirley was twenty-five, she had five children. Without much support from her husband, she turned to alcohol, leading to her early death at age forty-four.

In high school, my drafting teacher, Mr. McMurtry, asked our class to enter a state-sponsored contest to design a new intersection to reduce the flow of vehicles for the traffic circle that connected Memorial Drive on the Cambridge side of the Charles River to the Cottage Farm Bridge (now Boston University Bridge). Students from around Boston were invited to participate. A classmate and I sat at the junction of the bridge and Memorial Drive and counted cars, but most cars did not cross the bridge; they stayed on Memorial Drive. So instead of designing a new intersection, we designed an overpass so cars could continue over Memorial Drive without stopping. The state picked our design and built the overpass, and our names were engraved on a plaque that hung in the school lobby.

Good Money

Like most kids, Curtis and I would do almost anything necessary to earn money. In primary school, I built my own shoe shine kit with a hinged lid. On top sat a strip of wood, cut in the shape of a shoe. That way, when a customer put his foot on the lid, I did not bust my knuckles on the box while shining his shoes.

After school, I carried my kit to Central Square and called, "Shine, mister?" to people walking by.

"Sure," they'd say and put their foot on my box.

Then I'd get down on my knees and shine their shoes with brown, black, or cordovan polish.

Curtis worked for Teal Craft Handkerchiefs in Harvard Square. They purchased handkerchiefs from people who sewed at home. After the handkerchiefs were pressed, Curtis folded them and put them in packages. He suggested I work with him, so I did.

Later, my brother and I became projectionists like our father. Cambridge had three movie houses: Inman Square, Central Square, and the Olympia—all several blocks apart. Our house sat midway between Central Square and Inman Square, so during high school I got my projectionist license and worked at the Olympia Theater where my father first met my mother. A few miles east in Charlestown, I later worked at the Thompson Square Theater and the City Square Theater. It was a crummy job. I sat in a closed little room up in the ceiling with the projectors. The lights were hot, and no one else was allowed in the room because the films were highly flammable.

Back then, movies came in ten reels that we played on two projectors. To know when to switch between projectors, I had to watch for the little circles that came up on the film's upper right-hand corners. Before changing the reel, I felt along the edges of the film to make sure it was not broken. The older the film, the more banged up it got, and some of those films had been around for twenty years. Whenever I found a break, I cut the film and spliced the reels together. The edges were so sharp, I sometimes cut my fingers. In the projectionist's box, I often did my schoolwork, but I had to pay attention. If the film ran out before I changed the reel, everyone in the theater would shout and stamp their feet to get my attention.

Films were expensive, so theaters often shared them. One theater would start by showing the feature movie, while the other would begin by showing the Keystone News, followed by a serial, which came in thirteen chapters, that way theater-goers would have to buy another ticket to see what happened next. I would start a movie with the first five reels. Then a guy called a "juggler" would push a cart full of reels down the sidewalk as fast as he could to the other theater. Driving or taking public transportation was not allowed because the juggler couldn't risk being in an accident or getting stuck in traffic. When the juggler came back with the next five reels, I played them.

We showed the same movies several times a day, with the juggler running back and forth with the reels. One weekend all I saw was *King Kong* (1933), which had premiered at the Radio City Music Hall in New York City one year after I was born. Morning, afternoon, and evening, I watched Fay Wray scream as the giant gorilla carried her up to the top of the Empire State Building.

If an employee wanted to go home early, the manager might ask them to skip a reel. "We missed something here," people would complain, walking out of the theater. "How'd that guy get a gun in his hands?"

The truth is, we cheated them.

Mr. Brooks, or "Old Man Brooks," as we called him, owned the Olympia Theater. After having some work done on his house in Brookline, he hired Curtis and me to cart the rubble out of his basement in buckets. Then he refused to pay us, the same way he often shortchanged my father, who did electrical jobs for him. When I complained, my father said, "That's life." But I did not think that was right. If you work hard, you ought to get paid.

I also worked on a number of construction sites with my father. Since I did not have an electrician's license, I did the dirty jobs. After a heavy rain, when the trenches were full of mud and water, all of the guys would stand around grumbling, "Who's going to jump in?" Somebody had to guide the wires.

"Ken," my father would say, "get down in that trench and start pulling wire."

Because my father was in charge, the other guys thought I got favored treatment. Yeah, right! Any job that no one else wanted, my father asked me to do. I once had to empty an entire freight-train car filled with Orangeburg pipe, probably made with asbestos, and load it onto a truck by myself. By the time I finished, my eyes were so irritated I couldn't open them—but I was making good money, about twenty-five cents an hour.

When a three- or four-story building went up, my father did the wiring with the other electricians. While working for Kenworthy and Taylor Electrical Construction, Inc., he oversaw the electrical work at the Robin Hood Elementary School in Stoneham. The school was three stories tall, and I had to climb up and walk on the girders to carry up the materials, such as pipes, rolls of electrical wire, and various components. Climbing one floor and passing up the material, we brought it up in stages. One day, I was on the third floor with Bob Taylor, the son of one of the owners, while everyone else was down in the trench.

"Watch me," Bob said, drinking coffee. Then he pulled out his work shirt and shook the last few dribbles of his coffee on the guys underneath us so it looked like he had just relieved himself.

They did not have a good sense of humor. The men were so mad they started throwing hammers at us. To prevent them from reaching us, we pulled up the ladder and weren't able to go home until after all the other workers had left for the day.

On summer weekends I often rode with my father an hour or so north to Kittery, Maine, to stay with the Kenneys, a family who had previously lived next door on Prospect Street. They owned a turreted, three-story Victorian with a wrap-around porch on Gerrish Island, directly across from the bridge to Kittery over Chauncey Creek. To protect the Maine coast from enemy ships and submarines, their father, Russell Kenney, had contracts to install defensive guns at Kittery's Fort McClary and on Peaks Island just off of Portland in Casco Bay. My father helped. The Kenneys were good to me and liked having me around, so I stayed with them for a while. To earn extra money, I sometimes caught a ride to a local lumberyard and stacked slabs of wood all day.

I also went lobstering, which paid better, probably fifty cents an hour. During school breaks, a guy named Luther Witham would call me up, and I would hitch a ride to Kittery to work with him. His primary customer was Warren's Lobster House, beneath the bridge spanning the Piscataqua River between New Hampshire and Maine. In February, the deck on Luther's boat was sheer ice. While we pulled ropes to haul the traps, our gloves froze over. Luther kept a bucket of water on the boat's engine, and the heat warmed the water so we could soak the ice off our gloves. Being out on the water in February with the wind blow-ing was brutal. You won't ever hear me quibble about the price of lobster.

For fun, I played ice hockey at Lincoln Park in Somerville, less than a mile from our house. Sometimes I headed up to Spy Pond in Arlington. I really took to hockey.

I also rode my bike. In those days, we did not have ten-speeds. I had a one-speed Columbia bicycle from Sears & Roebuck. Twice I peddled to Montreal, roughly three hundred miles, just to get away. Each time I went with a friend to help carry my pup tent, which came in two pieces. Since there were not many highways, we took the back roads to Keene, New Hampshire. Then we picked up Route 91, a two-lane road, and followed it all the way to northern Vermont and Canada.

The first time, I went with a Greek friend, Alex. The second time, I went with Bobby Reid, a Black kid who lived right around the corner from me on Tremont Street. Bobby was a year ahead of me in high school and played on the Rindge football team. We were good friends. Because there wasn't any air conditioning, on hot summer days our family and his used to sit on the stairs outside our house with glasses of lemonade and talk. When Bobby and I bicycled to Montreal, we followed the same route I took with Alex the year before.

I also raised rabbits—more than thirty of them. Some were lop-eared, with ears that hung down like miniature buffalo. I don't remember how I got started, but once you get a couple, people who want to get rid of their rabbits give them to you. I liked animals, but I certainly wasn't buying them.

One day I rode my bike about nine miles north to Stoneham to buy rabbit food. When I came home, I discovered all my rabbits were dead in their cages. My mother told me a neighbor killed them. I never cried. Growing up, we were told, "Boys don't cry. Girls cry." That was a rule. So I learned to never show my emotions, even when my mother hit me with a wooden coat hanger—*Wham-wham-wham!* Because I did not cry, she hit me harder. Sometimes she would get mad at my father and take it out on me. But, more often, she hit me for getting in fights with some of the neighborhood guys who harassed my sister.

"I am not going to let guys think it is okay to say that in front of me," I'd argue.

"That's none of your business," my mother would yell, swinging the coat hanger. "Your sister has to learn how to take care of herself."

Decades later, my wife and I visited my mother in Florida, and she bragged about getting rid of those "damn rabbits," admitting that she had poisoned them. It was the first time I heard what really happened to my rabbits, but I did not let on. I had learned to keep information like that to myself.

Awestruck

Growing up, I enjoyed swimming, including in East Cambridge's Sixth Street Canal, which stayed warm even in winter because of the residue from the nearby soap making companies. I also swam in the ocean off Kittery. To stay under as long as possible, I took a sip of water, followed by a deep breath that I swallowed. Instead of exhaling, I then took another deep breath, packing my lungs with air the way pearl divers do. To hold as much air as possible, I repeated this process. Swallowing all that carbon dioxide gave me terrible headaches, but I could dive deep and stay underwater without equipment for three minutes, easy.

To conserve time on the way down, pearl divers carry a rock tied to a rope. To rise, they let go of the rock, but if they rise too fast, they can pass out and drown, so they pace themselves as they come to the surface by holding onto the rope. I did the same thing. After tying a one-hundred-foot rope to a cinderblock, I fastened the other end to my rowboat. Then I held onto the cinderblock and dove, timing myself so I would not run out of air. Unfortunately, paper mills dumped trash and chemicals into the rivers and harbors, which led to my getting frequent ear infections.

When I was about fifteen, a guy hired me to look for an outboard motor that had fallen off his boat near Gerrish Island, so I rowed out alone in my boat. Then I dove in to find the motor, but the water was too deep, with near zero visibility. I stayed under so long that on the way up I ran out of breath and feared I would not make it. When I finally reached the surface, I pulled myself onto the boat and lost my balance, struggling to stand.

As soon as I got home, I went to see Doc Levine in his office, an old brownstone on Massachusetts Avenue. That same day, Viola's fourteen-year-old niece, Nancy Berthold, happened to be helping around the office. Boy, was she pretty—tall and slender, with dark hair and eyes. I was awestruck. Going to school with only boys, I didn't know what to say; but after seeing her, I went to the doctor's as much as possible—which was pretty often.

Because of my diving accident, I ended up with a terrible ear infection. In those days, doctors really did not know what they were doing. Whenever there was a problem, they just took out parts. So a doctor at the Boston City Hospital surgically removed the inner parts of my left ear, including the cochlea. After that, I could only hear out of my right ear, which also affected my balance.

I discovered that Nancy liked to watch parades, so I made a point to suddenly have a great deal of interest in parades. After, Nancy and I often sat on the front steps of Doc Levine's office to watch all the parades.

Nancy's family lived in Rockville, Connecticut, just north of Hartford. To see her, I made a deal with my father. I would repair his old Dodge sedan if he would let me use it to drive two hours down to visit Nancy on weekends.

Cars were simple then. Open the hood, and you could lean on the fender and look down through the engine at the street. My grandfather Gene was an excellent mechanic. Some people say he put the first windshield on a car. I spent a lot of time with him. Since I was curious, he taught me to work on cars. Whenever I drove down to see Nancy, I carried fuel pumps, a carburetor, a timing chain—parts for the whole car—in my trunk. That way, I could fix anything if I broke down.

On one trip to visit Nancy, my friend Leo Henebury went with me. We played baseball together; I played second or third base, and Leo was the catcher. He weighed more than two hundred pounds and was the Golden Gloves heavyweight boxing champion for the Police Athletic League. Strong as a bull, Leo could lift a transmission into a car while lying on the floor of his father's garage. Well, when we arrived at Nancy's, another guy from her class, Franny, was already there. Leo asked if Franny was competition and offered to "take care of him."

"No, no, no," I said, knowing I had better head him off. "I don't have any competition." Franny turned out to be visiting Nancy's best friend, and I had just saved his life.

Nancy's father, Kurt Berthold, was very smart and charismatic. With only a high school education, he moved from Germany and became the technical director of the Plax Corporation, which pioneered many types of plastics. Kurt invented the method for lining thermos bottles with two layers of blown-in glass separated by a layer of air, and he helped pioneer polyethylene, which impressed me. Nancy's mother, Margaret, and Viola were sisters. Although she was nice looking, Margaret was not very affectionate. Once I was in the kitchen, fixing the cord for her vacuum cleaner when Kurt walked by and patted Margaret on the rear—and she whacked him. Nancy's younger sister, Carol, was also very pretty, but I only had eyes for Nancy.

I never did find the boat motor I was diving for that day off of Kittery, but as a result of my accident, I found something better—Nancy.

CHAPTER 2

MA HARTLEY

The most memorable years of my youth took place two hours north of Cambridge on my grandmother's fifty-acre farm. Born on August 8, 1892, Grace Amanda Walker and her younger brother, Elmer, grew up on a farm in Clinton, Massachusetts. Their father, Henry Walker worked in a local fabric mill and died of typhoid when Grace was nine. Their mother, Carrie, kept house in nearby Berlin for Charles and Mary Carr and often brought Grace to help with the work. In 1906, just after Thanksgiving, fourteen-year-old Grace married Charles and Mary's twenty-four-year-old son, Charles Lorenzo Carr. Nine days later, Grace's mother, Carrie, gave birth to a son, George, whose father she never named. Carrie eventually sent George to be raised by a family sixty miles away in Whitman, Massachusetts.

Together, my grandparents Charles and Grace Carr had seven children and raised crops and livestock on the Carr Homestead at the end of Carr Road. Their first six children—including one who was stillborn—were all born at home. My father, the oldest, arrived on February 16, 1908, when Grace was fifteen. Three brothers, Chester, Robert, and Ernest, and one sister, Grace Elizabeth, quickly followed.

Around 1918, Charles abandoned his family, leaving his pregnant wife with five small children and few options. The bank soon foreclosed on the farm, evicting the family.

After briefly visiting relatives in Canada, my grandmother loaded her belongings onto a train bound for Cambridge. Her youngest son, George Francis, was born the following January. Grace lived just across the town line in Somerville, where she and her children, with the exception of Chester, all came down with typhoid fever. On New Year's Day 1921, four-year-old Grace died in the Somerville Hospital. My grandmother was so sick, the state placed her remaining children in foster care—a trauma that haunted her for the rest of her life.

At the time, Grace and Charles were still married. Following their 1925 divorce, he headed to New York and remarried another woman named Grace, eventually moving to Olympia, Washington, where he continued farming.

When placed in foster care, my father, Lorenzo, was twelve. He and seven-year-old Ernest lived with a Carlisle family that worked them hard. If Ernest did not obey, the father hit him, so Ernest kept running away to be with their mother. However, nine-year-old Robert and two-year-old George apparently received good care from their foster families. Chester, eleven, stayed with the family of a friend, Billy Phelps, in Somerville.

While waiting for the state to return her children, my grandmother rented the top floor of a triple-decker apartment building on Antrim Street in Cambridge and worked as an upholsterer for R. H. White, a well-known department store in downtown Boston. She became the department store's chief interior decorator and bought a modest, two-story colonial on 142 Prospect Street. One at a time, my grandmother brought all her children home. Later, she took in blind lodgers. Growing up, I helped wash the windows in my grandmother's apartment house. Most of her tenants were very clean, but one lodger, Mr. Pierce, chewed tobacco and did not check to see if the window was open before spitting out of it. Somebody had to clean it up. I also took her lodgers on neighborhood walks so they could make a little money by door-to-door selling household items like brooms. While helping, I learned a lot—for instance, that some people who are blind prefer to drink from tall glasses. That way, when they pour a drink, they can hear the liquid filling their glass before it reaches the top.

Pop Hartley

At age thirty-seven, my grandmother married her second husband, Curtis Hartley, who grew up in Indiana. In 1913, he had joined the Navy at age eighteen, serving for thirty-two years and seeing plenty of action. Once, while on shore duty in Turkey during the First World War, Curtis was captured by Turkish forces. He and four other servicemen managed to escape. Three soldiers were shot and killed, but Curtis and the remaining soldier traveled to France, where they joined the Americans and continued fighting. In 1926, while patrolling the Yangtze River, Curtis's gunboat was captured by a provincial Chinese warlord. My grandfather and the crew were imprisoned for months before the United States paid a ransom to free them and their gunboat.

A Navy diver, Curtis often slipped out in a small boat at night and dove to measure the depths of harbors and chart the waters off the coast of Japan, inspiring me to learn how to dive. The Navy based much of its data on harbors on his work.

After returning home, Curtis met my grandmother in Boston. They married on June 25, 1930, at her Prospect Street home, and he became "Pop" to us grandchildren. By the time the Second World War came around, Pop had reenlisted—I suspect because he was married to her.

"Why did you reenlist?" I once asked him.

"I knew the war was coming," Pop said.

"Yeah, right," I replied. "It wasn't because of my grandmother?"

Ma Hartley, as everyone knew my grandmother, was tough. A strict teetotaler, she set the rules, and Pop had to follow them. One rule was that he could not drink any alcohol. But when you have been in the Navy for thirty-two years, I think you've probably had a beer or two.

Pop was tough too, but in a different way. During the Second World War, his ship was torpedoed and sunk in the Pacific. He survived twenty-two days in a raft at sea before the Japanese picked him up and transported him to the Philippines. Pop did not talk much about what happened, but after a forced march, he and thousands of other American prisoners were packed into the holds of Japanese merchant vessels, called "hell ships," where they were held without food and with very little water. Conditions were so bad, many prisoners died. Barely alive, Pop was carried off the ship on a stretcher as part of the first prisoner-of-war exchange between the United States and Japan. After recuperating, he returned to the Navy onboard a ship assigned to the Atlantic Fleet. Near the end of the war, his ship was torpedoed again. Thankfully, this time the British picked him up, and Pop returned safely home.

Band of Brothers

Growing up, my father's nickname was "Cap" because, as the oldest of five boys, he was the captain of the group. Unfortunately, he and his brothers did not always get along. Chester, who went by "Chet," was good-looking and a hard worker, but he was a ladies' man. His brother Elmer Ernest was a ladies' man too, but with a name like that, he automatically felt like he had to find another name. He would accept "Ernie," but never "Elmer." However, because he was stubborn and had a weakness for getting in trouble, everyone called him "Dutch," a nickname apparently associated with German immigrants who were considered strong-willed. Dutch married five times. The fifth time, he married his first wife all over again. I think he was trying to do the rounds and remarry them all. When it came to names, Robert, who went by "Bob," had it a little easier, and as far as I know, George stuck with the name he was given.

Five days after the bombing of Pearl Harbor, my uncle Robert enlisted in the U.S. Army Air Corps and became a technical sergeant and tail gunner on a Consolidated B-24 Liberator. His squadron, the Jolly Roger, flew the skull and crossbones as their emblem, replacing the bones that normally accompany the skull with bombs to signify that they were part of a bomber squadron. Like Pop, George enlisted in the Navy. Just nine when they left, I did not really know either of my uncles.

During the war, my father's skills as an electrician were critical for installing guns, so he worked along the coast of Maine in places like Kittery, Portland, and Peaks Island. He also served as an air raid warden, patrolling our Cambridge city block each night to ensure that our neighbors covered their windows in case of a bombing raid. In the evenings, we often sat around our kitchen table listening to President Roosevelt over the static on our old tube radio. To keep track of the war, I spread a map of Europe on my bedroom floor to chart the advance of the different armies.

In 1942, Robert's group, the 321st Bomber Squadron, 90th Bomber Group, arrived in Australia. From Port Moresby, New Guinea, they carved their own airstrips through the jungle. On February 16, 1943, Robert and the remaining members of his plane's crew received a citation and commendation for effective action against the enemy. Three days later, they flew a reconnaissance mission in the Southwest Pacific and spotted an enemy convoy near New Guinea. After reporting the convoy's position, their plane disappeared and the crew was reported as missing in action. Presumed to have been shot down, the plane and its crew were never found.

That was a tough loss, especially for my grandmother.

With Pop and George still fighting in the war, in 1944 my grandmother bought a farm out of the Strout Farm Agency catalog for something along the lines of $4,000—without telling Pop. The land abutted Province Lake, a clear pond of shallow water between southern Maine and New Hampshire. Because the state line ran right through the property, the house stood in Parsonsfield, Maine, but most of the land lay across the border in Effingham, New Hampshire. The red-painted house with white trim and a front porch overlooking the road was so rustic that instead of an indoor bathroom, it had a three-hole outhouse in the barn that you reached through the woodshed. Thankfully, the outhouse overhung a slope, so I never had to pull on hip boots and shovel it out, as some of our neighbors had to with their outhouses.

When Pop staggered home from the war and discovered that my grandmother had bought a farm in the middle of the woods, he was not too pleased. Running a farm was not his idea of retirement. "The only excitement here in the winter is when a car travels by—once in three weeks," he said.

Believe it or not, there were three cars a day. A sprawling farming community, Parsonsfield contained several villages and a prosperous woolen mill in nearby Kezar Falls. Up the road from the farm, in an area of Effingham known as "Taylor City," sat the old Trading Post store and gas station, which had once served as the town stagecoach stop. Every Fourth of July, the locals elected the owner, Earl Taylor, as the mayor of Taylor City. Just across the road, the town postmistress, Eva Downs, conducted business through a metal-grid window in a one-room shop by her house. Her wooden teeth often came loose, so her teeth stayed down while she spoke. One of the farm's nearest neighbors, Eva and my grandmother became good friends and enjoyed playing cribbage together.

Pop eventually came to like the place, particularly after Ma Hartley opened the Jolly Roger Village campground, named in honor of Robert's bomber squadron. Each Memorial Day when campers arrived, Pop enjoyed visiting with the families and telling stories about his time in the Navy.

After giving me three years to leave home, my mother pushed me into spending more time with my grandmother. My uncle Chet drove a delivery truck for Penn Oil, which had a facility in Boston. His farthest customer was Fisher's Gas Station across from Spaulding High School in Rochester, New Hampshire. On weekends and during school vacations, he drove me to Rochester in his truck. My grandmother picked me up in her 1939 Plymouth four-door sedan and drove me to the farm.

My brother, Curtis, and sister, Shirley, did not get along very well with Ma Hartley. They thought she was too blunt. Once, when my sister went up to the farm with me, our grandmother asked her to bring down her clothes on wash day. A pretty girl, Shirley enjoyed dressing nice and carried down her whole wardrobe.

"From now on you wear dungarees," Ma Hartley said and promptly bought her a pair.

Along with many other farmer's wives in the area, my grandmother helped make ends meet by hand-stitching baseballs for the Spaulding sporting goods company in Rochester. Every few weeks, a company representative delivered a box of leather ball covers to the farmhouse, and my grandmother spent her spare time sewing two figure-eight-shaped patches around a cork core to form each ball. Once she finished, someone from Spaulding picked up the balls and delivered more supplies.

My grandmother really made me work. In summer, one of my chores was hoeing about an acre of potatoes. To prevent the sun from turning them green, I covered them with dirt. Then I picked the bugs off the leaves and dropped them into a pail of kerosene. Ma Hartley also grew radishes, carrots, and other vegetables. What she did not eat or sell, she traded to her neighbor, Ralph Nutter, a farmer with a family of children whose names all seemed to begin with the letter 'R'—Roy, Ron, Roger ... Ralph worked hard and had tough hands from digging. He might be growing corn or turnips, and he and my grandmother would work out a deal so that they each had enough food to store for the winter.

Ralph Nutter and two of his boys, Roy and Roger, also harvested ice with Pop on Province Lake. In those days, the lake froze three feet thick. I helped cut the ice with a five-foot-diameter saw blade mounted to a four-cylinder, 1914 Buick engine that we hauled around on a sled. The saw blade had no guards, so if I slipped, I made sure not to fall toward the blade. While walking across the ice, we tilted back the sled, then lowered the blade to cut 200-pound blocks of ice that we marked in a grid. However, we did not cut all the way through the ice, or the water would refreeze around the blocks. Later, we cut out each block with a bucksaw. To remove the ice, we pushed the block down, and it popped out of the lake just like an ice cube. Then we grabbed it with tongs and pulled it up and out. Once I got the motion down, I could lift out the ice almost effortlessly.

Province Lake stayed frozen until April or later. In the coldest part of winter, the daytime temperature might be twenty degrees below freezing for five days in a row, so when we harvested ice, the water quickly formed a thin layer of ice. One day, as I walked backward from the ice we had just cleared, I fell through the surface. All I could see was a crystal ceiling above me with the sun hitting the ice. When you go down through the ice, you go down at an angle, so I could not find the hole. Being a Navy diver, Pop knew what to do. He jumped into the hole just far enough so I could see his legs. When I grabbed onto them, Pop pulled me out. Then he and the other guys carried me to the truck and drove me to the farmhouse. I don't recall being afraid, just plain cold. My clothes froze solid. Unable to move, I looked like a statue of a guy sitting down.

At the end of her woodstove, my grandmother kept a twenty-gallon water tank, which we used to bathe. As soon as Pop brought me to the kitchen, my grandmother soaked towels in the hot water and wrapped them around me to melt the ice off my clothes. I could not wait to get warm. Pop's legs were frozen too, but she temporarily ignored him to take care me.

The farm contained two icehouses—open bins without a roof; each measured about thirty feet long, twenty feet wide, and fifteen feet tall. Over the winter, we filled them with cakes of ice that we packed with sawdust, tight as a cork. On top we piled more sawdust, which kept the ice from melting. The sawdust also made it easier to drive a wedge between the ice cakes and pull them apart. But behind a loose board at the back of the icehouse, one cake of ice was always missing. That is where the booze was stored. Campers made little donations there for Pop to enjoy where Ma wouldn't catch him.

When I grew older, I sold the farm's ice to people who owned summer camps around the lake—as well as to several customers in Cambridge. Constance "Connie" Benzing, a local heiress whose Province Lake Country Club bordered the farm, leased the land to campers. Connie's uncle, Joseph Emery, was president of the New York City department store Lord & Taylor. A high-society man, Emery often vacationed with his family in Parsonsfield where he built the sprawling Five Chimneys estate with a wraparound porch overlooking the lake. Along with some friends, he also built the adjoining country club and nine-hole golf course. The locals thought highly of the Emerys, who helped keep the area alive during the Great Depression by employing people. After inheriting her uncle's property, Connie reopened the country club with her husband, Raymond, and ran the estate as an inn. While my grandmother sped around the lake on an Indian motorcycle, wearing a pair of leather strap goggles, Connie drove a classy maroon Chrysler Town and Country convertible with wooden sides.

"There she is," my grandmother would mutter, sitting on her front porch as Connie motored by. Then she would curl her index finger and flick it under her nose to indicate that she thought Connie was snooty.

Connie and Ma Hartley were like oil and water. They did not get along. Yet Connie employed my grandmother to manage the leases of ninety-two camps dotting the lake. Each summer, the camps' owners expected their iceboxes to be full when they arrived. When I grew older, my job was to fill them. I also delivered 55-gallon drums full of range oil, which required getting each barrel off the back of a big, rack-body truck by myself without a lift. I learned to spin the barrels a certain way to prevent them from splitting open when they landed. On Sundays, I drove back to each camp to pick up their trash.

The Year Maine Burned

In 1947, the summer after I turned fifteen, two hundred Maine fires destroyed more than a quarter of a million acres and nine towns. The largest fire, centered in nearby Shapleigh, burned more than 109,000 acres. Ma Hartley's neighbor Ralph Nutter served as Parsonsfield's fire warden, and my brother and I volunteered for emergency forest-fire duty.

"If I catch any of you at the Red Cross tent, you'll be arrested," Ralph warned us. If we even left the line of duty to get a cup of coffee, we would be considered AWOL. Ma was worse than Ralph. "I better not catch you breaking the rules," she threatened. She did not specify what she would do to us, but knowing my grandmother, I did not want to find out.

To feed the fire fighters, Wonder Bread trucks delivered boxes of bread to the local farm houses. Ma Hartley, who headed the local Order of the Eastern Stars, organized the other farmers' wives to make peanut butter and jelly sandwiches and baked beans, and Salvation Army volunteers ran the food down to those of us working on the fire lines.

We had no training. They just said, "Put out the fire."

With another volunteer, I rode along in an old Scanlon Oil gasoline truck full of water. On our backs we wore "Indian tanks," five-gallon tanks of water with hand pumps and a hose. When our truck ran out of water, my partner and I filled our tanks from streams. I was a little guy—five feet eight and 120 pounds. The straps from my tank bruised my shoulders black and blue.

We worked on many old logging roads. Sometimes the fire jumped across the tops of the trees without ever touching the ground. Have you ever seen a discarded Christmas tree when it burns? It explodes. Half the trees went up that way. At one point, the fire jumped through the treetops to both sides of the road. Behind us burned more fires, trapping my partner and me in our truck. Deer ran out of the woods, including one that was on fire. When the deer saw us, it startled and ran back into the flames. Then our water truck caught fire. My partner and I scrambled out. No one had told us what to do, but I poured the water from my tank over him. And he poured the water from his tank over me. Then, to protect us from the heat, we lay in the road with the empty water tanks over our heads like shields. With a tremendous roar like thunder and lightning, the fire raced overhead. I did not think we would get out of there, but the fire went by so fast neither of us got burned. Our truck did, though. The tires burned right off.

For seven days and six nights, we worked on that fire with no relief and no sleep. I do not recall being scared, just tired. When it was over, all that remained of some houses I saw in Shapleigh were bathtubs and chimneys. Thankfully, after a tremendous effort, the surrounding towns of Newfield, Limerick, Porter, and Parsonsfield were spared.

The Jolly Roger Village

A few years after the fire, my grandmother opened the Jolly Roger Village. On weekends, my uncle Chet drove up to the farm with his son, Richie, who was a few years younger than me. Together we built eight cabins in a field above the lake. I dug the holes for the cedar posts. Later, more families built their own cabins around the lake and Ma leased them the land. I also helped build a recreation hall with a small store that sold essential food items. On Saturday nights, campers carried their own pots and pans to the farmhouse, and my grandmother ladled them full of beans and franks. Truth was, she would open up gallon cans of B&M Baked Beans, made an hour away in Portland, and put them in a great big pot on the back of her woodstove. Then she spiked the beans with brown sugar, molasses, and salt pork to flavor them up a little. My job was to open the cans and take off the labels so no one saw them.

Every weekend Ma Hartley held Friday-night socials in the recreation hall. One guy played the back of a saw with a bow. When he bent the saw a certain way, it sounded like a bass violin. Another guy played a wooden broom handle with a string attached to a metal washtub. Ma loved to dance, but Pop did not. To stay out of Ma's way, he patrolled the farmyard, a quarter-mile up the road, checking cars to make sure the occupants were not getting into mischief. Earl Taylor's son Bill later recalled attending the dances. "We were allowed to go because our parents knew Ma would take good care of us," he said.

Years later, I restored an abandoned 1937 rack-body Chevy truck with help from Leo Henebury. We got the truck running with parts we rummaged in local junkyards. During the summer, before heading up to the campground every weekend, I would stop by the Penn Oil yard in Boston and load the truck with 55-gallon drums of range oil. At the end of the weekend, before driving home, I stopped in Rochester and unloaded the empty drums to hand shovel in a ton of coal. Then I set the empty drums on top of the coal and drove to Arlington, where I shoveled coal through the basement windows of several houses. The following Friday, I stopped at Penn Oil to exchange the empty drum for full ones. Then I drove back to Parsonsfield, but I had to get there by nine o'clock because the dances did not start until I waltzed my grandmother around the floor.

Several surrounding towns, including Freedom and Wolfeboro, New Hampshire, also held weekend dances. A bunch of us guys would pile into several cars—a half dozen people in each—and go as a group. I never dated anyone up there—just danced. Nancy was the only girl for me. When my brother, Curtis, was sixteen he met fourteen-year-old Corinne Peterson, the daughter of a family that owned a nearby summerhouse. In June 1952, Curtis and Corinne married while they were both in college, and I was the best man at their wedding.

As the Jolly Roger Village grew, my grandmother's interest shifted to the campground, and she decided to get out of farming. Because forestry land was taxed at a lower rate than farmland, she bought three thousand pine sprigs. The state dropped off the trees in big cartons. After separating the sprigs, I walked along and paced out a row. Every six feet, I drove a crowbar into the ground, wiggled it around, and poked in a spindly tree. Then I strapped on a metal tank, one like I had previously worn to fight the fire, and pumped water on them with a hose.

Later, my grandmother handed me a pickaxe and shovel. After a local dowser told us where to find water, Ma marched my cousin Richie and me over to the field at the top of the hill and told us to dig a well. To swing the pick-ax, the hole had to be five feet wide. While I dug, Richie pulled up each pail full of dirt and dumped it. Then he lowered down the empty pail. When the hole was deeper than my head, Ma threw down a hose so I would have some way to breathe if the hole collapsed. Truth was, if the well had collapsed, it would've crushed my lungs, and I would not have been able to breathe anyway.

Each day around lunchtime, Ma drove up to check on us. Planting her hands on her hips she would lean over the edge of the well and ask, "How you doing?" After satisfying herself that I was all right, instead of sending down a ladder, Ma would lower down a peanut butter sandwich in the bucket. Because he was younger, Richie ate up top.

Ma made me toe the mark. There was no such thing as a short work day, but I will tell you one thing, I developed good work ethics. When the well was finally finished, Ma covered it with a wooden lid and Pop installed a hand pump to draw water. Campers still use it today.

For fun, I played baseball in the nearby towns of Rochester, Eaton, and Conway, New Hampshire, which had some pretty good teams. The stands were small, just a couple of benches, and they had crummy fields. You would slide and leave your hide on the gravel, but we had fun. During the game, someone would pass around a hat and spectators would drop in a dollar bill or some change. If he got lucky, the pitcher might pocket fifteen dollars, while the other players took home ten. *Good money*, I thought.

One summer I stretched a sheet of watertight canvas over a row of wooden ribs and built myself a kayak. After shrinking the fabric with water, I slipped my boat into Province Lake, but it would not glide through the water in a straight line. The damn thing was bowed. The only way to go straight was by paddling to one side. Toward the end of summer, I often paddled across the lake by myself for a week or so, or I carried my kayak to a nearby river to fish for perch and pick blueberries or raspberries. All I took with me were potatoes, one for each day. I cooked the fish and potatoes right in the coals of my fire. The potatoes tasted wonderful, but the fish was terrible—really bony. At night, I slept on the ground. I had no plan. I just liked to get away and live off the land. Nobody cared where I went. My grandmother knew I'd be back.

As Pop grew older, I got to know him very well. At night, we sometimes sat by the ice house under the stars while he told me stories about his time in the Navy. But Ma did not volunteer information, particularly about family. If I asked about her first husband, she might say, "Well, why would you want to know about him?"

In the center of North Conway, about an hour north from the farm, stood a classy hotel, the Eastern Slope Inn, which had uniformed bell captains and a summer theater. I once asked my grandmother what it cost. "What do you care?" she said. "You're never going to stay there. That's a place for rich people."

Ask a question, and that is the sort of answer you got. But my grandmother had struggled so hard—being kicked off her farm, losing her children, moving into a tenement house—I understood her.

One summer day, a station wagon with New York plates pulled up in front of the recreation hall. Out stepped a woman who asked if we had a cabin available.

"I have four cabins down by the water for fifteen dollars a night," my grandmother said. Then she gave the woman sheets and pillowcases, which she did not leave on the beds for fear an animal might get into them. The woman took the sheets and walked back toward her car, which had a big box with holes sitting in the back.

"Get back here!" Ma barked. She would never say, "Excuse me, may I talk to you for a minute?" No, she said, "Get back here! What's in that box with the holes?"

"A cat," the woman said.

"No cat is going to piss on my sheets," my grandmother said. Then she snatched the sheets and gave the woman back her fifteen dollars.

"Granny," I said, "you can't talk to people like that."

"I'm Ma Hartley, not Granny," she said. "And I can talk to people like that. It's my place."

"Okay, Granny," I said, rubbing it in. "I understand."

I was the only person who could get away with calling her Granny. In her own way, I think my grandmother loved me. She never said so, and she did not show physical affection, such as ever giving me a hug. But she made me feel secure.

CHAPTER 3

THE BEST OFFER

For most of us, if we had to pick someone other than a relative who has had a tremendous influence on our life, I have always believed that person would be a teacher. For me, that person was my Sunday school teacher, Bill Linvill. My parents were not involved in church, but one Sunday morning while still in high school, I strolled up Prospect Street and walked through the doors of the Prospect Congregational Church. Bill led my brother's and my Boy Scout troop, which met in the church's basement. Once a week, a dance instructor also gave lessons in the church basement.

To avoid attention, I sat in a wooden pew near the back of the nineteenth-century red-brick building, which had a soaring bell tower and vaulted sanctuary. Young men do not usually show up in church on their own, and Bill and his wife, Bessie, were surprised to see me. Bill took a liking to me and asked why I joined the church. He assumed I had some inner feeling that going to church was important. I enlightened him by saying, "Your church has the best softball team in the church league, and you also teach dancing."

My other choice was a Baptist church, which was also nearby, but the Baptists did not allow dancing.

A religious person, Bill stood over six feet tall and taught math at MIT, as did his identical twin brother, John.* At the

---

* According to a memorial tribute on the National Academy of Engineering's website, William Linvill became a professor of engineering at MIT and helped develop the SAGE defense system at the institute's Lincoln Laboratory. Along with his brother, John Linvill, he later joined the faculty at Stanford University and became the Founding Chairman of the Department of Engineering-Economic Systems. A member of the National Academy of Engineering, he became a fellow of the IEEE and of the American Association of the Advancement of Science and served on a number of key advisory councils including the National Aeronautics and Space Administration's Advisory Council for Space and Terrestrial Applications. He and his wife, Bessie, had five children. https://www.nae.edu/30654/William-K-Linvill

time, Bill and Bessie, had no children, so they often invited me over to their campus apartment for dinner.

"I'm impressed," Bill said one day when I was about sixteen. "You're a really intelligent guy. What made you decide to go to trade school?"

"I have to leave home," I told him. Having completed all of my academic classes during the first half of my senior year at Rindge Tech, I stayed to work in the school's shop class until graduation.

Curtis had graduated from Rindge in 1948, one year before me, and enrolled in the engineering program at MIT, but I doubted I would get accepted. Trade schools are not the road most people take to get into college. I enjoy reading but never studied literature. Those sorts of classes were taught next door at Cambridge High and Latin. However, Bill encouraged me to sign up for the two-day college entrance exam, held in a local university gym. I aced the exam with almost perfect math scores, and MIT sent me an acceptance letter inviting me to tour the school. Thrilled, I showed the letter to my mother.

"That's nice," she said and threw the letter on the kitchen table. "You're not going to college. You are going to work."

I intended to leave home after high school at the age of sixteen, like my mother wanted. My good friend Leo Henebury's parents, Leo and Margaret, who often welcomed me for dinner, invited me to move into their house on Carlton Street in Somerville. They thought I was a good influence on their son, who got into even more trouble than I did. Leo had three sisters, Peggy, Muriel, and Agnes, and a brother, Jackie. Their parents offered to make room for me to move in. However, at the last minute my mother changed her mind.

"You can live at home," she said, "but we are not going to help you. You have to work. And we are not going to pay for your education."

Because they were easy to walk to, I also applied to Tufts University, Northeastern University, and Boston University. All four schools accepted me. Bill encouraged me to go to MIT, like

Curtis. So I visited. Expecting to leave home and go to work at a young age made me grow up fast, but when I toured MIT and saw more than one hundred students sitting in their lecture halls, I hesitated. I needed a place where people would pat me on the head and say "Attaboy!" I needed guidance.

Northeastern wanted me to play hockey and offered to discount my tuition. However, because labs took place in the afternoons, I knew I could not make the practices. That really bothered me. I love sports. But you have to know the difference between your work and your hobby, and I planned to be an engineer.

Since Boston University's engineering program was less recognized, I chose Tufts. In addition to being near enough to walk to, Tufts offered lectures with only fifteen to twenty students per class.

But first I had to graduate from high school. Because of a few schoolyard fights, the headmaster handed me a blank diploma at my Rindge Tech graduation ceremony. My father had to go down to the school and plead with the headmaster to give me my diploma. Ironically, more than three decades later, the Rindge Alumni Association selected me to receive the school's alumni award as the 1983 "Rindge Man of the Year."

In the fall of 1949, I started college at age seventeen. Because of the G.I. Bill, many soldiers returning from the war had enrolled in college. While a large number of my classmates were in their mid-to-late twenties, I looked about thirteen.

School cost about $650 a year—a lot of money, even though President Truman had recently raised the minimum wage from forty cents to seventy-five cents per hour. Over the years, I had saved about $600 from helping my father and working odd jobs, but since I did not have a bank account, I had asked my mother to hold on to my money. However, when I asked for it, she claimed I had never given it to her. To pay my first year's tuition, Leo, who worked for his father fixing cars in his family's three-bay garage, loaned me the money. The following year, I paid him back.

When I enrolled at Tufts, Nancy was still in high school. So I used all the money I had—a twenty-five-dollar U.S. Victory

Bond—to buy my first car, a 1929 Chevy sedan with wooden spoke wheels to drive down and see her on weekends. But the car was in Somerville. To pick it up, early one morning I removed the license plates from my father's car, planning to return them before he noticed they were missing. Then I walked to Somerville, put the plates on my new Chevy, and drove it home. However, by the time I returned, my father had already driven to work.

"How'd you get the car?" he asked later that evening.

When I told him, boy, was he mad. But I would have done it all over again to see Nancy. I thought she was just awesome. To show how I felt, I gave her my high school class ring to wear on a chain around her neck. Back then, that was a big commitment and meant that we were going steady. I really loved her. Although Nancy and I did not discuss marriage, I thought she knew how I felt and believed that she felt the same way about me. All Nancy ever wanted was to have a home and be a mother, but before starting a family, I wanted to finish college so I could get everything in order and provide her with a proper home. One day, I drove down to tell Nancy my plans. However, I did not ask her to wait for me, which is where I messed up. I should have said that my intention was to marry her.

Long Days

During our first two years of school, Tufts engineering students all took the same courses, such as math, drafting, and physics. Our final two years, we specialized in civil, electrical, or mechanical engineering.

My first week of class, I walked into an engineering shop and found my mechanical engineering instructor, Professor Hill, and the other students standing around a large cement-lined vault in the concrete floor. The school had dug the hole to install a heavy piece of equipment, which had a five-foot-square base. However, they forgot to allow room for ropes to lower the equipment into the hole. Embarrassed, Professor Hill stood there talking about what to do with a few burly riggers, who were scratching their heads.

"Professor Hill, may I make a suggestion?" I asked.

"Yeah, go ahead," he said, sarcastically. "Get it off your chest."

"Fill the hole with ice," I said. "It's cheap. Boston Ice is only a mile away. They'll fill the whole thing up. Then set the equipment on top of the ice and put a hose down in the hole and use a sump pump to suck the water out of the hole while the ice melts. If you set some stone and brick pads in the hole and leave a gap of about an inch or so under the bottom, the base of the equipment won't even get wet."

"The kid's got something." The riggers nodded. They followed my recommendation, and it worked just fine.

After class, Professor Hill pulled me aside. "What made you think of that?" he asked.

"I grew up on a farm," I said. "Ever seen a stone foundation with a house sitting on top? How do you think they put those huge granite stones in place?"

He shrugged.

"They built a ramp and pushed the stones up it on log rollers. Then they rolled the stones onto blocks of ice. As the ice melts, it acts like a disposable jack and lowers the stone into place. To place one stone on top of another, they would set it on lead balls so they could shim it up nice and flat as the stone settled down." As a kid, I was always curious and asked a lot of questions.

"That's very interesting," Professor Hill replied.

The guy already likes me, I thought.

"Go ahead. Get it off your chest." I got a kick out of that.

I figured I had this class made.

I attended college six days a week, including Saturday. My first class started at eight o'clock in the morning, and my last class typically finished around one o'clock in the afternoon. But three days a week, I also had laboratories or drafting classes, which ended around half past four in the afternoon. After that, I walked two miles to work at the city garage in Somerville. In high school, I had learned how to weld while working on trucks. Our grade was based on how many pieces were left over after we took apart a car and put it back together again. So we hid the extra pieces.

At the city garage, I received my first taste of politics. In winter, construction contractors leased their trucks to the city, and the city put snowplows on them. When spring came, we were supposed to return the trucks to the contractors in good running condition, but when the contractors first brought the trucks in, some were so beat up they dragged them in with tow trucks. We spent half the winter putting new engines in old trucks. Then, in the spring, when Somerville was done using it, the contractor would pick up his truck and say, "Good deal."

I also suspected that some city plow truck drivers intentionally ran their plows into the curbstone. That way, they got paid to sit in a warm room by the pot-bellied stove, playing cards while the other guys and I repaired their plows. Near Union Square, the city garage was close to Leo's house and the junkyards, where we hunted for spare parts. After fixing up the trucks, we sent them back out again. Between working on trucks, I did my homework in the back room.

For lunch most days, I bought a cup of hot chocolate and a couple of glazed doughnuts from a doughnut shop in Davis Square. The second doughnut I saved for dinner, along with a baloney sandwich, which I ate while walking to work. Around eleven at night, I walked one mile home—uphill both ways, as my children later teased—aiming to be in bed by midnight. Then I woke up by seven the next morning and did it all over again. Those were long days.

After my freshman year, I applied to work as a draftsman at the Raytheon Manufacturing Company, which had facilities in Waltham and Watertown. After producing magnetron tubes and radar systems during the war, Raytheon developed and manufactured military weapons systems. Hoping one of the company's facilities would hire me, I applied to work at both and was surprised when they both offered me a job. Because of the Fair Labor Standards Act of 1940, I couldn't work more than forty hours a week. However, since I needed money to return to college, I accepted both jobs without telling anyone. During the day, I composed production drawings at the "Bleachery," a former Waltham textile mill that manufactured missiles. At night, I worked for Raytheon's engineering division in Watertown.

Soon after, the International Brotherhood of Electrical Workers held tryouts for the company's fast-pitch softball team, and I signed up. So I could make the games, the Bleachery let me out early from my day job, and the engineering facility in Waltham allowed me come in late. Our team did so well we made it to the playoffs. I was a good infielder and played third base, positioning myself in front of the base so I could grab the ball quick. Everyone thought I was aggressive. The truth is, I had a terrible throwing arm, but I was very fast on my feet. So, when it was my turn at bat, I'd poke these shots to the infield and run like hell to beat everybody to the base. As a result, I had the best batting average in the playoffs, earning a write-up in one of the local papers. Unfortunately, the article said I worked for Raytheon's Waltham facility. After reading the article, the division manager in Watertown called the Bleachery. "Excuse me," he said, "Ken Carr works for the engineering division."

"He works for us," the manager at the Bleachery insisted.

After discovering that I worked at both facilities, the head of personnel came to fire me.

"I knew it was wrong," I admitted. "But I needed the money to pay my tuition, or I would not be able to go back to school."

Both division managers were very nice about it. Instead of firing me, they let me resign, and I went back to school with enough money to pay my next year's tuition, plus some.

The following summer, my uncle Frank Hogan, who married my mother's sister Althea, called me up and asked me to run a baseball clinic in Medford. Frank co-owned Hogan and Van, a big auto body paint shop, and managed the city's Park and Recreation Department.

"You're a disciplined guy," Uncle Frank said. "I want you to teach these kids how to play ball."

The first day at the ballpark, I lined up half the players on the infield and the other half on the outfield. Then I instructed the coaches to hit fly balls to the outfielders and ground balls to the infielders. Each player had to catch five balls before moving to the next position.

"C'mon, for Chrissakes, catch the ball!" the other guys would yell if a guy missed the ball.

There is no such thing as nice try. You either catch the ball or you don't. After a guy in the outfield caught five balls, he'd move in halfway to relay the throw from the outfield to the catcher. The catcher hung back with the coaches who were hitting the fly balls. I liked to keep everyone moving.

"Stare at the ball," I told the kids who turned to the side when the ball came at them. "Keep the ball in front of you. Charge the ball. Attack it. It doesn't matter if the ball hits you. You can still make the play."

Frank called me one day and said, "Ken, you're really pissing off the parents. You're making the kids cry."

"Well, you asked me to teach them," I said. "You know I love to play, but I play tough."

Frank relieved me of my duties. The coaches continued to use the drills I taught them, but they did not insist that each player make five successful catches before moving on. They liked my technique, but not my attitude. They played a little gentler.

Private E-2, United States Army Reserve

On September 20, 1951, during my junior year at Tufts, I enlisted in the United States Army Reserve without telling anyone—not even my family. The Korean War had started one year before, and I wanted to go to Korea and fight. As a college student, I knew I would not be drafted, but because of Pop Hartley's stories and my uncle Robert's death, I have always been patriotic and felt bound by duty to serve my country. I hoped to join the combat engineers—the Army's version of the Seabees—building runways and other infrastructure for land troops.

After one year at MIT, Curtis had transferred to Tufts and repeated his freshman year, which put us in the same classes. Because we studied together, we intentionally did not sit together at school. If we made the same mistakes on tests, we worried it would look like we were cheating. Curtis was a good student. However, he received a student deferment. So, when my brother discovered that I had enlisted, he asked, "What are you doing?"

"I want to serve my country," I said, embarrassed someone might accuse me of enrolling in college to avoid the draft.

However, because I was so skinny and could hear out of only one ear, I feared being rejected as unfit for duty. Before signing up, I ate as many bananas as I could. Then, during the hearing portion of my medical exam, I concentrated on reading the examiner's lips to see what he was saying. It worked, and I got accepted.

The following summer, I reported to active reserve training at Fort Devens Army Base, thirty miles away in Ayer. Three days after arriving, I tried to catch a metal ammo box that fell off a truck. I got a double hernia. The Army sent me to the Murphy Army Hospital in Waltham for surgery. Six weeks later, they assigned me to teach evening classes in math and airfield construction and wiring to other reservists at the South Boston Army Base near the Boston Fish Pier. Although I remained in the reserves for eight years, I felt like a draft dodger. For many years, I did not tell anyone about my time in the service and left it off of my resume. It was a terrible war, and the more I heard about what happened, the more ashamed I felt for not being sent to Korea to fight.

Decades later, when I requested my service records, the National Personnel Records Center sent me a letter stating that my records were most likely destroyed in a fire. A 1973 blaze at the military personnel records building in St. Louis, Missouri consumed 16 to 18 million military record files for people who had served in the Army between 1912 and 1959.[8] As a result, I have my Army identification cards and my October 30, 1959, discharge papers, but not my enlistment papers.

Meanwhile, Nancy graduated from high school and briefly worked as a secretary for an insurance company, putting together policies. About the time I joined the reserves, she took a job as a hostess at a Rockville restaurant run by Fred Fluckiger, a former Merchant Marine and Navy veteran. Four years my senior, Fred swept Nancy off her feet, and in September 1952, she married him. When I found out, I was crushed.

During this same time, my parents' marriage fell apart. They were constantly at odds with each other. Neither one was happy. It is hard to live in a house where people scream at each other over everything, and they divorced. My father kept the house on Gardner Road, and my mother moved to Somerville. After taking a government procurement job in Japan, ordering supplies for the Air Force, she later married John O'Neil, a master sergeant in the Air Force. Sometime later, my father married Nancy's aunt Viola, and they invited Doc Levine to live with them. It turned out better for everybody.

"A Tree in the Meadow"

In the spring of 1953, while preparing to graduate from Tufts, I filled out more than a dozen job applications and interviewed with companies like Otis Elevator (named for Elisha Otis, who invented the safety break on the elevator) and Sylvania (which manufactured television sets and radios). But I honed in on Philco, a big company in Pennsylvania that made washing machines, refrigerators, and radios, along with radar systems and televisions.

Sometime prior, two classmates and I had taken summer jobs at the Johnsville Naval Air Development Center in Pennsylvania. A small farming community, Johnsville had little more than a diner, but during the Second World War, the Brewster Aeronautical Corporation purchased 370 acres of farmland and constructed a $9 million plant to build Allied bombers and fighter planes.[9] After a series of problems, the Navy transformed the plant into the Naval Air Development Center and the Naval Air

Facility—one of the top aeronautical research and development centers in the country.

Commonly known as "Johnsville," the base contained thirty aviation electronics and equipment laboratories. While there, I met Fritz Blom, an engineer who worked as a Philco "tech rep." Along with other tech reps from Philco's Contract Engineering Division, Fritz traveled the country teaching servicemen how to operate and repair equipment, including radar systems. Taking me under his wing, Fritz introduced me to radar.

At that time, radar systems were very simple and had few active components, such as diodes (an integral part of the downconverter) and TR tubes (which alternately connect the transmitter and receiver to a shared antenna and protect the receiver). A basic radar system consists of five components: a transmitter, a receiver, a display screen, a transmit antenna, and a receive antenna. Through the use of a passive switch, or duplexer, the transmit antenna and the receive antenna are typically combined to create a single antenna. The ferrite duplexer, also known as a "circulator," is a passive, non-reciprocal switch that allows the high-power transmit signal to couple to the transmit antenna with negligible attenuation, or loss. In turn, the return signal passes from the receive antenna with negligible loss to the receiver.* Usually a four-port device, the duplexer can be formed by using two three-port circulators in tandem.

To transmit microwaves, we did not yet have much in the way of sophisticated microwave integrated circuits. We had

---

* The receiver is normally a superheterodyne configuration in which a mixer is used to combine the received microwave signal with a low-power microwave signal (a local oscillator at a different frequency from that of the received microwave frequency). The semiconductor diodes are an integral part of the mixer. The mixer downconverts the received microwave signal to a lower or intermediate frequency where it can be more easily amplified and filtered, producing a video output proportional to the received signal's amplitude and timing. The TR (transmit and receive) tube, a gas-filled spark gap device located in a sealed glass waveguide, is a receiver protection device placed in the receive port preceding the mixer. It allows the low-level receive signals to pass with minimal attenuation and reflects energy strong enough to damage the sensitive receiver.

waveguide transmission lines made of hollow metal tubes,* so microwave engineers were often called "plumbers." However, I saw that microwave engineering was the future, and I wanted to be part of it.

During my interview with Philco, the company representative asked how much of my education I had paid for myself.

"One hundred percent," I said.

"You went to school, got good grades, and paid for your own education?" the man asked.

"That's correct," I said and offered to show him my tax forms.

I ended up getting the best job offer in my class. Philco even offered to pay my tuition at the University of Pennsylvania, which had accepted me to earn my doctorate of engineering degree. I planned to take classes during the day and make up missed time by working at night. The Army reassigned me to teach at the Schuylkill Arsenal in Philadelphia, and I rented a house in the Germantown section of Philadelphia with four other guys from Philco. For fun, we all went out to the movies as a group. They were trying to fix me up with nurses or other girls, but I did not date again for five years.

All that time, Nancy never contacted me, and I never asked how she was doing. Viola suggested I date Nancy's sister, Carol, a good-looking girl. But if I got involved with Carol, it might seem as if I was trying to keep track of Nancy, which did not seem proper. So I never visited. But, boy, did I wish that I had asked Nancy to marry me.

I can't carry a musical note in a basket, but to stay awake while driving back and forth from Philadelphia to Cambridge, I

---

* Transmission lines connect the transmitter to the antenna (or radiating element), and connect the return (or receive signal) to the receiver. All signal processing was done by detecting and downconverting to a lower or intermediate frequency. At the higher frequencies, signal losses became serious, necessitating replacing coaxial transmission line with lower-loss, hollow-pipe waveguide, basically eliminating the need for a center conductor and its dielectric support. At the microwave frequencies, there were few active components. The conversion from waveguide to coaxial transmission line involves a passive coax to waveguide transition, which is, basically, an antenna—a connection between waveguide interfaces and coaxial cables.

used to sing. About the time I had first met Nancy, one of the top songs on the radio was "A Tree in the Meadow," sung by Margaret Whiting. It always made me think of Nancy, and although I had not seen her in a couple of years, I often sang it to myself in the car.

There's a tree in the meadow
With a stream drifting by,
And carved upon that tree I see
"I love you till I die."
I shall always remember
The love in your eyes
The day you carved upon that tree
"I love you till I die."
But further on down lovers' lane
A silhouette I see
I know you're kissing someone else.
I wish that it were me.

However, I changed the lyrics from "the day you carved upon that tree" to "the day I carved upon that tree, I love you till I die." Nancy had gone off and married someone else, and the song fit the situation.

CHAPTER 4

STRIKE!

While working at Philco, I helped develop color television. RCA produced the first commercial color television set in the spring of 1954. Featuring a fifteen-inch screen, it sold for $1,000—roughly the equivalent of $7,500 today.[10] My own family had purchased a seven-inch, black-and-white tube TV while I was still in college. With few stations to choose from, viewing options were limited—although I avoided watching them. TV was not conducive to doing homework.

Philco soon selected me for their management training program and assigned me to work in various production areas developing refrigerators and radios, but I really wanted to work on radar and asked to join Philco's microwave program.

When most people hear the word *microwave,* they probably picture a microwave oven, invented by Percy Spencer, a self-taught engineer from Maine. In 1945, while working on a magnetron for Raytheon, Percy discovered that it had melted a peanut cluster bar in his pocket.[11] After determining that microwaves could also pop corn and explode an egg, Spencer helped Raytheon produce the first microwave oven, the 750-pound "Radarange."*

Microwaves themselves were first predicted in 1864 by the Scottish mathematician and theoretical physicist James Clerk Maxwell, who presented a set of equations suggesting the presence of unseen waves of energy (including millimeter waves) that traveled at the speed of light.[12] His equations are the basis of understanding microwaves (in the frequency of 1 gigahertz to

---

* In 1965, Raytheon later bought the appliance company Amana and retained me as a consultant to redesign their microwave oven to make it more cost-effective and last longer. To do this, I invented and patented a plug-in waveguide ferrite isolator, a necessary device that extended the life of the ovens' magnetron tubes. My design also improved safety by absorbing unwanted reflected power and reducing electromagnetic leakage.

110 gigahertz [GHz]), the upper end of the radio-wave portion of the electromagnetic spectrum. Soon after, German physicist Heinrich Hertz produced and detected these invisible waves of energy, leading to their eventual use in radio communications. And in 1935 British physicist Sir Robert Watson-Watt developed the first practical radar system, employed by Britain during the Second World War. After the war, with increasing tensions between the Soviet Union and the United States, radar quickly became part of our country's national defense system as well.

At Philco, I developed microwave-based components for radar systems, which transmit and receive microwave signals. Despite safety concerns regarding the use of microwave energy, we never feared microwaves. To monitor our exposure, technicians carried a neon bulb clipped to our shirt pockets. If the bulb glowed, we knew someone had turned on the radar. When we climbed up on the roof to work on the antenna, we deliberately hung our badges on the radar switch so nobody would turn on the radar while we were up there. Sometimes while working on the antenna, the back of my neck would get hot. *Oh, Christ*, I would realize, *someone turned on the radar*. During the holidays, we spelled out *Merry Christmas* with lights in the laboratory window and scanned them with the radar system to light them up.

While working as a full-time engineer in Philco's Government and Industrial Division, I also took graduate classes during the day at the University of Pennsylvania. Using textbooks from MIT's Rad Lab series, I studied radar systems and low-frequency amplifiers and antennas. At night, I made up the time spent in class by developing microwave ferrite devices.* My early work on ferrite devices involved designing four-port waveguide components that were used as duplexers, or passive switches.** An

---

* A ferrite device involves placing a "ferromagnetic," or non-conductive ceramic material, in a transmission line surrounded by an electromagnetic field. Although they operate on different principles, most ferrite devices are non-reciprocal and only allow the microwave signal to exit through a specific port, or opening. Initial designs were used in waveguide transmission line.

** A ferrite isolator is a non-reciprocal waveguide, two-port component that

important component in radar and communication systems, the duplexer eliminated the need for a mechanical switch to circulate the microwave signal.

Because the transmitter could be coupled to the antenna, and the antenna coupled to the receiver, we often referred to them as "circulators." The received signal entered the antenna and was circulated to the receiver port. Any unwanted reflection was directed to the terminated port of the duplexer and isolated from the other ports. The major advantage is that the duplexer enables the transmit antenna and the receive antenna to be combined into a shared antenna. As a result, a single antenna could simultaneously transmit and receive a microwave signal. Known as "timesharing," this system saved space and allowed aircraft to carry a single antenna.

As a single guy without a family to worry about, I signed up for all the Philco jobs that required taking risks. This included volunteering for assignments on aircraft carriers to try out radar systems, such as the Gilfillan FPN-16 automated landing system we were developing to help land planes on the deck of a ship.

In earlier times, the British used catapults, which resembled a crossbow, to launch Sopwith Camels and other small fighter planes from the decks of aircraft carriers. During the First World War, this allowed the British to launch aircraft close enough to destroy German blimps or airships. But after returning from a mission without a way to land back aboard their ships, pilots often intentionally crashed their planes in the water then waited for a ship to retrieve them.

Later, the United States designed a tailhook and weights to catch the plane with a steel cable strung across an aircraft carrier's deck. For this system, a pilot had to come in fast, so if he missed

---

transmits microwave signals with low loss in the forward direction, but will absorb the signal in the reverse direction. Eventually the ferrite isolator took the form of a three-port circulator. The third port terminated in a microwave-absorbing material. This new form of isolator, which was smaller and more conducive to high-level integration, improved microwave performance. Frequently used in strip transmission line and in microwave integrated circuits (MIC), it later led to my development of "suspended substrate" transmission line.

the wire, he could take off and do a go-around. But if the pilot missed the wire and was flying too slow to take off again, the plane would fall off the end of the ship into the water.

Philco's aircraft-landing system used radar to guide a plane in. My responsibilities included building the system's receiver. To find out if it worked, I sat in the back seat of a Navy fighter plane over the Atlantic while the pilot, seated in front, came in for a landing on the ship.

While the plane's radar system landed the aircraft, the pilot was prohibited from touching the controls. To ensure we tested the system properly, the plane's wings had special "chicken lights." If the pilot touched the controls during final approach, the chicken lights flashed on, invalidating the test.

From that high up, the aircraft carrier looked like a postage stamp. As our plane came in high and fast, I peered over the pilot's shoulder. *We're going to land on that?* I thought.

"Aren't you worried about the landing system?" I asked the pilot. "You won't touch the controls?"

"I won't touch the controls," he said. "The chicken lights will go on."

"Aren't you concerned about whether it'll work?" I asked.

"Hey, sonny," he said. That's what he called me, "sonny," like I was a kid. "These guys know what they're doing."

He did not realize that I was heading up the receiver portion of the project. Early radar systems relied on tubes with filaments that had to be warmed up, so I had been up all night trying to keep the system running. If something went wrong, I did not want to be embarrassed—or worse. Despite testing the hell out of the system and doing preventative maintenance, parts sometimes failed. Of course, I did not tell the pilot that.

Anyway, the landing system worked, and I am still here. In fact, taking those high-risk jobs saved my life. In the fall of 1955, I was returning from a Navy snorkel hunt on a seaplane. To test Philco's APS-44 radar system, we were competing with another Navy plane using General Electric's APS-45 radar system to see which system could first locate a submarine snorkel in the water. Snorkels are very difficult to see on a radar screen, especially when the water is choppy. The unwanted interference makes it difficult to pick out the snorkel from all the background noise, or "clutter." Philco had originally designed the APS-44 system for another use. However, at that time the United States was not very friendly with the Soviets, so we were running multiple tests to modify the system and make it more sensitive for hunting submarines.

On November 1, 1955, one particular test took longer than expected, and our plane returned late to Maryland's Naval Air Station Patuxent River. As a result, I missed a flight to the West Coast with another Philco engineer, Marion Hobgood, who was headed to Portland, Oregon, to work on the Bonneville Power Administration Communication System. I was scheduled to fly on the same plane, United Airlines Flight 629, to consult with Boeing in Seattle, Washington. After departing from New York, the plane stopped in Chicago before continuing to Denver, Portland, and Seattle. After missing the flight, I caught another plane to Chicago where I learned that a plane flying from Denver to Portland had just exploded in midair and crashed. Sure enough, that was Marion's plane, and I was supposed to be with him.

Eleven minutes after taking off from Denver, the DC-6B airliner with thirty-nine passengers and five crew members blew apart and crashed in a farmer's beet field, killing everyone onboard. An FBI investigation later found that the plane had been destroyed by twenty-five sticks of dynamite attached to a nine-volt battery and a timer. Twenty-three-year-old Jack Gilbert Graham later confessed to wrapping the bomb as a Christmas gift and placing it in the suitcase of his mother, Daisie King, who unknowingly carried it onboard.[13] Hoping to get rich, Graham had taken out a $37,500 travel insurance policy on his mother. During the trial, he showed absolutely no remorse, appearing to care only about the money. Graham was quickly convicted and put to death without ever apologizing for what he had done.

After I returned to Philco, the company asked me to drop out of graduate school and take over as the company's Microwave Special Products Section Head, developing ferrite devices. I agreed, hoping to later pick up my classes. But when you make a decision like that, your whole life changes and you often are unable to go back to the original plan. That is what happened to me. So instead of completing my graduate education, I developed a whole series of ferrite devices, including isolators and four-port circulators.

When I was just twenty-four, Philco selected me to receive its Outstanding Engineer Award, which came with a stock option in the company. On the night of the award, I dressed up in a suit and tie for a company dinner held at the banquet hall of a local hotel. The company VIPs were sitting together at a table, and when they announced my name to receive the award, I felt great.

Thorn Mountain

Although I enjoyed working at Philco, I did not like living in Philadelphia. At the time, the city had no professional hockey teams, and in the winter they got ice and rain instead of snow. On weekends, I often drove seven hours north to visit Ma Hartley and would moonlight as a ski instructor at Thorn Mountain in nearby Jackson, New Hampshire. An aggressive mountain with twenty trails and two chairlifts, Thorn Mountain was one of the state's popular ski areas and boasted an impressive view of Mount Washington. However, it lacked a full-service restaurant and other amenities. Those of us who went there, did so to ski.

I hoped to become a professional ski instructor, like Egon Zimmermann, the well-known Austrian Olympic gold medalist who taught Olympic hopefuls at nearby Mount Cranmore. Although not nearly as good a skier as Zimmermann, I was better than the average guy. So, hoping to spend more time skiing, I bought a burned-out farmhouse on a seven-acre parcel near Crystal Lake in Snowville, New Hampshire, planning to rebuild the house.

My cousin Richie, also a very good skier, worked with me. A real daredevil, he hoped to become a naval fighter pilot. We were both pretty fearless. Neither of us thought we would ever get hurt. After a full day of skiing, the other instructors and I joined the ski patrol and swept the slope for stragglers to make sure no one was stranded on the mountain. One day, before sweeping the slope, Richie said, "See you at the bottom."

I took that as a challenge. Racing down the mountain one last time, Richie took one trail and I took another, veering across a bend in the trail to take a shortcut through the trees. It was risky, but the important thing was to win, not to be safe. I was going like hell when my right ski cut through the snow's crust. Back then, skis did not have automatic-release bindings. We strapped our boots onto our skis with leather strips called "long thorns." When my right ski cut through the crust, that ski broke off, but my left ski kept going. It spun me around so fast that I twisted my right leg inside my ski boot, breaking the bones in my foot.

Meanwhile, everyone was waiting for me to check in at the bottom of the mountain. When I did not show up, Richie swept the mountain with the ski patrol. They spotted me off the trail between some trees and dragged a toboggan up on the ski lift.

"No, I'm all right," I told them, too embarrassed to get on the toboggan. Then, very slowly, I skied the rest of the way down the mountain on one foot.

Richie drove me to Memorial Hospital, twenty minutes away in North Conway, and rolled me inside on a gurney. Although I cannot remember the first name of the doctor on duty that night, I can't ever forget his last name: Twaddle. A contract guy who practiced orthopedics at the Boston University Medical Center Hospital, Dr. Twaddle drove up to Memorial Hospital to help on weekends. Before the invention of the safety binding release, doctors got a lot of practice setting skiers' broken limbs while making a little money on the side. Anyway, Dr. Twaddle took one look at my leg and said, "We've got to cut your boot off."

"Can you give us a little time to try to get the boot off without cutting it?" I asked. "Boots are expensive."

Dr. Twaddle doubted we could get the boot off, but since a few guys were waiting in line behind me, Richie pushed my gurney to the back of the line to give us more time. We kept working that boot a little bit, and a little bit more. It hurt like hell, but I could not afford a new pair of ski boots. By the time my turn came up again, my foot was free.

"I can't believe you got that boot off," Dr. Twaddle said.

It turned out, I had broken my ankle, my arch, and the metatarsal joints, which connect the toes to the arch. I broke them all.

After Dr. Twaddle placed my foot in a cast, Richie drove me to the farmhouse, but I still had to get back to Pennsylvania. Back then, cars did not have automatic transmissions. Operating the clutch, the brake, and the gas with one foot was going to be a problem. So, Richie removed the gas pedal from my old Chevy. (Actually, it was two Chevys. During my senior year of high school, I had combined a 1935 Chevy Coupe and a 1936 Chevy Standard to make one decent car. My mother made me cut up the parts I did not use with a hacksaw. Eddy Weisberg, a classmate and friend, who lived a block away, helped me load the pieces I did not need onto a horse-drawn wagon, and we dumped them at his family's junkyard business.)

After removing my gas pedal, Richie took an old cane and drilled a hole in the bottom. Then he set the bottom of the cane on the pin that connected to the gas pedal. This allowed me to work the gas with my right hand rather than using my foot, which is how I drove back to Philadelphia.

I made it all the way down Route 1 to near Trenton, New Jersey, on the Pennsylvania border, when at about three o'clock in the morning a state trooper pulled me over.

"Please step out of the car, sir," the trooper said as I rolled down my window.

"Okay," I agreed. "But step back, because I need to open the door wide."

Puzzled, the trooper bent down to look in my window. "What've you got in there?" he asked. "What's this?"

"I broke my leg today," I said.

"Where are you coming from?" he asked.

"New Hampshire."

"How'd you get here?"

"I had to drive, so…" I showed him the cane.

"Geez!" The trooper shook his head. "You made it this far. Do me a favor. We never met. Right? I never saw you in my life. Get out of here. Go get some sleep."

He let me go. After driving the rest of the way to Philadelphia with a broken leg, I went to work that same day.

Stalling for Time

Working at Philco's engineering lab one day, I got a call from the production manager about a problem with the APS-44 radar system. Although the system was already in production, we were modifying the construction to make it more sensitive to hunt for snorkels. After changing several components, I knew the problem was in the intermediate frequency amplifier, contained in a metal chassis about the size of a cigarette carton. Rather than give the amplifier to a technician, I wanted to change the components in the receive path and solve the problem on my own. So early that morning, I drove the faulty amplifier a couple of blocks over to Philco's engineering facility, "the Factory." As an engineer, I was not allowed to use the tools in the production area. Production was unionized. Engineering was not. So I asked the factory worker assigned to me to remove the mixer diodes and TR tubes and to change the IF amplifier, components in the receiver path.*

---

* Properly called semiconductor diodes, crystals detect the radar return and down-converted the microwave frequency signal to the intermediate frequency. A TR tube, or transmit and receive tube, protects the receiver by preventing high-level energy from entering and damaging the sensitive receiver. The reflected energy, or echo, should only represent a very small percentage of the transmitter power output. Exceptionally strong signals may be received by inadvertently operating the radar adjacent to a large reflecting surface or in close proximity to another radar. The receiver protection device, or TR tube, allows the passage of weak echoes from the duplexer to enter the receiver with negligible loss, or attenuation, but rejects any signals strong enough to damage the sensitive receiver.

In the receive path, following the TR tube, a mixer converts the receive signal to an intermediate frequency (IF), which can be more easily filtered and amplified. The mixer contains two replaceable 1N23C diodes. The output of the mixer is amplified to an intermediate frequency and filtered to eliminate interfering signals and background noise. The output of the IF amplifier is detected, creating a video frequency which is further amplified and coupled to the radar's display screen.

After taking his time warming up the system and fooling around with the equipment, the guy said, "Well, it's time for my coffee break."

"Hurry back," I said, growing impatient.

When the guy returned, he had to use the bathroom and disappeared again. All this time, I kept waiting. By lunch, we were getting nowhere. Then he shut down the system and said, "We're going to have to start over after lunch."

After he left, I turned the system back on. "To hell with this," I said and swapped out the parts myself while everyone else in the factory sat around watching with their arms crossed. *Geez*, I thought. *This sure isn't a very productive place. Don't any of these guys work?*

That afternoon I drove the faulty IF amplifier back over to the engineering area and found an entourage of executives waiting for me outside on the front stairs. I thought they were going to compliment me for doing a good job. So, being a confident guy, I said, "You didn't have to come over. It was nothing."

"What the hell did you do over there?" one executive asked.

"I found the system problem," I said.

"The whole company's on strike," he replied.

They were not there to greet me. They were angry.

My father belonged to The International Brotherhood of Electrical Workers, so he dealt with unions all the time. The union shop stewards would show up and bring out workers that my father was supposed to take on. They would take these cronies—people with poor work ethics who were only on the job because they knew somebody—and you had to give them a job. Even though he was a union man himself, my father felt the same way I did about unions. While once serving a useful purpose eliminating sweat shops and improving wages, unions are now so political, they do not really accomplish much. Working under those conditions was not something I wanted to do.

"I didn't do anything wrong," I said. If somebody was going to be fired, I figured it would be the production guy. Didn't anybody care about meeting the production schedule? It sure did not seem like it.

"No, no," they said. "You made a mistake. There's going to be a grievance committee. Don't argue. Just say you're sorry."

The grievance committee consisted of four or five "bozos" sitting at a table. They were not interested in the fact that the system was not working right or in finding out what was wrong. They were like broken records. "You realize you could have jeopardized that person's job," they said. "You took that man's job away from him."

I did not want his job. I had my own job to do too, but they did not seem to care. They only wanted to gripe.

"I'm sorry." I kept apologizing, just as I was asked to do, but they kept repeating the same thing, over and over.

The strike went on for four days, and the company did not back me. Worst of all, some striking union workers ruined my car, a two-toned, blue and buff 1953 model 210 Chevy. Just prior, while driving back to Philadelphia, I had tried to pass a truck carrying concrete cinder blocks. As I pulled up to pass, the chain holding the blocks gave way and the cinder blocks fell into the road. I hit them, sending my car onto its side. When the driver pulled over and saw I was okay, he was really apologetic.

"What can I do for you?" he asked.

"Well," I said. "I need a new car."

The trucking company could not find me a car fast enough. My uncle Frank Hogan, in the auto collision business, knew the people at Davidson Chevrolet in Medford and helped arrange for me to get a new car, which the truck's insurance company paid for. I was ecstatic. My first decent car!

Then the striking union guys slashed my tires. They hammered nails into boards, like spikes, and ran the nails up and down the sides of my new car. I wanted to fight them, but in the end, I went to the division manager.

"I'm leaving," I said.

"No, no." He reminded me of my recent promotion and award, trying to convince me to stay. "You don't want to leave. This will blow over."

I was their youngest executive, but I said, "My work ethic is getting me in trouble."

The company would not even repair my car because it would look like they were backing me, not the union. Right then I decided I would never work for a union company again, and I didn't. I gave Philco six weeks' notice and assisted them in finding my replacement. They thought they could get me to change my mind, but I am as stubborn and principled as Ma Hartley. So I left Philco and Philadelphia at the same time, and I never looked back.

CHAPTER 5

A NORMAL GUY

After renting a house with four guys, I wanted a place of my own. So I bought a small, newly-built cape on Wilson Road in Bedford, just northwest of Boston. A nice, quiet place to live, Bedford had an A&P supermarket across the road from a small shopping center with a post office, a dry cleaner, and a package store—Genetti's Wine and Spirits.

On April 19, 1775, local Minuteman Nathaniel Page had carried the town's flag in the first battle of the American Revolution at the battle of the Old North Bridge in neighboring Concord. Woven more than a century before, the crimson-painted flag portrays an armored arm bearing a sword and the Latin words for "Conquer or Die." It is now preserved at the town library.[14]

Like the area's colonial militiamen who had to be ready to fight at a minute's notice, during my time in Bedford, America also had to be ready to fight at a minute's notice. The development of the atomic bomb toward the end of the Second World War launched the United States and the Soviet Union into a Cold War marked by the rapid production of nuclear weapons. After moving to Bedford, I briefly worked at Sylvania's Electric Products Division Avionics Laboratory in nearby Waltham, helping to develop the radar system for the B-1 bomber. A long-range military stealth aircraft, the bomber was designed to carry nuclear bombs and short-range attack missiles. My brother, Curtis, also worked at Sylvania and had encouraged me to join him.

After marrying during his junior year of college, Curtis and his wife, Corinne, had a daughter, Lawnie. Corinne had graduated from Boston's Wheelock College the same year my brother and I graduated from Tufts. My brother and his family briefly moved to Buffalo, New York, where Curtis worked for Sylvania and Corinne taught at a nearby elementary school, sometimes bringing Lawnie with her. I often drove up to visit. After moving back to Massachusetts, Curtis continued working for Sylvania, and Corinne taught in Melrose. However, a few months shy of their fourth wedding anniversary, Corinne died at Mount Auburn Hospital in Cambridge from blood clots in her lungs, possibly the result of heart problems related to rheumatic fever, which she'd had as a child. At the time of her death, Corine was six-months pregnant with their second child.

Devastated, Curtis and Lawnie moved in with our sister's family above the first-floor apartment where our father still lived on Gardner Road. They slept in a small bedroom under the third-floor eaves. While Curtis and Frank worked, Shirley cared for Lawnie along with her own young children. Shirley's life was very hard. The big claw-foot tub in the bathroom was often filled with dirty clothes, which she washed and hung out on the backyard line to dry. However, Lawnie recalls how kindly Shirley treated her, like one of her own children. While I did not stay at Sylvania long enough to get much accomplished, Curtis worked there for nearly twenty years.

During my short time at Philco, I had met Richard "Dick" Kirchberger, an older sales representative for Airtron Inc., a microwave component company in Morristown, New Jersey. Dick enjoyed talking with me and often took me out for lunch when he swung by Philadelphia. After learning that I no longer worked for Philco, he spoke to Airtron's president, Dave Engel, and the company's technical director, Tore Anderson, who had been an influential engineer at MIT's Rad Lab.

"You've got to hire this guy," Dick told them.

A key microwave company, Airtron had pioneered flexible waveguide, which bends without attenuating (reducing) the microwave signal. In early radar systems, a simple, forward-looking parabolic-shaped dish often served as the antenna. On land, the dish is usually located in a tower. However, to protect it from the weather, the radar equipment is housed inside a shed or other covering on the ground. On ships, the equipment is below deck. But because microwaves travel in a straight line-of-sight path and do not bend to follow the curvature of the earth, radar systems must scan to receive the microwave signal. So Airtron developed a flexible waveguide that moves. In search mode, the antenna scans to sweep across a target area, much like scanning the ground in the dark with a flashlight. To achieve this motion, the rigid rectangular waveguide must be replaced with an equivalent flexible rectangular waveguide, i.e., a bellows. A flexible jacket, normally made of rubber, contains the waveguide and retains the shape of the beam while preventing it from damaging the thin-walled bellows.

The development of commercial and military radar systems was instrumental in detecting submarines, mapping terrain, blind landings on aircraft carriers, air traffic control, search and rescue missions, identifying targets, developing gun and missile control systems, strategic bombings, and more. The type of antenna varies depending on the application. However, to transmit and receive microwave signals from a shared antenna, these radar systems required ferrite duplexers.

While reading technical journals, I had become interested in ferrite devices. A ceramic compound made of iron and other metals, ferrite was first mass-produced for use in radio equipment. On Dick's recommendation and because of my preliminary research on the technology, Airtron asked me to co-found a new division making waveguide microwave components for the military. However, after living in Philadelphia with its wet, icy winters, I had no interest in moving to New Jersey. Enrolled in day courses to complete my doctorate of engineering at Northeastern University in Boston, I wanted to stay in the city that had become a leading center for microwave engineering. I also wanted to ski and play hockey. At my insistence, Airtron located the new division on Vassar Street in Cambridge, behind MIT's former Rad Lab, and in 1956 I became the co-founder and technical director of Airtron's ferrite material and component division.

While driving to work one icy morning after sunrise on February 1, 1957, I pulled out of Henry Street, near the Memorial Drive overpass I had designed in trade school. As I followed several cars onto Brookline Street, the car in front of me abruptly stopped to pick up a passenger. Unable to stop, I veered left, bumping the car ahead of me. After pulling over to the curb, I climbed out to inspect the other vehicle, which appeared undamaged, when a passing car slid on the ice and rammed into the stopped vehicle, pinning me between them. After hitting me, the driver backed up and sped off, leaving me lying in the street. The pain was excruciating. My left leg was broken, and the skin flapped open. My right leg was completely crushed, exposing my bones. Only bloody tissue held my right leg together.

The other driver and his passenger must have run for help, because I never spoke to them. In shock, I looked up to see a young girl, who appeared to be six or seven years old; she must have been walking to school and stopped to see what had happened. Somehow, I pulled a pen and paper from my shirt pocket and wrote down Doc Levine's name and telephone exchange. "Call this number," I said, handing the paper to the girl. "Tell him I've been hit by a car, and I'll be at the Mount Auburn Hospital."

Whether she made the call or someone else did, I do not know. All I remember is the girl, who ran off with the paper. Unknown to me, the rescue wagons only went to Cambridge City Hospital, which is where they brought me. All alone, I waited in the emergency room. Then in walked a doctor, accompanied by two young interns. With barely a word to me, the doctor, whose last name I later learned was Lundgren, marked both my legs with a pen.

"Here's where we want to amputate," he told the interns.

I had a comminuted compound fracture, combined with a broken pelvis and internal injuries. Worried I might get an infection, the doctor wanted to remove my legs below the knee joints and fit me with prosthetics. By then the pain had returned full force, but when I realized the doctor planned to cut off my legs, I said, "My doctor should be here." I did not want them operating before Doc Levine showed up. That was my biggest concern, *Where is my doctor?*

"We can't wait for him," Dr. Lundgren said. "This is an emergency."

"My doctor's on his way," I repeated, hoping to stop them. "I know he's on his way."

Meanwhile, Doc Levine and Viola were at the Mount Auburn hospital, trying to figure out where I was. After learning I had been taken to Cambridge City Hospital, Doc Levine called a colleague, Dr. Sullivan, across the Charles River at Massachusetts General Hospital. Still wearing an apron covered in plaster from his last patient, Dr. Sullivan arrived at the emergency room and looked me over.

"Let's see what we can do before we talk about cutting off his legs," Dr. Sullivan said.

"If he gets an infection, he is going to lose the whole leg," Dr. Lundgren argued.

Thankfully, by then Viola had driven Doc Levine to the hospital and described my injuries to him.

"No," Doc Levine said. "We are not going amputate."

Instead, an ambulance drove me directly from the emergency room to Longwood Hospital, several miles away in Jamaica Plain.

"We are going to try something new," Dr. Sullivan informed me, visiting my room. "Can you handle what I'm about to suggest? We are going to repeatedly re-break your leg while it heals."

When you do that, the leg kind of knits itself back together. Each time you break the bone, it grows a little more as it heals. So every other day for six weeks, the nurses carried a metal rail into my room and clamped it onto on the side of my bed. The rail was for me to hold onto because I had elected to forgo pain medication.

"All set?" they would ask.

"Okay." I would grab the rail and grit my teeth. Then they would pull my right leg apart and break my bones all over again.

For several months, I lay in traction with my legs stretched out, unable to move. I got painful bedsores and blisters that the nurses had to spread with a salve. I remained in the hospital so long that I became a fixture. Everyone on my floor knew me, in part due to my calculator.

At Airtron, I had hired a young engineer, James "Jim" Regan. About six feet three, with a thin build, Jim would have been taller, but as a child he had contracted polio. Jim was studying engineering at MIT. Although he had never previously worked with ferrite technology, Jim was meticulous about data—very precise. After my accident, he and another guy I worked with, Don Rich, shortened the legs of a drafting table and slanted the top so it straddled my hospital bed. I owe those guys a lot. Being able to work was really important to me. That table saved me.

Jim and Don also brought me a Monroe calculator, a heavy, old-fashioned, mechanical adding machine with columns of numbers and a crank handle that made a distinct clunking sound whenever I cleared the counter or register. In fact, the machine made so much noise that at night the nurses would rush into my room with their hands raised over their heads and ask me not to use it.

"Ken," the head nurse explained, "you can't use the calculator at night. We can hear it all over the hospital—*kajunk, kajunk, kajunk*..."

Unable to get out of bed, I amused myself by reading through my *Machinery's Handbook*, a reference guide for mechanical engineers and draftsmen. I experimented with various ways of folding a dollar bill to use as a measuring tool. I even calculated the outside diameter of various screw sizes, such as a number 2 or a number 6, to figure out how they derived the different numbers.* If I was going to be there that long, I thought I might as well learn something.

The drafting table allowed me to keep designing and sketching. While in traction, I invented a dual-mode transducer, al-

---

* It turns out that a number zero screw is 0.060 of an inch in diameter, and every screw size above that moves up by 0.013 of an inch. So, what you have to do is take a number 2 screw and say it is 0.060 plus N multiplied by 0.013 (where 'N' is the screw size). When N is 2, you have $0.060 + 2 \times 0.013$ or 0.086 inches in diameter. That gives you the outside diameter of the screw. But I could not figure out where the 0.013 came from. It should be noted that catheter diameter increases by 0.013 inches. A 6 French catheter is .078 inch diameter, whereas a 7 French catheter is 0.091 inch diameter. I was curious that both are related to a factor of 0.013 inches.

lowing for the design of a four-port switchable ferrite circulator. Capable of combining or separating two waveguides (one with a horizontal polarization, the other with a vertical polarization) into a common circular waveguide, the dual-mode transducer could transmit microwaves in both horizontal and vertical polarization.* By adding a dual-mode transducer to each end of a ferrite-loaded circular waveguide section, I could create a switchable four-port duplexer. This allowed a transmitter and receiver to share a single antenna in which the heating frequency and the detection frequency share a common antenna.**

The dual-mode transducer turned out to be a very important device, particularly during the Cuban Missile Crisis. But at the time, I was more concerned about whether I would be able to skate or ski again. When it comes to achieving something, I am a nut. Having turned twenty-five just two weeks after my accident, I wanted to get back on my feet and go to work and do the things I enjoyed, like playing sports, so I kept asking the doctors and nurses, "When can I go home?" and "When will I be able to skate and ski again?"

They were not very encouraging. One doctor said I would never walk again without braces, but I could not accept that. *As soon as I get out of here, I'll exercise my butt off*, I thought. *I am going to make it.*

---

* Signals come in one of two polarizations, horizontal and vertical. The polarizations can be separated by switching the field of the ferrite from horizontal to vertical. There is a transducer on both ends of the circular waveguide/ferrite section. So, you can put the transmitter and the receiver ports on one end, and two antenna ports on the other end.

** To accommodate the electromagnetic field, hollow, round circular waveguide was used. The circular waveguide contained a ferrite rod centrally supported in a low-loss dielectric sleeve (quartz), which was supported in turn by a length of conductive circular waveguide. On each end of the circular waveguide/ferrite assembly, a dual mode transducer was attached. The dual mode transducer mated to the circular waveguide and transitioned the horizontal and the vertical polarized signals to the mating orthogonal rectangular waveguides, creating, in essence, a switchable four-port circulator.

While I recovered, Jim Regan often came by the hospital to talk about business and keep me up to speed with work. He also brought me drafting paper and my textbooks, which I stacked all over my bed; to change the sheets or feed me, the nurses had to move everything. I do not recall having many visitors, not even family, but after a couple of months, the nurses wheeled a familiar face into my hospital room on a gurney—my uncle Chet. He had been driving an oil tanker truck for Penn Oil when the truck's flywheel shattered, busting through the floorboard and breaking his leg. While recovering from surgery, Chet ended up in the bed next to mine. Unlike me, Chet had lots of visitors—all his lady friends. One suggested putting a ladder up to the window so she and Chet could elope. After they left, the two of us would joke around, like about the big metal bed pans that the nurses used to slide under us. They were so cold, we thought they stored them in the refrigerator. When Chet left, I was sorry to see him go.

Late that spring, a team of doctors came into my room with the head nurse and the president of the hospital, a lady named Mrs. Courtney. A radiologist, general practitioner, and Dr. Sullivan accompanied them.

"I'm the spokesman for the group," Dr. Sullivan said, "but what I am going to say has been agreed to by everyone in this room. You've been asking everyone the same question, 'Am I going to skate or ski again?'" Then he looked me straight in the eye and said, "You will never, ever, ski or skate again. Be happy if you learn to walk without a brace." He was very emphatic.

"I can't accept that," I said.

"That's what we are afraid of," he replied. "You can't get despondent. You have to accept it, because that is a fact."

"Geez," I said. "I want to be a ski instructor. I play hockey and baseball. That's an important part of my life."

Life had been kind of tough—being told at age thirteen that I would have to leave home, believing that I had lost all hope of marrying Nancy, leaving Philco after the strike. But not being able to ski or skate for the rest of my life was unthinkable.

Then three days later, into my hospital room walked Nancy.

"Well, now maybe you'll be a normal guy," Nancy said when she saw me.

I was stunned. I had not seen Nancy in five years and never expected her to come, but Viola had told her where to find me. Two weeks prior, Nancy had filed for a divorce from Fred, with whom she had two young children. Soon after she became pregnant with their first child, Fred had run off with a waitress from the restaurant where they both worked. When he apologized and came back, Nancy accepted him. A couple years later, she became pregnant with their second child, and Fred ran off with another waitress—or it might have been the same one again. The third time he ran off, Nancy refused to take him back.

How could her husband have been so mean? So cruel? When I found out how Fred had treated her, I wanted to kill him. If only I had asked Nancy to marry me. My feelings had not changed toward her at all. She was the missing part of my life. I just worshipped her.

A few days after Nancy's visit, the hospital released me in a full-body brace. The treatment put well over an inch back into my right leg, but it remained one inch shorter than my left leg. The tibia had grown back together, but the fibula never rejoined. A two-inch gap, where the smaller bone is rounded off, limited my range of motion. To stand, I had to strap a brace around my chest. A hinged cuff circled each knee. A pair of steel rods extended all the way down my legs to the heel of my shoes. With crutches, I could finally hobble around, but Dr. Sullivan cautioned me not to get my hopes up about sports. "Just be happy that you can walk again," he said.

As soon as I got out of the hospital, Nancy and I resumed dating, but after nearly half a year without pay, I was broke. Two days after my accident, the police had caught the driver of the car that hit me. An escaped convict serving a life sentence at the Concord Reformatory, the state's oldest prison for men, he had stolen the car that hit me. So the car insurance company was not liable for the accident. However, because they had never seen something this bad, they wrote me a check for $5,000. Unfortunately, I never received it. The insurance company had a deposit record for the check, which was cashed, but I never got the money. My lawyer explained he could not do anything—particularly as the guy who had hit me was married to two different women at the same time and was not supporting either of them.

"It's a dead issue," my attorney said. "Forget it. You're not going to get any money out of a guy who can't support his families."

When you are in the hospital, you have more things to worry about than a check, so I let it go. Airtron's sick leave policy provided one week's compensation for each year served at the company. At the time of my accident, I had worked there less than a year. Although the company let me keep my job, they cut me off with one week's pay and did not resume paying me until I returned to work. I never asked my family for help. I owed the hospital so much money I had to take out a mortgage on my house to repay my doctors. Beacon Medical Supply, which made my braces, agreed to cut my bill in half if I returned my leg supports each time they fit me with a new pair. Even so, I was unable to make mortgage payments on my ski property in Snowville and lost the house without ever getting to fix it up.

I eagerly anticipated returning to work at Airtron. However, because I could not climb stairs in my braces and buildings were not required to be handicapped accessible, this created a problem. To solve it, Jim Regan and Don Rich asked the construction crew modifying the building for our laboratories to secure a winch on top of the three-story roof. Then they rigged up a metal T-bar connected to a steel cable. Each morning when I arrived at work, I held onto the bar like I was doing a chin up, and Jim or Don would crank the winch to hoist me through a second-story window. At the end of the day, I did the same thing in reverse.

That June, my brother married his second wife, Janet Evensen. After moving back from Philadelphia, I had invited Curtis to a dance at the University Club of Boston, where he met Janet. My brother wanted me to be the best man at their wedding, but because of my leg braces, Janet said no. So they made me an usher. Instead of using crutches, I walked down the aisle with two canes, which looked a little more dignified. However, my canes got caught in a floor register, which had been covered by a white runner, and I did a face plant. Everybody in the adjacent pews jumped up to help me and retrieve my canes, which were sticking out of the register, but Janet made a loud comment about not wanting me there. My brother and Janet later bought a house near mine in Bedford at the other end of Wilson Road. Together they had a daughter, Diane. However, Janet never liked me, and after their marriage, Curtis and I drifted apart.

Although my doctors said I would never ski or skate again, I proved them wrong. I have always been determined, like when my mother told me I had to be out of the house at sixteen and I became intent on learning a trade. Sometimes things happen along the way that you cannot control or predict, like Bill Linvill encouraging me to go to college, which is why you can't plan too far ahead. At the end of five years, I would ask myself, "Did I achieve what I wanted to?" Then I would set my goal for the next five years.

After getting hit by the car, my goal was to learn to walk again without crutches. For one, I am very competitive. I also wanted to regain my strength so I could marry Nancy and support a family. When she came to the hospital, that was the turning point. The summer after getting out of the hospital, I went up to my grandmother's farmhouse and stayed for a month. I still needed leg braces to walk, but every day I hobbled down to the lake on my crutches. At the water's edge, I unstrapped my braces and swam one and a quarter miles to the other side. Unable to stand without my braces and with no one to help me, I sat in the water to rest for a bit before swimming back.

Nancy often met me at the farmhouse to help with my exercises, but Ma Hartley got a little nasty. "You couldn't keep your marriage together, and now, on the rebound, you're going to take my grandson to raise your kids?" she asked Nancy.

"I would appreciate it if you did not say that again," I told her.

My grandmother had a lot of good characteristics. One was that she always told you where she stood, but that was a double-edged sword. She thought Nancy only wanted someone to raise her kids. Ma had been in a similar position when she had married Pop, but my grandmother was tough. Nancy was gentle—a real lady. I never heard a foul word out of her, but after the way her previous husband had treated her, Nancy's self-esteem was wiped out. Having gone through something similar, my grandmother should have been a little more aware, but the next time Nancy came up to the farmhouse with me, Ma said it again.

"She's taking you on the rebound," she said.

After that, Nancy and I did not go up to the farmhouse for many years. To be with her was all that mattered. After Nancy's divorce was finalized, I proposed. When Nancy said yes, I felt like I was sitting on top of the world, but we still had to work out some details.

"Nancy, I have some personal questions for you," I said. "Do you want a refrigerator or a ring?"

"I'll take the refrigerator," she said.

I knew she would say that. I actually owned a refrigerator but did not have much furniture. My dining room table was a card table, but I like to make things. So I set up a basement woodworking shop and began building my own furniture.

On Monday, April 7, 1958, I married Nancy in the front parlor of my father's house on Gardner Road in Cambridge. I wore a blue suit and had to pull the pants on over my leg braces. In those days, they did not have Velcro, so I was all buckled up. By then, my mother was living in Japan. The few who came to the wedding were my father, Doc Levine, Viola, my cousin Richie (who stood up for me), and Nancy's sister, Carol. That was it. The minister from Prospect Congregational performed the ceremony, and I went back to work the following day.

At the time, Nancy's daughter, Randee, was four, and her son, Michael, was nearly three. Their father, Fred, had moved to the West Coast and showed no interest in them. He made no child support payments and never sent cards for birthdays or Christmas. Wanting to start anew with Nancy, I hired a constable to track him down. Then I went to court to adopt his children, which Fred readily agreed to. While still wearing leg braces, I used some of the money from the mortgage I had taken out to build an addition, doubling the size of our house so Randee and Michael could have their own rooms. After finishing, I built a two-car garage. The remaining money I put toward my hospital bills, which took a decade to repay.

Inheriting a family was hard. That first year or so, Randee did not want me in her room. At bedtime, I would walk up to her door and say, "Goodnight," but I would not go in.

"You're not my dad," she would tell me.

Nancy did not want Randee to say that, but I told her, "Don't say anything. It's up to me to get to know her better. Let her get to know me."

I am not a person who hugs somebody. Growing up, I had never been hugged by my family. We did not do that, but to be cordial, I said goodnight to Randee through her door. I did not expect Nancy to tell Randee to like me. I never said, "I adopted you. You're my child now." I would not do that, but as Randee got a little older, she warmed up to me, saying that I would always be her father.

Nancy was a wonderful wife. Her whole life, all she wanted was to have a family. She loved to cook and sew. She made potato pancakes that you would not believe—thin and crispy. Put a little apple sauce on them, and they were great. Nancy was a natural mother, and she was so beautiful. On Saturdays, whenever I dropped off my shirts at the dry cleaners, the two older ladies who worked there would ask me not to bring them in.

"It's nothing against you, Mr. Carr," they would say, making a little joke of it, "but we wish your wife would come instead of you. We just love to watch her walk across the parking lot."

Nancy was so classy. She had a nice way about her. It was not intentional; it was her nature. She was just terrific.

When the doctors said that I would never walk or ski again, I was really down, but the day that Nancy walked into my hospital room was the most important moment of my life. She turned my life around.

CHAPTER 6

BREAKING THROUGH

Being in a full body brace made life difficult. Unable to attend class, I reluctantly dropped out of graduate school for the second time. Since Airtron had declined to pay me while I was recuperating in the hospital, I chose not to give them ownership of the dual-mode transducer. However, when I returned to work and described the transducer to them, they offered to make up my pay in exchange for the design details.

"You can never make it up," I said. I had lost everything except my house in Bedford.

During my hospital stay, I had written a paper explaining my design for the transducer, which involved a ridged "finline" waveguide with a very thin ridge and a small gap between the ridges. The full technique included the circular waveguide equivalent, but I kept these details to myself.

The technical review committee for an annual engineering conference, WESCON, accepted my paper and invited me to present it at the conference in San Francisco. Due to my leg braces, I was unable to attend, so the co-founder of Airtron's ferrite division presented the paper for me. When I later received a copy of the conference digest, my name was not included as the author. Instead, the digest listed the name of the man who had presented my paper. Because I had not patented the technique for the transducer, it was already in the public domain. However, after the way that Airtron had treated me, I had no intention of staying with the company.

In 1958, Litton Industries acquired Airtron and Monroe Calculator, which had a facility in Morris Plains, New Jersey. At the time, Monroe Calculator's Morris Plains workers were on strike. To break the strike, Litton planned to relocate Monroe Calculator's facilities elsewhere. They also planned to consolidate Airtron and move the entire company, including the new ferrite division in Cambridge, to the Morris Plains facility. After learning of the move, I talked with some of the guys at work.

"Look," I said. "I am not moving to New Jersey." The skiing and skating there were just terrible, and I wanted to stay near Boston. Although I was still in braces, I hoped to skate and ski again.

At the time, Jim Regan and his wife, Marie, were on their honeymoon, so I sent him a telegram. "Don't worry about your job," I wrote. "We are not going to move. We are going to start a new company."

Forming Ferrotec

In 1958, the same year I married Nancy, two partners and I started Ferrotec Inc. Located in the vacated Boston Knitting Mills, a skinny, three-story building at 217 California Street in Newton, we developed ferrite devices such as isolators and duplexers for commercial, military, and space systems. Thankfully, since I still required braces to walk, the mill was equipped with a freight elevator, so I did not have to enter and exit through a window. Don Rich and I started the company with another Airtron engineer, Charles "Chuck" Carson. Don was the president. Chuck managed marketing and sales, and I was the technical director, later becoming president.

In any business, finding the right people to work with is key. It is not only about knowledge. It is about attitude. One of the first people I hired was Jim Regan, our senior engineer, who had completed four years of a five-year program at MIT and had a great attitude. One of the finest engineers I have ever known, Jim did most of the testing and worked as hard as I did. With Jim, I knew I could build a team.

To get us started, Henry J. Riblet, a key player in MIT's Rad Lab, invested $20,000 in our new company. An inventor and former math professor, Henry Riblet had co-founded Microwave Development Labs (MDL) in 1948 in nearby Needham Heights. The company quickly became a global leader designing and developing microwave waveguide components and microwave waveguide subsystems used in both commercial broadcasting and military systems (including radar). MDL's sales manager, Nat Tucker, and its chief engineer, Edward Salzberg, also invested in Ferrotec. However, without enough money to pay our own salaries, Jim, Don, and I, along with several Ferrotec technical staff members, all worked for Henry Riblet during the day. He gave us a tough but fair deal. During the day from eight until five o'clock, we did math calculations, designing microwave cavities and filters for MDL. Then we drove back to the knitting mill and made ferrite devices for Ferrotec until eleven at night.

Don, Chuck, Jim, and I were about the same age and willing to work hard. We were also all newlyweds with great wives who were very supportive. We took great pride in building components for radar systems and were very successful. If it involved microwaves, we were capable of designing it. We even made our own ferrite material. In its uncured state, ferrite resembles sludge. You can cut it like butter, but after you fire it in an oven at a very high temperature, it becomes as hard as ceramic. After compounding, curing, and cutting the ferrite blocks into slabs, we polished them with a diamond wheel or sent them to another company for grinding.

I would go to any extreme to make the date, to get the job done. Nancy was impressed. She knew I was going to be successful. It was just my attitude. I never had a problem getting a design contract. I was very confident, and she appreciated that. I was getting a salary from MDL, and I was making money. But like the rest of the guys, I did not get a lot of sleep.

In the beginning, only two employees worked at Ferrotec's facility during the day: Edward Antoon, the chief chemist who made our ferrite material, and Chuck Carson, who answered the phone. When a customer called with a question, Chuck would say, "The person you need to talk to is with a customer, but let me check with my technical staff. I'll have them look over the problem, and we'll call you back tomorrow."

At night the rest of us came in and wrote down the answers to the customers' questions. The following day, Chuck would call them back. To hire additional technicians, we got them on MDL's payroll. However, to attract contractors we needed photos of our operation. We owned laboratory instruments and had built our own workbenches, but because our employees worked for MDL during the day, we lacked people to sit at them. Our building adjoined the Willis Tent Company, so one day Don Rich and I walked next door and asked the owner if we could borrow his employees. In exchange for a free lunch and one hour's pay, the tent company's employees dressed in rented lab coats, and we photographed them sitting at our benches. Although it was cheating, it worked. The photos helped us win our first production order, building two-port waveguide ferrite isolators for the first long-range anti-aircraft missile system: the Bomarc.

Designed to protect North American airspace, the three-story, supersonic Bomarc missile had an 18-foot wingspan and could carry a conventional explosive or a nuclear warhead. It also had a range of more than four hundred miles.[15] Boeing produced the missile but contracted Westinghouse Electric Corporation in Baltimore to make the radar system for the airborne target seeker, which guides the missile toward its target. Westinghouse contracted us to build the isolators.

I wanted our servicemen to have the best products and became very involved in military weapons systems. However, when we shipped our first batch of isolators to Westinghouse, all one hundred were rejected because the threads were incorrect. We were devastated, and the mistake almost sank our company.

Thankfully, the guys we worked with at MDL said, "Oh, we know how to fix that."

They took a clamp and put a ball bearing on the tapped hole of an isolator to tighten it up. Then they squeezed the ball bearing and pushed in the thread, so the thread gauge went in properly. After our machinists spent a couple of days fixing all of the threads, we shipped the same batch of isolators back to Baltimore, and they all passed. As additional contracts started coming in, Henry Riblet allowed us to resign from MDL and work full-time for our new company. Within four years, Ferrotec quickly expanded, more than quadrupling the size of our facilities and employing 110 people to become one of the largest U.S. companies that specialized in developing ferrite devices.

New Techniques

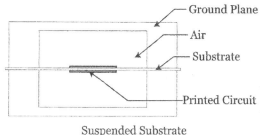

Suspended Substrate

At Ferrotec, I invented a new transmission line: suspended substrate. In a conventional integration technique known as strip transmission line, or "stripline," a printed circuit center conductor is sandwiched between a pair of non-conductive dielectric plates. This involved bonding a thin copper film under compression at an elevated temperature to each of the non-conductive surfaces of the dielectric plates. Using a milling machine, I channeled out the ground planes supporting the integrated circuit assembly and replaced the dielectric material with air, which is very low loss. My technique improved the performance and reliability of the transmission line, which made it function better than any other technique available at the time. The creation of suspended substrate was a significant advancement in microwave integration. Replacing the non-conductive dielectric plates with lower-loss air dielectric eliminated the connectors and circuit interconnections and resulted in a performance approaching that of a waveguide assembly, at a fraction of the size and weight.

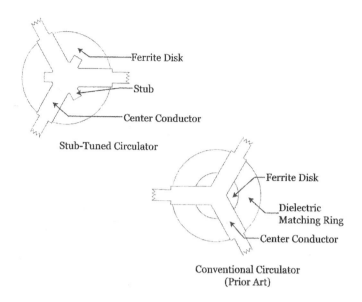

Stub-Tuned Circulator

Conventional Circulator
(Prior Art)

Using this same technique, I invented additional devices including the stub-tuned, three-port ferrite circulator. A stub is a protrusion of the center conductor. Normally, this type of circulator had a large dielectric ring around the ferrite disk. The ferrite disk in the stub-tuned circulator is the same diameter as the disk in a conventional circulator; however, the ferrite in the stub-tuned circulator is slightly thicker. The increased thickness of the ferrite plus the addition of the stubs (which inherently match the circulator), eliminated the need for the dielectric ring. The substrate is actually a thin printed circuit etched on both sides of the substrate, the copper film forming the 50ohm transmission line. The inherently matched stub-tuned circulator operates over a broader frequency band than the conventional circulator. Eliminating the quarter-wave ceramic matching ring, or transformer, further reduced the size, weight, and cost of the circulator while improving reliability.

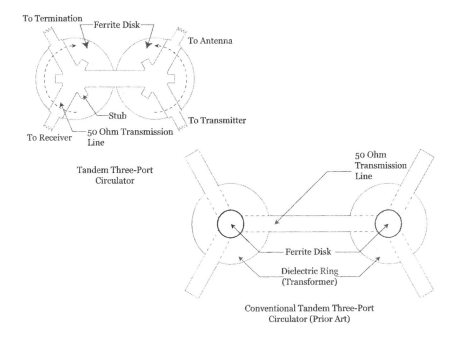

Tandem Three-Port Circulator

Conventional Tandem Three-Port Circulator (Prior Art)

This, in turn, led to the invention of the tandem-connected ferrite circulator: two three-port circulators in a series or on a common substrate. If the frequency of the receiver is different from the transmitter frequency (as with the use of radiometric sensing), the antenna must share the same (or a common) aperture. (This later satisfied the promise I made to the FDA and the American Association of Blood Banks to always measure temperature at the same point that energy (heating or cooling) is applied.) The diplexer, located in the receiver port, separates the receive frequency from the transmit frequency and directs unwanted energy to the terminated port of the four-port circulator. The direction of circulation is shown on the tandem three-port circulator.

With radar, you usually transmit a microwave signal and receive a reflected return signal, or echo. By reducing circuit loss, suspended substrate increased radar range and significantly improved the system's sensitivity, enabling it to detect smaller targets at a greater distance. The return signal also came back with less clutter. By eliminating the dielectric matching transformers, solder joints, and connectors, my transmission line had fewer parts, which made it smaller and more reliable. This was a major breakthrough.

In addition to using suspended substrate to improve the performance of ferrite devices, we used this new transmission line to improve the performance of a whole series of microwave components, such as diode switches, filters, terminations, and DC blocks. Later, the U.S. Navy and Air Force also used it extensively in the fire-control radars of the F-14, F-15, and F-18 fighter planes, which employed radar-guided "fire-and-forget" missile systems to direct a missile toward its target. I eventually used this same technique to develop medical products.

During the Cold War, the Soviets obtained much of their weapons know-how by spying on the United States, but their missiles lacked the fire-and-forget advantage. To illuminate the target, their aircraft had to remain in the vicinity of the target. If an aircraft left the target area too soon, their missiles had no guidance. Because missiles are shaped like a bullet with just enough of a wing to keep them stable, they fly up to ten times faster than planes, which are vulnerable to being shot down—particularly if they are under attack and have to stick around to illuminate a target. But fire-and-forget missiles have the ability to track the target on their own. The fighter aircraft can fire the missile but does not have to maintain contact with the missile or the target, hence "fire-and-forget." This is better for the military and for the pilot, because it takes longer to grow a pilot than to build a plane.

Using suspended substrate as a transmission line gave Ferrotec a distinct advantage over other companies competing for military contracts. Our technique lowered production costs, reduced size, and improved reliability. It also improved performance. As a result, we could guarantee characteristics no one else could match. The circulator alone won us contracts. The only way to beat it was to duplicate it. I received patents on the components, including the circulator, but as with the dual-mode transducer, I did not patent the suspended substrate technology for the transmission line. I used it as a trade secret. I received a lot of criticism for giving away the goose that laid the golden egg. Should I have applied for a patent? In retrospect, yes. But, like the Shakers, a Christian sect founded in the late 1700s, I felt that knowledge—particularly for a new transmission line—should be shared.

Ever since beginning to build my own furniture, I have admired the Shakers. Well-known for crafting simple, well-designed objects, their motto was, "Hands to work, and hearts to God." Nancy and I visited several of their communities, including Canterbury Shaker Village, just north of Concord, New Hampshire. Everything they made was designed for efficiency and built to last. They also shared everything they made. Like the Shakers, I believe that if you make something it should be functional and long-lasting. You should also make it simple by eliminating extra parts. And some things should be general knowledge, which is why I felt everyone should be free to use my new transmission line.

A Special Delivery

At home in Bedford, while still hampered by leg braces, I worked to finish the addition on our house with extra urgency. Nancy and I were expecting our first child, and I was thrilled. Whether the baby was a boy or girl did not make a difference. Nancy's and my first child together, the baby's arrival felt extra special. On January 10, 1959, I drove Nancy the twenty miles from Bedford to the Longwood Hospital, the same hospital where she had walked back into my life nearly two years before.

"Don't speed! Don't speed!" Nancy gasped between labor pains.

I tend to drive fast, but I was a basket case. When we got to the hospital, the staff wheeled Nancy into a delivery room while I waited outside. About half an hour later, at 8:40 a.m., our daughter Kirsten arrived. She weighed eight pounds three ounces—a good size—but the first time I held her, she seemed so fragile. The day that I drove Nancy and Kirsten home, I was so happy.

Randee, then five, took very well to having a baby sister. Later, the girls shared a bedroom. Michael, just three and a half, had a harder time adjusting, but Nancy made sure to include him. After I'd lived alone so long, having three children filled our home with activity.

Project Mercury

In April 1959, the newly established National Aeronautics and Space Administration—today simply known as NASA—launched a test program to send chimpanzees into space. Part of Project Mercury, the program aimed to discover whether humans could survive the rigors of space travel. To test the high g-forces endured while re-entering the earth's atmosphere, some chimps endured a ride on a giant centrifuge at Johnsville's Aviation Medical Acceleration Laboratory. Dubbed a "gruesome merry-go-round," the centrifuge spun the chimps and would-be astronauts in a gondola-like capsule at the end of a 50-foot arm.[16] On January 31, 1961, the first "astrochimp," Ham, was buckled inside the nose cone of a space capsule attached to a Mercury-Redstone rocket at Cape Canaveral in Florida. Sixteen minutes after blast-off, the capsule splashed down in the ocean, making Ham the first hominid in space.[17] A second chimp, Enos, rocketed into space on November 29, 1961, orbiting the earth 2.5 times, before landing in the ocean three hundred miles south of Bermuda.[18]

Stationed aboard naval ships, NASA observers successfully retrieved the chimps. However, as the capsules re-entered the earth's atmosphere, NASA momentarily lost track of them. Since the capsules traveled at a velocity of up to seven miles per second during re-entry, if NASA lost track of one for even a few seconds, it could land in a completely different ocean. After reading an article in which NASA described the problem. I wrote them a letter, confident that we could help.

To provide contact with the recovery ship, each space capsule employs multiple antennas. This allows the recovery ship to detect the capsule, regardless of its position or orientation during re-entry. The antennas transmit microwaves in patterns that partially overlap. If the overlapping portion of the signal being transmitted is in phase, or coherent, it is considered additive beam forming, which strengthens the signal. However, if the overlapping antenna patterns are out of phase, the resulting pattern is considered subtractive, which produces a void, or a blind spot.

Assuming that NASA had a blind spot (a *null*) occurring during re-entry, I suggested that we could solve this problem by making a microwave ferrite phase shifter to wobulate, or wiggle, the antenna pattern during re-entry. Aiming a radar signal is a little like aiming the beam of a flashlight. If it is dark and I aim two flashlights in a fixed position, I may not see you if you are standing in the space between where the two beams are shining. But if I wiggle the flashlights, I will see you. NASA wrote back and asked if I could build the proposed phase shifter. So I worked in the lab with Jim Regan, who was my right arm, and we built it.

A ferrite phase shifter is reciprocal, meaning that the signal can transmit between any two ports regardless of the direction of the applied field. So we ran a center conductor back and forth along the length of the ferrite slab. You have three separate lines. This created a meander line between the ferrite dielectric slabs, which reduced the overall length of the phase shifter.

Next, we sandwiched two flat, rectangular slabs of ferrite (each approximately four inches long and half an inch wide) between a pair of thin conductive ground planes. Around this assembly, we wrapped a coil to produce a longitudinal magnetic field. Finally, we wound the center conductor back and forth to create three separate paths, or transmission lines. This allowed us to wiggle the microwave signal on the capsule so the recovery ship could continuously track it during re-entry.

The microwave phase shifter worked so well NASA asked Ferrotec to make twelve additional units. However, doing so would have required us to develop a space-qualified facility, which would have been costly and time consuming. Instead, I donated the design to NASA by giving them a paid-up patent license. This allowed the agency to use my invention to build additional units on their own at an existing facility, which they did. Two decades later, in 1983, NASA thanked me for my "creative development of a scientific contribution determined to be of significant value in the advancement of its Aerospace Technology Program" and awarded me its Certificate of Recognition. It was the second such certificate I received from the agency. The first, in 1980, was in recognition for a brief on a Dual-mode Microwave Antenna, which allowed two widely separated radiometric frequencies to enhance cancer detection. Jim and I took great pride in solving problems, and assisting NASA was very gratifying.

Project Dogwood

In the fall of 1962, Westinghouse contracted Ferrotec to develop a 150kW millimeter-wave four-port waveguide switch for a top-secret military spy program code-named "Dogwood." Westinghouse needed the ferrite switch to enable two antennas to "timeshare" a common transmitter and receiver for a radar system it was developing to allow a high-altitude aircraft to take high-resolution images, even in bad weather.

At the time, the Soviets were bringing all kinds of equipment into Cuba, and the U.S. government wanted to know what was going on. To gather data, surveillance aircraft, such as the U-2 high-altitude jet and the Vigilante all-weather bomber, flew high on the verge of space, out of range of most anti-aircraft missiles. However, they needed our switch for a special radar system to take microwave images of activities on the ground, such as trucks moving dirt or building silos to hide missile sites. Our switch would be installed in a particular plane.*

In a radar system, the transmitter generates an electronic pulse that the antenna sends out as a focused beam. The aircraft's

---

* On the electromagnetic spectrum, millimeter frequencies are part of the radio frequency spectrum and occur above the microwave band, but below infrared and visible frequencies. Frequencies below the visible spectrum are non-ionizing. The transmitter power is 150 kilowatt at a frequency of 35 GHz. At this frequency, the radar produces high resolution images approaching optical quality, but more importantly, it can be used at night to see through rain and fog.

mission defines the shape of the antenna and the microwave frequency being transmitted. A narrow beam, used for spotting aircraft, will transmit farther, illuminating distant targets. A wider down-looking beam for mapping and taking pictures will cover a larger area, particularly when transmitted from a supersonic aircraft flying at a high altitude near space, where there is less interference. The receiver then picks up the reflected signal, which depends upon the shape, size, and reflectivity of the target.

Viewing a target with a radar system is a little like driving past a picket fence in a car. By glimpsing small slivers of what is on the other side of the fence, your mind fills in the missing details. When a radar antenna switches from transmit to receive mode, the transmitter briefly shuts off between pulses during the listening period while waiting for the reflected signal to return. A row of blips consisting of echoes (called "radar returns") for a truck looks different from the blip pattern for a tank. So when the antennas pick up a particular pulse shape in the field of view, you know it is a tank rather than a truck in the same way your mind puts together the missing pieces while driving by a picket fence.

To make the four-port ferrite switch for Westinghouse, I used the dual-mode transducer that I developed at Longwood Hospital while recuperating from my car accident. We based it on the Faraday Rotation Principle. First observed in 1845 by the English scientist Michael Faraday, this principle relates to the rotation of the plane of polarization of an electromagnetic beam when affected by a magnetic field. In a circular guide, you can rotate the plane of polarization to switch the microwave signal between two ports, one horizontal and one vertical. My device allowed the transmitter to alternately switch between two antennas, so that the return signal reflected back to a common receiver. Prior to this, you needed two separate transmitters and two separate receivers, sharing the same frequency for two separate antennas. Our switch made the system more compact and enabled the radar system to collect more detailed images, particularly through clouds and fog.

Westinghouse originally gave us a time frame of six months to one year to build the switch. We were just beginning to work on it when I received an urgent call from Tom Van Rankin, manager of the Dogwood program for Westinghouse.

"Ken," he said, "we've got a problem. We are getting information about missile activity. The Soviets are putting missile sites in Cuba, and we need the switch *right now*."

I assured Tom that I would phone him back in one hour and let him know how fast we could make the switch. Then I called for a company technical review meeting.

"Look," I said. "I need five volunteers. First, I need one engineer." When I said that I was looking right at Jim Regan. "Then I need a mechanical guy and a draftsman, because we are going to draw the parts and make them on the spot—that is how fast we are going to do this. And I want a machinist, but he does not have to be full-time because I don't want him falling asleep at the machine and getting injured. The rest of the volunteer team is not going home until we complete the switch."

Then I told the guys my story about fighting fires near Ma Hartley's farm nearly fifteen years earlier.

"I stayed up for six nights and seven days," I said. "I was really tired the first day, but after that you become almost like a robot and just go through the motions. It is hard, but it can be done. I am not telling anyone to do something that I won't do. I would never do that. I am going to be here every day, but I need some volunteers."

To work as a team, it is important to know that the guy next to you feels the same way you do. I would never tell people that they "have to" stay. They had to volunteer on their own.

Jim Regan's hand went up first. "I'll be here too," he said.

"Good," I said. He was the engineer I needed.

Dan Binder, our shop foreman and supervisor, volunteered as the machinist. Gino, an Italian-American Korean War veteran who had been awarded a Purple Heart, volunteered as the draftsman. We kept other machinists on standby, alternating them, so they could work at the spur of the moment as needed. The fifth volunteer was me. We each got in touch with our families and told them we would not be coming home for a while. Then I called Tom at Westinghouse.

"I've got the guys we need," I said. "We're going to stay here twenty-four hours a day, seven days a week to complete the switch as fast as humanly possible."

Quartzite Processing, in nearby Malden, typically ground, cut, and polished our ferrite material. "We need full cooperation," I told the shop owner, Julius Westerman, who went by the nickname "Babe." "This is a top priority government job and needs to interrupt any other work you've already got going."

After Babe agreed, I called Westinghouse again and asked Tom for a transmitter to generate the kind of power we would need to test the switch. Typically, to test a unit we would fly back and forth to Baltimore with the switch, but on this occasion, we did not have time.

"I have a guy who can test the switch right here," I said.

The guy was Jim. We were a small company, but we were very capable. So, the following day an engineer from Westinghouse drove the transmitter up to our facility, set it up, and instructed Jim in how to use it. That way, we could test the switch on site while developing it. By working with the customer and involving them in the problem, we found the solution faster. We did not require a purchase order or change order. When you have that kind of rapport, people trust you. We had the same kind of an understanding with Quartzite. With the missile crisis, it was more important just to get the job done. We could settle the details later.

To do the testing, we devised some really new techniques, which we later used to develop even more high-powered switches. I worked on the problems, and we solved them as we went along. For instance, to protect the ferrite rods, which were about the size and shape of a pencil, we put each rod inside a quartz sleeve. To center the ferrite in the circular waveguide, the quartz cylinder provided the impedance matching the ferrite rod to the circular waveguide. The cylinder had to be polished and rounded to give it a fine surface; this kept the electric field from arcing. When the ceramic sleeve broke down, it arced across the waveguide. So, we used a small torch mounted to a lathe to flame spray the quartz cylinder.

Instead of machining and polishing the material with the lathe, we spun the quartz-ferrite assembly in front of the torch, which is mounted in the tool rest, while moving the flame in and out to polish the quartz sleeve and round the corners. We developed that technique on the spot. To lengthen the path of the electric field, the ferrite is recessed. That way, the quartz does not arc and deform. The switch we were making could pass 150 kilowatts of power. At a frequency of 35 gigahertz, that is a tremendous amount of power.

To my knowledge, it was the first time anyone had made a four-port ferrite switch operating at this frequency and power level. In our previous attempts, the electric field would arc from the high power and produce a loud bang followed by a lightning-like flash. However, when lightning occurs, it is far enough away that it takes a while for the sound to reach you. When it happens right in front of you, the bang occurs at the same time as the flash, and the electric field breaks down. If you have the beginning of breakdown—it is called a "corona," a sort of glow, or blue light—then it zaps. To create a conductive path and deform the ceramic sleeve, we drew a flame right across the whole waveguide. The intense heat turned the device we were working on into carbon particles like soot. It would just vaporize. Then the machinist, Dan Binder, or the guys over at Quartzite would start making up some new parts quick.

We did not have time to make a part and stop. We had to make another part right away so that by the time we tested it, the next part would be ready. The big problem was getting the quartz cylinder machined and polished. Flame spraying solved the problem. Because it is a ceramic, quartz has a low dielectric constant and a low-loss tangent, which makes it an ideal transformer material for this application. Using Ed Antoon's formula, we produced the ferrites ourselves. Then somebody had to drive to Quartzite to pick up the machined ferrite rods and the quartz hollow cylinders. To save time, we ordered extra parts. We probably went through half a dozen. It is machining, so you have to bore the quartz cylinders to insert the ferrite rods. We also gave Quartzite a drawing of the component we were making. We labeled each section of the drawing with letters. That way, when we changed a dimension, all we had to do was call and tell them what section we were changing. Then Dan or someone else would drive over, and the new part would be ready. To make the switch, we had our customer, Westinghouse, as well as our vendor, Quartzite, and our own microwave team working together as one *big* team. That is how you should approach things: Get the job done. Without time to run back and forth between Baltimore or to call other guys in, we worked around the clock without going home. We dozed at our desks, and could be quickly woken up when needed. We were all fairly young and very committed, and our families supported us. No one was getting a ration of ill will from our wives. Nancy had the patience of Job.

We completed the switch in eight days and immediately delivered it to Westinghouse, which was really pleased. Tom's team installed the switch in the high-altitude spy plane, mounted with two antennas and a shared transmitter and receiver. Then the crew used our device to take secret, high-resolution images of nuclear missile sites that the Soviet Union was building in Cuba. Equipped with this information, on October 22, 1962, President John F. Kennedy gave a nationally televised address.

"This government, as promised, has maintained the closest surveillance of the Soviet military buildup on the island of Cuba," President Kennedy said. "Within the past week, unmistakable evidence has established the fact that a series of offensive missile sites is now in preparation on that imprisoned island. The purposes of these bases can be none other than to provide a nuclear capability against the Western Hemisphere."[19]

Kennedy's announcement sent the country into a panic. People emptied grocery store shelves and hid in backyard bomb bunkers. Until the Soviets removed their missile sites, President Kennedy called for the Navy to blockade Cuba and cut off supplies to the island. Should the Soviet Union fire any nuclear missiles at the United States, the president pledged to retaliate.

What most people did not know was that at the time the president made his speech, several Soviet submarines were stationed in the 90-mile belt of water between Florida and Cuba. In fact, one Soviet captain, overwhelmed by intense 120-degree heat and running out of oxygen, ordered his crew to fire a nuclear torpedo at the American fleet. Fortunately, cooler heads prevailed, and Vasili Arkhipov, the Soviet naval officer responsible for the flotilla, prevented the captain from launching the torpedo. That is how close America came to nuclear war.[20]

The thirteen-day Cuban Missile Crisis was finally resolved when Soviet Premier Nikita Khrushchev agreed to remove his country's missiles from Cuba, and America lifted its blockade.

Throughout the crisis, Nancy was home taking care of Randee, Michael, and Kirsten. I do not really remember how she reacted. We did not talk about it. But I was proud of my team, including our customer, Westinghouse, and our vendor, Quartzite, for delivering the switch on time. In the end, Jim and I and the rest of our team were all just glad to get the job done so we could finally go home and get some sleep.

CHAPTER 7

THE MOST TRAGIC DAY

Despite my doctors' predictions that I would never be able to ski or skate again, I became very active with local sports and started the Bedford Recreation Department hockey program. We skated on a little rink in the middle of town, just across from the softball field on Loomis Street. About two-thirds of the standard-sized rink, it was hard to free skate. On a rink that size, hockey becomes more of a checking game, with lots of pushing and shoving. But I held weekend classes, teaching kids from as young as three all the way up through high school how to skate.

I also played fast-pitch softball. As a youth, I had played both baseball and fast-pitch softball, but as an adult I stuck with softball. Because the bases are closer together, you have to move the ball fast to throw a person out at the base and the game moves much faster than a baseball game. With seven rather than nine innings, you can play a game in a little over an hour. To save time, I tried to only play sports that required an hour to complete, including hockey.

For the first five years following my accident, I wore leg braces and required crutches to get around. While still working for Airtron, I got so good with crutches that I would plant my crutches on the ground and vault over the railroad tracks on Vassar Street. I also learned to walk on my crutches without putting my feet down. To get my strength back, I practiced picking up marbles with my toes in a pail of warm water filled with Epsom salts. I did that for hours every day until I was finally able to walk with just a brace that grabbed my leg above the knee.

Nancy admired the fact that I had got back on my feet and came to watch some of my softball games. Because it hurt too much to bend my foot, I had to put a steel plate in the bottom of my shoe. Soon after I returned to the field, I played a game of volleyball while wearing my leg brace, and I broke my leg inside the brace. When I got to the hospital, the doctor said, "What are you doing playing ball in a brace?"

"I wanted to play," I said.

Here I was, the executive of a company, but everyone remembers me for breaking legs and playing ball.

At that time, people took their softball seriously. Many people in town came to watch the games. I especially liked it when Nancy came. Seeing her sitting in the stands made me so proud. The other guys would say, "Wow! That's your wife?" She was just so pretty.

In Bedford, I played softball for the Dodgemen, sponsored by Dodge Tire, a local auto parts dealership. Our main rivals were the Genettimen, sponsored by Genetti's package store. Joe Genetti, the owner, was a good ballplayer and sponsored his own team. The Dodgemen and Genettimen always fought for first place in the town softball league. We played at Page Field, right across the street from the hockey rink. The field lacked lights, preventing us from playing at night. So I went to the town hall and got a motion to install lights in the ballpark. The power company offered to put in the electric poles for free, but we still needed $8,500 to cover the lights.

The warrant for the next town meeting contained an article for the lights. I prepared to give a presentation at the high school gymnasium, where the meeting was held. But the article right before ours asked voters to buy a new ambulance, which cost the same amount as the lights. For an ambulance, the town was using a Volkswagen bus—a ridiculous vehicle. To slide patients in the back of the bus, the crew had to lift them on stretchers. Right in the middle of the town meeting, a group of firemen climbed on the stage with a stretcher and a couple of sawhorses the same height as their bus. Then they asked for a volunteer to sit on a stretcher.

"I'll do it," said a heavy lady, the wife of one of the firemen.

They got her up on the stretcher and intentionally swayed her back and forth as they struggled to lift her onto the platform. They nearly pitched her right into the audience. People were laughing like hell. Of course, it was all a setup. After they sat down, everyone voted, but the town did not want to spend the money, and the fire department did not get their new ambulance. *No way am I going to get lights for the ball field after that*, I said to myself. If the townspeople were not willing to buy a much-needed ambulance, they certainly were not going to buy lights for a ball field. So when it was our turn, I stood up and said, "We've decided to table the article."

The only way to convince the town to give us the lights was to enlist all the ballplayers and their wives to show up early and fill the town hall to vote. The next year, that is what we did, and we got the lights.

The Santa Claus Route

I also helped coordinate the Bedford Community Santa Program. In 1946, after the end of the Second World War, a town selectman, Clayton Morrill, decided to make sure that every local child received a Christmas gift. More than three generations later, volunteer Santas—each accompanied by a driver and a "checker," or helper—still drive all over town on Christmas Eve, handing out gifts. We even covered the nearby Air Force base at Hanscom Field.

A couple weeks before Christmas, Nancy and the other parents would buy one present for each of their children and deliver the gifts to the high school gymnasium. Additional gifts were donated by Davidson's Pharmacy, Genetti's, the hardware store, and other little shops in town. That way, if a family had a kid visiting when Santa arrived, Santa could hand out an extra toy in the bottom of his sack. Volunteers wrapped each package and marked it with a child's name or with a code indicating whether the extra gifts were for a boy or a girl, and the particular age.

Everyone took it very seriously. When I became involved, the town had forty-seven volunteer Santas. Organizing all those Santas and gifts was like organizing a troop movement. Each team provided its own station wagon, which were all numbered—one through forty-seven—with signs on their dashboards. A team of ladies did each Santa's hair and makeup and did a great job, very professional. They powdered their faces and beards and even their eyebrows, but they were fussy. Each Santa had to be a certain height. Too short to qualify, I went as a "checker," checking the Santa Claus route and ensuring the gifts were loaded into the car in the right order. I also volunteered my Chevy station wagon.

On Christmas Eve, the cars lined up in the high school parking lot. Each driver pulled up to the gymnasium where volunteers loaded the wagons full of packages. Then we drove around to the front of the building to pick up Santa.

Each station wagon covered thirty to thirty-five houses. If a car broke down, the local Chrysler dealer, Gould Motors, sent out a tow truck at no cost to the driver and delivered an extra wagon. Because my wagon was not exactly a sleigh, we taped the headlights and left just enough light so the driver could see. That way, we could slither along undetected. So the kids would not see Santa getting out of a car, the driver dropped Santa off a little way past each house.

My job was to fill Santa's sack with the right gifts. I also told Santa the names and ages of the children in each house. Then Santa would knock on the door. After being invited inside, he would go up to the youngest kid in the room and say, "You must be Jimmy" and hand him his package. He only needed to know the name of the youngest child in the family before handing out the remaining gifts.

The Santas also did little favors. For instance, I always bought something for Nancy, like a snow shovel that I left with a ribbon on it outside our front door. We never went to our own houses. But when the Santa on our route rang the front door and Nancy opened it, he would grab her and say, "You must be Nancy! A snow shovel!"

"Oh, how nice," Nancy would say. "A shovel with a bow."

And everyone would laugh.

Families always wanted to take photos before Santa left. However, because we used flashbulbs, they were only allowed to take one picture. Otherwise, Santa would be blinded. Every family wanted a picture of each child sitting on Santa's knee, so by the time Santa stepped outside into the dark, his eyes were completely dilated. Standing just out of sight, beyond the door, I'd grab Santa by the shoulder so he would not fall down the stairs.

"I'll be back later tonight," Santa always said before leaving, while the kids tore into their presents. "I'll be watching. You had better behave yourselves, because Santa knows when you've been naughty or nice."

Randee, Michael, and Kirsten loved it. The only drawback? I missed spending Christmas Eve with my children.

Kirsten

While I worked, played ball, and helped around town, Nancy stayed home. When she moved from Connecticut to Bedford, Nancy did not know anyone. Shyness kept her from getting to know our neighbors, but soon after we welcomed Kirsten, Cynthia and Ted Houston bought the house next to ours on Wilson Road. Ted taught elementary school in Newton, and their three children were similar in age to our own. Soon after the Houstons unpacked, Nancy carried over a plate of cookies. A couple days later, Cynthia knocked on our door to return the plate, and the two of them became good friends.

Nancy loved to garden. Cynthia invited her to join the Bedford Garden Club, where Nancy made more friends. While the older children were in school, she and Cynthia often packed up Kirsten and went shopping or out for lunch at Grover Cronin, a popular, three-story department store in nearby Waltham. Nancy always brought a little something home for the girls. Connecting with Michael was harder. I blamed the rough beginning he'd had after losing his father. Whatever the cause, there was a lot of conflict at home, which increased as Michael got older. At one point, I tried talking to Ted Houston about it because he had married Cynthia and adopted her son after her first husband's death in the Korean War.

While working long hours at the office, I spent as much time as I could with my family, including taking the kids trick-or-treating at Halloween. When Randee was little, she dressed up Kirsten's stroller and pushed her little sister around. Another year, I wore a dress stuffed with a pillow and went as a pregnant lady, carrying an empty wine glass. Nancy's father, Kurt, went along as the father-to-be. We got along great. While I introduced my father-in-law to our neighbors, they poured a little brandy in Kurt's and my drinking glasses.

At the time, Nancy and I had a big St. Bernard, Samson, "Sam," who weighed a whopping 220 pounds. One Halloween when Randee was about seven, we were going house to house when she was attacked by a neighbor's dog. Sam chased the dog off. When the owner called his dog inside and slammed the door, Sam hit the door so hard, he broke it. I ran up to the house and apologized, offering to pay to fix his door.

"Don't worry," he said. "I'm glad your daughter's okay."

For a while, Nancy and I raised St. Bernards, but I was a failure at the dog business. Whenever someone wanted to buy a puppy, I would ask, "Where do you live?"

"Boston," they'd say.

"In an apartment?"

When they nodded, I would say, "You don't get a puppy. St. Bernards belong on big pieces of property."

Although I was not the kind of father who read books to my children—Nancy did that, along with taking them to the Bedford Public Library, which Kirsten loved—I taught my children to skate and ski. In Bedford, the Paul Little Farm had a long hill on the property, owned by Paul Little, the town's dog officer. Nancy worried that the children might get hurt, but when they are small, they don't have much distance to fall—not to mention the padding they are wearing. So when Kirsten turned five, Nancy bundled her up in a jacket and hat and mittens, and I took her to the hill. After we hiked up, I made a V with my feet, like a snow plow, and we skied down together, with me skiing backward. Kirsten skied toward me, and I caught her at the bottom.

Kirsten was a natural athlete. I often took her to the ice rink for open skating. Shy and quiet like her mother, Kirsten looked like Nancy too, with soft, light-brown hair cut short in a bob and eyes that sparkled. She was so pretty, and she loved attention.

Some mornings, Randee would hide behind the boulder at the end of our driveway to avoid getting on the school bus, and Nancy would let her stay home. But Kirsten could not wait to go to school. In the fall of 1965, she started first grade at Nathaniel Page School, two miles down the road from our house. That Columbus Day, October 12, began as a nice day. Since I had the day off work, I climbed out of bed early to work on finishing the back of the house and garage. The kids had the day off school. Randee, then eleven, remembers that she and Kirsten were in the kitchen that morning with Nancy, having breakfast. Kirsten wanted to go out and play, but we had a rule: You had to eat all your breakfast before leaving the table. If you did not like what you had on your plate, you had to sit there until you learned to like it. Kirsten was a picky eater, but Nancy was a great cook and tried to make things the children liked.

Later that day, Kirsten asked to play at the house of her first-grade classmate, Jackie Healey, whose family had just moved to a new house on a quiet cul-de-sac, a few doors down from ours on the corner of Ledgewood and Lido Lane. Although there was not any traffic, Nancy must have walked Kirsten down.

As I finished working around dinnertime, a siren wailed up our usually quiet street. I hurried around the front of our house, where someone informed me that a newspaper delivery boy had found Kirsten lying by a large boulder near the end of the driveway. I jumped in our station wagon and chased the ambulance to the hospital. When I got there, Kirsten was dead.

There were no signs of injury. No bruises. Not even a scraped knee. The hospital did an autopsy and found there was no water in Kirsten's lungs. No heart defects.

"There has to be a reason," I said to the doctors. "What happened?"

Two additional autopsies could not explain why Kirsten died. As a result, Kirsten's death was initially under investigation.

Eventually they attributed her death to "Pulmonary and cerebral edema of undetermined etiology. Sudden death—natural causes."

The toughest part of the whole thing was that I could not talk to Nancy about what had happened. She was so fragile. In fact, I worried so much about Nancy and what the impact of losing Kirsten would have on her, I did not talk to anyone. I could not even remember if I had taken Nancy with me when I drove to the hospital.

"Was Nancy in the car with me?" I asked Randee, decades later, but she did not remember.

I sure hoped I had taken Nancy with me to the hospital. I could have never forgiven myself if I had left her behind.

Kirsten's death was the most tragic day of my life. Losing a child is a horrible thing to go through, but I think it is a lot tougher on a woman than on a man, especially when the woman is a stay-at-home mother.

We had a private ceremony with a closed casket. My brother and his wife and daughter came to the funeral. My sister came. So did Ma and Pop Hartley. Lawnie, Curtis's daughter, later recalled that it was the only time she ever saw Ma Hartley cry, but to take care of Nancy I thought I had to hold all of those emotions inside.

I could lose myself in playing hockey or softball or going to work and doing research, but I cannot imagine how Nancy felt. She was close with Jim Regan's wife, Marie, and Dan Binder's wife, Pat. But even with her closest friend, Cynthia Houston, Nancy could not bear to talk about losing Kirsten.

I played softball with a fellow who was hiking through the woods, carrying his one-year-old child in a pack on his back when a limb fell off a tree and struck the child, who died. As a result of the accident, he and his wife divorced. I do not know how people can blame someone else for a situation like that. I had a lot of questions, but I did not want to put Nancy through more pain. So instead of talking to Nancy, I went to the military people I worked with through Ferrotec, and they arranged for me to meet with a group of Army doctors in their trauma unit.

"Could a person die of fright?" I asked them.

"Yes," they said and explained how that could happen. During the First World War, they conditioned soldiers for battle by having them imagine the enemy while sticking bayonets in sacks of sawdust or straw. "You have to be conditioned for what you fear," they said. Otherwise, when commanded to "fix bayonets," some soldiers would die in the trenches without a mark on them. They were so afraid, their hearts would just stop.

"Was Kirsten afraid of anything?" the doctors asked.

"Yes," I said.

Kirsten would come out of her room at night and say, "Dad, can you come in? The bogeyman might be in my room." So I would go and look under her bed and check the room to make her happy. Before Kirsten died, I thought that was a normal thing for a kid to worry about. After, I wondered whether someone might have tried to scare her by jumping out from behind the rock where her body was found. But I never told Nancy that I met with the trauma doctors. I thought it would just add more grief. So I kept it to myself.

Before Kirsten's death, Nancy and I had a portrait taken of our three children sitting side-by-side. There must have been a larger one, but I laminated a small one to carry in my wallet. I have carried it in my wallet ever since.

After losing Kirsten, Nancy was in bad shape. I had my work, but Nancy spent all her time at home. Without anything to fall back on, she became withdrawn and lost interest in socializing. Some days, I would come home and find Nancy holding Kirsten's hat or a mitten and crying. We could not even talk. Bringing up anything personal was too painful. It was just so sad. Sometimes when you knock a person down, they stay down. Nancy's first marriage was so tragic. After the cruel way she had been mistreated by Fred, her self-esteem was crushed. Going through one more loss when Kirsten died caused Nancy to collapse.

I could not understand why God would take Kirsten. What did I do wrong? Searching for answers, I went back to the Prospect Congregational Church in Cambridge.

"Why did God allow my daughter to die?" I asked the minister.

"God must have wanted her more than you did," he said.

I did not buy that answer. Nobody wanted Kirsten more than I did. That was not the right thing for a minister to say. Before that, Nancy and I occasionally attended the Congregational church in Bedford, but after the minister's answer, I lost all interest in church. If God makes a selection—like when it is someone's time to die—why does he choose one person instead of another?

I still considered myself a Christian, but I looked at life on Earth as out of God's control. So, I left the church and walked away. I made a mistake in doing that. If I had encouraged Nancy, and if the two of us had stayed in church, I think maybe she would have found some solace. Things might have been different, but I let her down.

For a while, Nancy and I went to counseling together.

"If you have more kids, it would be nice," the counselor said.

Eleven months after losing Kirsten, we had another baby, our son Christopher. Four years later, we had another son, Jeffrey. Two boys.

Then Nancy said, "No more children." She did not want to get pregnant again.

So we stopped.

CHAPTER 8

A GOOD TEAM

Soon after Christopher's arrival, Nancy met another woman named Nancy who had also recently delivered a son at Emerson Hospital. At first, neither realized that the other Nancy's husband, Harlan Howe Jr., was my competition at Microwave Associates, Inc., a Burlington microwave and radio frequency technology company with roots reaching back to MIT's Rad Lab. A microwave engineer working on stripline circuit design, Harlan and I often wrote competing proposals for the same contracts, which Ferrotec frequently won thanks to my technique of using suspended substrate as a transmission line.

One day, Harlan's Nancy informed my Nancy that her husband's business was about to merge with another company.

"They have this great guy, a technology guy," she said. "It's a guy Harlan really likes, and he's looking forward to working with him."

"I think you're talking about my husband," my Nancy said.

The other Nancy looked at her and asked, "Your last name is Carr?"

The merger between Ferrotec and Microwave Associates had not yet been made public, so we were not allowed to talk about it. But some months before, Larry Gould, the president of Microwave Associates, had traveled to Hughes Aircraft Company and met with Richard "Dick" Jamison, the head of the Hughes Aircraft Radar Systems Group.

"One small company is getting all of your business," Larry told Dick, referring to Ferrotec. "What do we need to do to get your business?"

"You have to get Ken Carr," Dick said. "He does everything he says he's going to do."

After returning to Boston, Larry approached Henry Riblet and asked about buying Ferrotec.

"It's up to Ken," said Henry Riblet, who had taken a real liking to me and appreciated the hard work my team and I had accomplished. By then I was president and technical director of Ferrotec. Although I owned only 15 percent of the company, Henry Riblet left it up to me whether to accept the deal. It felt like I was the one being sold, not Ferrotec.

Two decades before, four engineers—Vessarios Chigas, Louis Roberts, Hugh Wainwright, and Richard Walker—had founded Microwave Associates in a rented laboratory above a Boston toy shop. All four had started out at MIT's Rad Lab before briefly working for Sylvania. Notable for the time, Richard Walker, who contributed to the Rad Lab's book series, and Louis Roberts, who later became chief of NASA's Microwave Optics Laboratory, were both Black. Thanks to a strong emphasis on research and development, Microwave Associates helped lead the industry in manufacturing microwave and millimeter-wave semiconductors, components, and technologies for aerospace and defense-related industries and had quickly expanded to fill a 50,000-square-foot facility in Burlington.[21]

Rather than competing, I felt the merger would be good for both companies. By combining our resources to create a larger company, we could accomplish more together. Wanting to build the best group I could, I agreed to the sale.

In early 1970, Microwave Associates acquired Ferrotec, later changing its name to M/A-Com to reflect its increasing involvement in developing microwave communications components and systems. I became M/A-Com's group vice president and technical director—the key incentive to get me there. Harlan Howe, the engineering manager of the microwave assembly portion of Microwave Associates, became one of my key staff members. Instead of resenting each other, we became close friends.

I treated the merger like playing hockey. At the time, I often skated with the Massachusetts State Police hockey team, which got my name and phone number from a bulletin board of available skaters at the Assabet Skating Rink in nearby Acton-Boxboro. Whenever the team needed an extra player, they called me.

"Can you get down here in a hurry?" a team member would ask. "We need you tonight."

By then, I had bought a second-hand Porsche that I fixed up myself, so they could hear me coming. I carried my skates in a cooler with a small lightbulb that plugged into my car's cigarette lighter. That way, my skates would be warm when I laced them and did not loosen while playing. They were so tight, I did not even wear socks. The game mattered more than my comfort.

Although you cannot win every game, you have to want to win; otherwise, you never will win. But it is also important to learn how to lose with grace and congratulate the opposing team on their game. After a match, our team frequently went out for a beer. Often our opponents would be there, and we would get to like them. I felt the same way about merging with Microwave Associates. With Harlan Howe and the guys from Microwave Associates and Ferrotec working together, we had a great team. Instead of competing, we got the benefit of both companies and could accomplish more by working together. As a result, we probably had the strongest microwave group in the world.

Like many companies that grew out of MIT's Rad Lab, Microwave Associate's new facility in Burlington stretched along the Route 128 corridor, known as the "Electronic Highway" for its large number of technology businesses. After the acquisition, Ferrotec moved to Burlington. The main facility, Building 1, made semiconductors. We moved to Building 2, a single-floor office space out back. As the company grew, M/A-Com acquired and built additional facilities, eventually operating out of eleven buildings along Route 128.

When I first arrived, Richard "Dick" Walker handled patents, which I later took over. Although he no longer played an active role in the company, Vessarios "Vess" Chigas served as a board member. Both Dick and Vess liked me.

Another key player from Microwave Associates was the company's chief scientific officer, Marion Hines. An absolutely brilliant mathematician and great microwave engineer and researcher, Marion had previously developed microwave electron tubes and other devices for Western Electric, the manufacturing division of Bell Telephone Laboratories (the research arm of AT&T). As the chief scientist of research and development, Marion helped build the first all-solid-state microwave communication system. This made Microwave Associates an early leader in developing the first semiconductors, which offered much better performance and reliability than transmit and receive tubes.

Two other important players from Microwave Associates were Rick Kelley, a mechanical engineer who led the company's involvement with computer-controlled machining, and Bob Bielawa, a resourceful engineer who took night classes at Northeastern University in Boston to complete his degree in electrical engineering. For many years I worked closely with Rick and Bob.

The main people who came with me from Ferrotec included George Hemple, who originally worked with me at Airton and became head of ferrite production at M/A-Com; Jim Fallon, a young engineer who began working at Ferrotec as a co-op student from Northeastern; and the person I was closest to, Jim Regan, who originally followed me from Airtron to Ferrotec. Every morning I would walk into the lab and sit at the bench with Jim for fifteen or twenty minutes, enjoying a cup of coffee with him. Jim and I just communicated so well. On Fridays, whenever I was not travelling, I joined him on the bench and we would work together. I never wanted to become an executive. I wanted to be part of the team and keep my touch with the technology so that when I was talking with the team, I still understood the equipment and measurements and could explain how to use it.

Unfortunately, Larry Gould, the president of Microwave Associates, and I did not get along. An excellent executive, Larry had a doctorate in physics from MIT. We respected each other, but I did not like working with him because of the way he handled people. As a condition of the merger, I informed him, "I will never report to you."

Larry ended up restructuring the company, and Richard "Dick" DiBona, a former Microwave Associates manager, became the chief operating officer. Larry played a tough game, and Dick served as the interface between Larry and me. Whenever Larry and I got into a disagreement, Dick would rush in to calm everyone down. He was the glue that held the company together. Dick also played hockey, which in my book made him a great guy.

Any time you meld two companies together, there are casualties. To avoid redundancy, Larry thought we should downsize both groups, but I did not want to lose any talent. To me, combining groups was a situation where one plus one equaled three. Most people thought I should be a hard businessman, but it was not necessary. If you put together a strong team with more staff, you can bring in more business. However, Larry saw things differently and gave me a list of people he thought should be eliminated.

"I'm not following anyone's list," I told Larry. I kept people the company was going to let go, and I let go or transferred people the company wanted to keep.

One day, Larry fired a tremendous guy, Arthur "Art" Blaisdell. A senior staff engineer, Art had worked with Microwave Associates and understood mixers better than anyone I knew. If I had a ferrite problem, I went to Jim. If I had a mixer problem, I went to Art. But one day Art was on the phone with a customer and kept a friend of Larry's waiting in the lobby, so Larry fired him.

"You're not going anywhere," I told Art. "You're staying right here."

Then I walked down the hall toward Larry's office. Dick saw me and came running with his hands up.

"He fired me," I said to Dick.

"What do you mean, he fired you?" Dick asked.

"Larry must have fired me," I said, "because if he is going to fire one of my people, he first has to fire me."

Larry apologized, and Art never left the company. But I wanted more than an apology.

"From now on," I told Larry, "if you do this again, we go to the board of directors and we are going to discuss it. I do not want to hear from you that someone's fired. I want to hear from the board."

Nobody touches my people.

At Ferrotec, our staff was so lean I did not even have my own secretary. My secretary, Georgie Burton, also came from Microwave Associates. We had great respect for each other. Georgie was very protective of me and could keep a secret, an important characteristic considering the many military contracts I was involved with. Georgie could also type like gangbusters. During the 1960s, IBM had come out with the Selectric typewriter, which replaced type bars with a metal ball covered with raised characters that rotated and tilted to print individual letters on a sheet of paper. "This is the best thing that's happened to typing since electricity," claimed a television ad.

But Georgie typed so fast the ball jammed. They thought Georgie was abusing the machine. So IBM sent out an engineer and a typist with a new, specialty typewriter for her to try.

"I'd like to see you type this," the IBM engineer said, handing her a printed sheet of paper.

Georgie typed the paper so fast, the ball jammed right in front of them.

"I've never seen anyone type that fast," IBM's engineer exclaimed.

In compensation, IBM gave Georgie, for free, a brand-new electric typewriter: their previous model, with traditional keys.

Georgie worked so hard, I had a room built and moved her into an enclosed office. She was a great asset. I depended on her. Whether helping me write a letter or a grant or taking dictation from an airport payphone during a layover between flights, she took care of the details and made my words look great.

When Georgie finished, I would often look over what she had written and ask, "Did I write that? That's a very nice letter."

Georgie stayed with me for nearly fifty years. To this day, we remain good friends.

New Divisions

Following the merger, I created a ferrite division. It included George Hemple, Paul Rutledge, and Lou Forny, a young technician who had come to Ferrotec from Quartzite.

Babe, the owner of Quartzite, had called me up one day. "Can you help this guy?" he asked. "If he can work with you, he's really going to go someplace." Just seventeen at the time I hired him, Lou stayed with the ferrite division his entire career.

Instead of operating as a service group to me, the ferrite division now had its own identity and production line. The Ferrotec engineering group worked closely with Harlan Howe and Karen Goodburn, who typed the division's proposals. Like me, they all worked long hours. If we faced a deadline to get out a proposal, they stayed until it was done. Years later, Harlan became the editor and publisher of the *Microwave Journal*, an industry trade publication. In an article regarding the history of microwave passive components, he named me as a microwave pioneer, citing the technique I had invented at Ferrotec using suspended substrate to integrate ferrite circulators in stripline subassemblies.[22]

Running their own division gave everyone a new opportunity. Later, we sent some of the division's key production people an hour or so north to Sanford, Maine, where I had occasionally raced my old '35 Chevy on the ice at the defunct Sanford Airport. My uncle Dutch maintained the mechanical equipment at a Sanford fabric mill that had recently relocated down south where the labor market was less expensive. The labor market around Boston remained tight, as did the workspace. So, when Dutch told me about the empty mill and unemployed workers, I mentioned the mill to the other members of our site committee, and we moved our ferrite production facility there.

I also created M/A-Com's Advanced Program and Technology Center, which developed new products. The "Tech Center" is where I had my key technical people. About one hundred engineers worked with me in the center, developing entire radar systems and subsystems. Jim Fallon became the center's grant writer. With Harlan Howe and me, he led the proposal and bid preparation. After winning a program to develop a system, the Tech Center also built the prototypes.

Because of my past experience working on components for the military, we submitted many of our first grant proposals to companies in the defense industry. We sent bids to Hughes, Westinghouse, Ford Aerospace, and Boeing and won contracts such as developing the seeker heads for fire-and-forget missiles, expanding the capabilities of fire control radars in the F-14, F-15, and F-18 fighter planes, and making components for communications systems.

A missile contains at least three radars—a fire control, a proximity fuse, and the beacon, which emits a tracking signal. One radar subsystem we helped develop, called a "proximity fuse," measures the closeness of a missile to a target and tells the missile when to detonate. If the missile gets within twenty feet of the target, it will release the weapon, or fragmentation bomb, to puncture the fuselage of a supersonic plane. Often missiles do not hit the target. They are not expected to. When a jet is flying at high speed, the missile puts holes all over the fuselage and actually tears the plane apart. Another radar subsystem, the beacon radar, allows the missile to track the target. An additional radar seeks and identifies a target.

We brought in business on all fronts, including working on special projects such as Terrascan, a downward-looking radar system designed to locate underground pipes. Columbia Gas, a utility company in Columbus, Ohio, sponsored the project, and we worked in collaboration with the electromagnetics lab at Ohio State University. At that time, pipes were made of plastic and other non-conductive materials. When burying them in the ground, utility companies commonly laid metal wires alongside the pipes so metal detectors could find them. But locating the pipes often proved difficult, particularly when the wires were damaged during repairs. To address this problem, Columbia Gas put together a user committee of town officials, engineers, and utility workers. The committee gathered data, including the diameter of the pipes (which ranged from two inches to twenty-four inches) and the maximum depth at which they were buried (which turned out to be ten feet). Behind M/A-Com we dug a field of trenches covered by a garage so that we could work year-round.

"What are you building?" people asked.

"A pipe farm," we said.

However, our radar could not find the two-inch pipes we buried.

"How deep did you bury them?" asked the committee, when we reported back to them.

"Ten feet."

"Who the hell buries two-inch pipes ten feet deep?" they asked.

It turned out two-inch pipes are buried just beneath the ground's surface. After we corrected our mistake, the system worked just fine, thanks in part to Bob Bielawa and Bob Williams, an electrical engineer who designed microwave and electronic circuits. Because the underground radar system detects objects that are long and narrow, in addition to pipes it has since been widely used to locate historic artifacts, building foundations, and in criminal investigations even dead bodies. In 1978 our team won an I-R 100 award from *Industrial Research* magazine (now *R&D World*), which annually chose the top one hundred technologically significant products of the year from a pool of international applicants.

Another special project involved designing the components of a radar system for tractors. DICKEY-john, which supplies electronics to major tractor manufacturers, including John Deer and Massey Ferguson, contacted me about a problem. Whenever a tractor spreading grain or fertilizer got stuck in a field, it continued scattering material so that the seeds or fertilizer piled up. To correct this problem, I made a motion detector that measured the tractor's ground speed, as opposed to the speed of a tractor's wheel. That way, when a tractor got stuck, the spreader stopped shooting out seed. To my knowledge, it has been used on every large tractor since.

We also developed radar systems used by police to detect speeding cars. Inevitably, this later included systems used by drivers to detect police radar signals. However, because M/A-Com did not want to be involved in work considered anti-police, we freely gave the designs for the systems to the companies that manufactured them. Then we priced the components with a fair markup so the companies had to buy the components from us. Eventually, we did more business with those companies than with developing units for the police, but this arrangement kept us from directly aiding speeding drivers.

Because the Tech Center had its own machine shop, we could modify a component or complete a project without making a purchase order. Thanks to Rick Kelley, M/A-Com was very active in programmable computerized numerical control (CNC) machines, which made it much easier to route channels, rather than guiding the machines by hand. This was important to the fabrication of suspended substrate. As a result, M/A-Com probably had more CNC machines than any other business in the area.

The Tech Center was so successful that we won programs even when we were not the low bidder. After a company gave us the requirements for what they needed, we made sure our proposal included a design that was more reliable, less expensive, and outperformed our competitor's. Working with our engineers, I would agree to change the specifications of a project to give the client a better product. To enable companies to award us a contract, even when our design cost more, I always gave them a little justification. We would also request a technical representative from the customer to be a member of the design team. Involving the customer was very important. When making changes to improve a product, you should always include someone from the customer's team.

Often the products we created resulted in the creation of a new company. As part of my agreement with M/A-Com, I would manage a new company for eighteen months. Then I would transfer the new technology to an existing division within M/A-Com or form a new division of the company. Anyone who worked with me in the new entity had a choice. They could either stay with the new company or division, or they could go back to the Tech Center with me. They all wanted to stay with the Tech Center. Every one of them.

One such division at M/A-Com was the Integrated Circuits Division. M/A-Com was one of the first companies to transition from using waveguide-based transmission tubes, such as magnetrons and klystrons (a specialized vacuum tube developed after the magnetron), to solid state microwave integrated circuits, also called a "MIC."[23] To connect the chips together and form a microwave integrated circuit, we often used very thin, 0.001-diameter gold wire, which is as soft as lead. The chips are so small that during development women did most of the work using vacuum picks under a microscope in a laboratory. In production, the chips are assembled by machines. The use of discrete components and circuit functions later gave way to monolithic microwave integrated circuits, called an "MMIC."

These labs, once called "white rooms" after the white lab coats and booties technicians had to wear while working in them, were spotless. We could not even carry in a pad of paper. Bob Bielawa, a senior engineer, was such a skilled technician he could work under a microscope as good as anyone. At his suggestion, I insisted that every M/A-Com engineer learn how to bond chips. By understanding how complicated it is to assemble these microwave circuits, I hoped our engineers would find ways to make them easier to build, such as by putting a chip on a flat ceramic ground plane where it is easier to reach, rather than putting it down in a hole or channel. When engineers learn how difficult something is to assemble, they learn to put it together better. So Bob taught our entire team of engineers to bond chips.

Part of what made the Tech Center successful was that we took a technically diverse group of people and turned them into a team. When people work for me, I never say, "I'm the boss." Who gets the credit is not important. It is about getting the job done, and we were good at that.

Dick DiBona provided me with talented and capable business support, particularly in the financial and contract area. M/A-Com also provided me with leadership training. At Ferrotec, I had been too busy running a company to complete my doctoral degree, but while working for M/A-Com, I earned an Executive Certificate in Management and Leadership from MIT's Sloan School of Management. Later, while serving as a member of the Board of Bar Overseers of the Supreme Judicial Court of Massachusetts, I attended law classes (such as patent law) at the New England School of Law.

Years later, at a M/A-Com reunion, one of the guys made a comment about being part of the Technical Center.

"You weren't part of the Technical Center," I said.

"Yeah," he said. "I wasn't. But I tell everybody I was because it sounds good."

That is how highly thought of it was to be part of M/A-Com's Technology Center.

Finding Solutions

My greatest expertise as an engineer was my ability to find a solution to a problem. When you have a problem, you have to first identify and understand the problem or you will not find the best solution. Sometimes people settle for an acceptable solution instead of the best one. Before you propose a solution, understand the whole problem. In my opinion, the difference between a physicist and an engineer is that a physicist is working on basic theory, while an engineer is using their knowledge and experience to find a solution.

In addition to being good at finding solutions, I fully engaged my team. With each group that reported to me, I held meetings and conducted design reviews in which we critiqued each other's work. That way, everyone learns together. Even if I did not quite agree or thought they were making a mistake, instead of saying, "I don't think your idea is going to work. Do it this way," I would say, "You have to have a plan B."

Why? Because if I had said, "You have to do it this way," then they may argue, "My solution would have worked."

I would have to tell them, "Maybe, but you need to have a plan B in case plan A does not make it. That way, you skirt an issue that could have caused the program to fail and hone in on the solution."

If you ask an engineer, "Is there any reason we can't solve this thing? Is there any reason why this solution may not work?"—most engineers will say, "No, no, no. We thought it all out. We are convinced it is going to work."

"In any event," I would say, "I want you to name three things that might cause your solution to fail."

One of those problems might be the environmental conditions. For instance, if you are putting a missile underwater, what is the water pressure at forty fathoms? If an engineer works with missiles in space, he might mention that as a concern. So whenever I put together a design review, I included an expert in that area on the design review team. Rather than waiting until the last minute to see if their original plan worked, I allowed the engineer to express what he really thought about the problem—but did not want to say—by listing upfront those three things which could be a weakness. Whether he knew it or not, I got him to concentrate on the solution.

Rather than telling everyone I was the boss, I let people do their own thing. In my opinion, that is why people like Jim Regan, Rick Kelley, and Bob Bielawa stayed with me for so many years. I did not tell them what to do. In my own way I did, but I let them figure it out so we got the solution faster. At the Tech Center, we were good at that.

As technical director and group vice-president of M/A-Com, I traveled a great deal, supervising several operations in Massachusetts, including M/A-Com's Advanced Semiconductor Operation (which later moved to Lowell) and a microwave assemblies and components facility in Chelmsford. In a suburb west of Los Angeles, I also oversaw M/A-Com's antenna facility, Microwave Design and Manufacturing (MDM), which made most of the country's commercial airline antennas. And in southeast England I supervised Microwave Associates Luton (MAL), which primarily made components for communications and military systems and subsystems. With customers all over Europe, MAL was like a mini Microwave Associates.

Every six weeks I traveled to Luton, staying for one week each time.

"You know, guys," I would say, starting off each of these meetings, "your accents are really improving. I can understand you a little better each time I come over."

They looked at me like, *Who's got the accent?*

Bob Bielawa and I often traveled together. At one well-known hotel in London, we checked into our rooms before meeting downstairs at the bar.

"My room is great," Bob said.

I could not figure out what he was talking about. My room was about the size of a bathroom with barely enough room for the mini bar and a chair. The windows overlooked an alley full of trash cans, with lids that slammed up and down all night long.

A few days later, Bob stopped by my room before checking out.

"I think the hotel made a mistake," he admitted. "They must've accidentally given you my room and given me yours." His room had a hot tub and stained-glass windows overlooking a cobblestone street.

Although working for M/A-Com kept me very busy, Nancy never complained. While I worked and traveled, she raised our children. On every trip to England, I caught a train to London and picked out a fine English bone china teacup and saucer at Harrods to give Nancy when I returned home. Whenever she had Cynthia Houston over for tea, Nancy used the cups. I also bought her Lismore Waterford crystal from Ireland. Whenever possible, Nancy joined me on trips, including to visit my mother, who had retired to Florida. Later, I took Nancy on a vacation to England and Scotland—just the two of us—to make up for the honeymoon we'd never had. The guys at MAL insisted I bring her over so they could meet her.

Nancy enjoyed the trip, but ever since losing Kirsten she had suffered from depression. I knew she was struggling, but talking about Kirsten's death was too painful for either of us. I had been in weapons systems for most of my life, and when two parties can't talk, it is the worst of all worlds. You cannot find a solution to a problem that you are unable or unwilling to discuss and address.

CHAPTER 9

A FRESH START

In 1970, my fast-pitch softball team won a regional tournament. Sponsored by Davidson's Pharmacy, our team included Steve Shea, who grew up in Bedford and spent several years playing for the Houston Astros and the Montreal Expos; Joseph "Joe" Bellino, this first United States Naval Academy football player to win a Heisman Trophy and who was later drafted by the Patriots (I believe he also played baseball for the Boston Red Sox); and William "Bill" Tomlinson, who played for the Chicago Cubs before becoming an industrial artist and designing packages for many well-known products, including Junior Mints.

With teammates like that, all I had to do was throw the ball over the plate, and they would save me.

Bill Tomlinson and his wife, Priscilla, owned a house on the Cape in North Eastham, near First Encounter Beach where the Pilgrims first landed on the *Mayflower*. The coastal resort community borders Orleans to the south and Wellfleet to the north. South Wellfleet once featured a Marconi wireless telegraph station. Invented by a young Italian, Guglielmo Marconi, on January 19, 1903, the system used radio waves to send the first public, two-way transatlantic wireless communication from President Theodore Roosevelt to King Edward VII of Great Britian.[24] Ships later used it to communicate at sea, saving many lives, including those of the 706 people rescued after the 1912 sinking of the *Titanic*. But due to erosion, the South Wellfleet station and its towers were dismantled in the early 1920s, removing the area's link to the early days of microwave engineering.

To celebrate our team's victory, the Tomlinsons held a cookout down on the Cape. While Nancy and I were there, Bill's neighbor, an old guy named Ernie Soule, stood by the road pounding a "For Sale" sign in the ground beside his oceanfront property. I walked across the road with Nancy.

"How much do you want for the land?" I asked.

"I was hoping to get twenty thousand," he said, explaining that he was selling half of his double lot to pay for his wife's medical bills.

I did not hesitate. "If you will accept a handshake and take the stake out of the ground, I will make an arrangement with the bank and bring you a check next week," I said.

Nancy loved the Cape. With some of the money I had made from selling Ferrotec, I wanted to build her a house. Someday, I hoped that we could retire there. So Ernie pulled out the sign, and I bought the land with a handshake.

Before starting to build, I laid a half-sheet of plywood on a pedestal to create a sundial. Over the following year, I tracked the sun's location to make sure that in the heat of the summer the back deck and big windows I planned would be facing away from the sun. Then I dug a five-foot square, surrounded by a plywood frame, and used a posthole digger to install the first section of the well pipe, which came in five-foot lengths. I then welded a second, narrower pipe to the bottom of a two-foot-square, cast-iron engine block. To guarantee I always hit the ground in the same place, I climbed atop a plank suspended between two sawhorses and lifted the engine block to slide the narrower pipe into the well pipe. Bringing the engine block down like a sledgehammer, I drove the well pipe into the ground. After pounding in the first section of pipe, I attached a coupling to the next five-foot section and raised my platform. Then I started pounding all over again.

For four straight days, I lifted and dropped the engine block, over and over. By the time I finished, I had pounded in about nine sections of pipe. The pipe went into the sandy ground easily enough, but when I turned on the pump, it sucked in sand. All that pounding had fractured the drill point, which draws in water through a filter. So, I drove to the Sears, Roebuck catalog store in Orleans where I had bought the parts on sale as a package.

"I'd like to replace the drill point," I told the salesclerk, wanting to only purchase the part I needed

"You can't do that," he said, insisting that I either bring in all of the other parts I had bought, which were now at the bottom of the well, or I would have to buy another complete package.

"Are you refusing to make a sale?" I asked.

Not wanting a confrontation, he called a manager in Boston.

"Find the part in the catalog and sell him the point," the manager said.

I began drilling all over again, boring a new hole beside the first one. Thankfully, the second time, the pump worked and clean water came out.

Although I have never taken a course in construction, I love to build—a skill I learned while helping build cabins on my grandmother's farm. Over the next seven years, I built a three-bedroom Cape with an interior balcony, overlooking the ocean. I framed, plumbed, and wired it. In my basement woodworking shop, I even built the hickory kitchen cabinets. Each weekend when I drove to the Cape to work on the house, I took several cabinets. At night, I rolled up in a sleeping bag on the floor. In the morning, I washed and shaved in a public bathroom at the Cape Cod National Seashore. Then I began building again.

I hired only one person to work on the house, a guy named Woodchuck—at least, that's what he said his name was. A drifter with a little facial fuzz and dingy clothes, he was not even carrying a change of clothes the day he walked by the house and saw me working.

"Hey," he said. "Who's building your fireplace?"

"I am," I said, stopping to chat.

Woodchuck said he was working his way up to "P-Town," otherwise known as Provincetown, an artists' enclave at the outermost tip of the Cape. Then he pulled out a few pictures of fireplaces he'd built. Since I could tell the guy knew what he was doing, I hired him to build the fireplace. Woodchuck stayed with me for a few months. During the week, he caught a ride into Provincetown, and each weekend, he came back to work and slept on the deck.

The bricks for the fireplace I bought from Gonic Manufacturing, an old brick mill in Gonic, New Hampshire. On weekends, I drove up to Gonic in my old Chevy truck and load it with used bricks before heading back down to the Cape.

One day while walking down at First Encounter Beach, I spotted a big beam about the length of a long railroad tie lying in the middle of the marsh. Since it was too heavy and waterlogged to drag, I stood the beam up on its end and flipped it. Then I flipped it again. An hour or so later, I managed to flip it all the way back to my Cadillac, sitting in the parking lot.

Then I drove home for a couple of sawhorses and hoisted the ten-foot-long beam on top, one end at a time. But when I slid the beam into my trunk, it hung out the back and lifted the front wheels of my car right off the ground. So I hauled it out and drove home to get my chain saw. After cutting off the rotten end pieces, I slid the remainder of the beam back into my trunk and crept slowly home—this time with all four wheels touching the ground. Unfortunately, the sea grass in the marsh was full of poison ivy. Having waded through the marsh with bare feet in only a bathing suit, I ended up with poison ivy all over my body. But the beam made a fine mantle.

Even when I had hockey or softball games, I worked on the house every weekend and during vacations. After I finished, Nancy named the house *Sea Broom*, after the tall, willowy grass that grew in masses along the shore. When the wind blew, it shimmered like waves. As a housewarming gift, Bill Tomlinson painted us a large watercolor of the house that still hangs on my wall fifty years later.

Nancy and I spent a lot of time down on the Cape with the kids. I taught them to sail in a small boat called a Sunfish. We also had a 17-foot Boston Whaler, a power boat with a 115-horsepower outboard motor, and we did a lot of fishing. Often we took Randee and the boys out to Billingsgate Island to dig clams. We watched for squirt holes in the sand, then dug up a mess of clams using the shells of larger sea clams as a rake, which were better than traditional rakes because they did not break the clams' shells. Then we sailed home and Nancy boiled clams for dinner.

The sixty-acre island once held a lighthouse and homes, but as the island eroded, the last houses were hauled onto barges and floated to shore in the 1850s. Later, the lighthouse was dismantled. The Cape is constantly changing. At high tide, Billingsgate Island, now known as Billingsgate Shoal, becomes completely covered by water. Some people would sail out to the island to dig clams and then get stranded when the tide went out. Then they had to wait for the tide to come back in and float their boats. I often sailed out in our Sunfish, which was easy to drag across the sand. I also trolled for bluefish, but the Sunfish had no place for me to put my feet except in the well where I stored the fish—and bluefish tend to bite.

We had a good time down on the Cape. Nancy loved the place. She liked to go out with me on the water, or she would sit in a low canvas chair on the beach with her eyes closed and lean her head back, listening to the waves.

But the drinking down there was kind of heavy, and I did not want Nancy to get caught up in it. Before Kirsten's death, Nancy did not drink. Not at all. When I came home from work, she would always have a cocktail waiting for me—she made a terrific Old Fashioned—and we would sit and talk about our day. I never saw Nancy drink. But after Kirsten died, she began taking medication to treat her depression. Because Doc Levine was blind, Nancy's aunt Viola was his legal signature and signed everything for him. She wrote whatever prescriptions she believed would make Nancy feel better. I never saw the bottles she gave Nancy and did not ask what was in them. The subject was too sensitive to talk about.

Harvard

One decade after losing Kirsten, Nancy continued to struggle. At school, another girl named Kirsten Carr had been in the same first-grade class as our daughter. The similarities between our two families were uncanny. This classmate's father, Paul Carr, also happened to be a microwave engineer who lived in Bedford and worked at MIT's Lincoln Lab. His daughter's magazine subscriptions and mail often got accidentally delivered to our house. Or people would call Nancy while I was away, wanting to share some theory on why Kirsten had died, and Nancy would be crying when I got home.

Wanting to protect Nancy, I bought a colonial reproduction house in Harvard, a quiet town along the Nashua River about twenty miles west of Bedford. Harvard was best known for its Shaker Village, the second community of its kind in the country, and for the Fruitlands, the family home of Louisa May Alcott. A well-known transcendentalist, the writer's father, Bronson, advocated living close to nature, which the town provided plenty of. When we got there, Harvard had no night life. No liquor stores. No restaurants. Nothing except the town hall and the town common, where people once grazed livestock. Harvard did not even have a hockey team, but it had the one thing our family desperately needed—a fresh start.

I bought an unfinished saltbox modeled after a 1740 house in Connecticut. The builder, Macdouni "Mudd" Sherrigan, was selling it while going through a divorce. A real craftsman, he later made a name for himself producing knives. In fact, you are not considered a real sailor unless you have a Sherrigan knife. However, Mudd's wife had so many unbroken housecats that before moving in I had to rip up and replace the wood floors and carpets.

Whenever I built something, I researched the construction techniques from that time period. In colonial days, instead of seasoning lumber, they used fresh cut planks, which shrank as they dried. So they laid the thick-sawn floor boards while the wood was still green and did not nail them down. Six to eight months later, they took up the dried planks, squared off the edges, and nailed them in place. This prevented gaps from forming between the boards. I thought you should do things the old way, so I laid the floor in the same way. Nancy was very patient. However, in the months the planks were drying, they bounced so much when we walked on them that Nancy thought I should have bought kiln-dried wood instead.

Meanwhile, I finished the cherry paneling and built cherry cabinets for the kitchen. I even made my own pewter lighting fixtures with cups to hold the candles. Since Nancy liked to sew and had a good sense of color, she made the curtains.

One October day in 1978, while working in the basement, cutting wedges with a table saw to lay down the floor, I got careless. A six-inch spear caught the back of the blade and shot toward me, shattering my glasses and piercing my left eye. To prevent Nancy from seeing what I had done, I pulled out the wedge and held a washcloth over my eye. Then I ran upstairs and asked her to drive me to the hospital.

"Let me look at your eye," she said.

I would not show her. "Just take me to the doctor," I said, concerned that if she saw my eye, she would not be able to drive.

Nancy drove me to Emerson Hospital in Concord, about twenty minutes away. The doctor who saw me could not believe I could handle the pain. My eye was not even in place; it had been pushed way down in the socket and flattened like a squished grape. He sent me to Mass Eye and Ear in Boston, which kept me overnight for surgery to re-inflate my eye.

"Do you want an old guy like me doing your surgery, or do you want a young guy with steady hands?" asked Dr. Henry Allen, the doctor treating me. He was accompanied by a younger doctor, Dr. Robert Bellows.

"I'll take both," I said. "The young guy with steady hands and you looking over his shoulder."

A good friend, Ed White, the manager of the Union Oyster House in Boston, heard about my accident and sent a lobster Newburg dinner up to my hospital room.

"You're going to come back later and get the dishes?" I asked the waiter.

When he said yes, I requested that he also bring me a nice bottle of wine. He returned with a bottle of Robert Mondavi

Cabernet Sauvignon tucked under his jacket, and I hid it under the bedsheets.

The next morning, after reconstructing my eye, Dr. Allen came to check on me. "You did a great job," I said.

"We haven't got the bandages off yet," he replied, since both of my eyes were still bandaged and I could not see.

"Regardless of the outcome," I said, "I've learned to always say thank you." Then I handed him the bottle of wine.

"How'd you manage to get that?" he asked.

So I told him.

After that, I could not see very well out of my left eye. My doctor barred me from physical activity for six months, but a few weeks later, one of my teammates on the Acton Bears called and said they needed me to ensure they qualified for the playoffs. Not wanting to let my team down, I agreed to play. I ended up getting the butt of a hockey stick in my eye, which sent me back to Mass Eye and Ear for a repeat surgery. Although my eye injury made it hard to play sports, I did not let it stop me.

When we moved to Harvard, I was in my mid-forties and joined the local fast-pitch softball league. Sponsored by the *Times Free Press* in neighboring Ayer, our team played surrounding teams from Tyngsborough, Townsend, Shirley, Littleton, Groton—all over. However, after my eye injury, I had trouble balancing, particularly as I could only hear out of one ear, which also affects balance. Playing hockey was fine; the puck never comes from up high. But in softball, if I leaned back to catch a pop ball, I fell over backwards.

Whenever I can't do something, I compensate. So I bought a book to learn how to pitch. Then I painted a line for the pitcher's mound at the correct distance from my garage and rolled up the door to hang a sheet of canvas from the top. I cut a hole in the sheet the width of home plate. Every night after work, I stood in the driveway with a couple of buckets full of softballs and threw them at the hole until I got quite good at hitting the target.

"Don't you ever quit?" Nancy asked, watching me.

The next year I was the starting pitcher. When you pitch, you are supposed to keep both feet on the rubber, bring the ball back, and snap it underhand. I could almost sidearm the ball and could pitch at 70–80 mph—not very fast, but I was accurate. However, I stood sideways on the mound and stepped off, which gave me an advantage and was considered illegal, but the league took my injury into account and the umpire looked the other way.

Later, I also pitched for a team that played in the state prison league. Organized by various correctional facilities, the league often held games in Concord and Shirley. We also played at Walpole, a maximum-security prison regarded as one of the most violent prisons in the country.

The rules were very strict. One hour before the game, our whole team had to arrive at the prison together. The guards opened a gate and let us into the prison yard, which served as the ball field. Prohibited from mingling with the other players, our team had to stay in a chalked-in area with a bench. Before taking our positions, we had to wait for the other team to leave the field. The prisoners liked to play ball and took their games very seriously. We played against some good teams, and none of their players ever missed a game due to scheduling conflicts, so they had an advantage.

In my younger days, I played ball with the fathers of my current teammates. By now my former teammates had mostly retired, and I was playing with their sons. Because of work, I sometimes arrived without enough time to warm up, which caused a shoulder injury. Eventually the pain got so bad, I had trouble finishing a game. So I went to Brigham and Women's Hospital, and they put a silicone pad between the bone and the tendons in my shoulder so they would not rub. After recovering, I could pitch doubleheaders.

During one prison league game, the guards at the Concord correctional facility told me about a couple of inmates whose good behavior had earned them appointment as trustees. One man was getting out of jail soon. I did not know what he had served time for, but he had woodworking experience in a machine shop. He also had a good attitude, so I hired him as a machinist.

Meanwhile, Nancy joined Harvard's garden club. I helped her get into bird watching and went with her on bird counts. She went to area Audubon meetings and learned the sounds of all of the birds. Nancy was so good, she could tell the sounds of the birds with her eyes closed, and I often joined her on birding expeditions. An avid gardener, she also planted crocuses, daffodils, and roses around our house so that something was always blooming—especially for the hummingbirds. Chains of lavender wisteria hung from the garden arches that I built in my basement workshop, and Nancy planted wavy clusters of sea broom, which reminded her of the Cape. But her favorite flowers were the big, sweet-smelling peonies with their multi-layered blooms. Because they were too weak to stand on their own, Nancy supported them with a big round disk to cradle the stalks. That way, when the blossoms came, the flowers did not fall over.

By then, Randee had graduated from Plymouth State University in New Hampshire with a degree in education. The day that Nancy and I dropped her off at college, Randee did not want to stay. As we started to drive away, she held onto the door handle, begging to go home.

"Stop the car! Stop the car!" Nancy said.

"I am not going to stop the car," I said and kept driving. "If we stop the car, she will come home and never go back to college."

Nancy was upset the whole ride home, but Randee stayed. She had a very nice roommate, Mary, and that made all the difference. Later, Randee thanked me for not stopping the car. When she finished school, there were very few local teaching jobs. She ended up teaching in Australia and loved it. I was proud of her— particularly when I remembered the little girl who used to hide behind the rock at the end of our driveway to avoid getting on the school bus.

Growing up, Michael continued to struggle. When he was in grade school, I had often attended counseling with him because of trouble he was having in the classroom. Later, when he was a teenager, my Porsche keys went missing and a neighbor called to say that he had seen Michael—who did not have a license—driving my car through the middle of Bedford. In high school, he threw a desk chair through a second-floor window and decked his high school principal, Bob Biggio, who happened to play in the same softball league with me.

When I went in to see Bob, I told him, "If Michael hits you again, hit him back."

"I can't do that," he said.

My fault is, I am a straight-arrow guy. I do not see any excuses for bad behavior. I think everybody should toe the line. Be a decent person. Do the right thing.

Before the school allowed Michael back, they required that I take him to see a counselor. The counselor had us sit on pillows on a wooden floor, which hurt my back. When I asked to sit in a chair, the counselor called me uncooperative, saying I needed to sit down at Michael's level. Then he blamed Michael's problems on me because I was not his real father. To me, that sounded like an excuse. I am not sure why Michael never warmed up to me. It is a question I cannot answer, but soon after graduating from high school, Michael joined the Air Force and left home.

While all of our children were going through school, I attended their parent-teacher meetings with Nancy. Nancy would ask how they were doing over all, and I would ask what courses they were taking.

When Jeff was in grade school, he got into the local 4-H club with his pet rabbits. He had around thirty, about the same number I had at his age. He left their pens open so they were free to hop all over the backyard. In winter, they slept bunched all over our giant Newfoundland, Tiffany. Unfortunately, a couple of the neighbor's Dobermans came over one day and killed them. What a mess. I made sure to clean them all up before Jeff came home, so he would not see it.

Later on, Chris and Jeff both had snakes. We even had a couple of wild pet raccoons that ate out of our hands. In fact, Jeff was so good with animals that I hoped he would become a veterinarian.

Chris was a free spirit. In high school, he played guitar and formed a rock band with his friends. They all brought their instruments over to our house to practice. Randee also played guitar. In Bedford, she and two friends had formed a band, The Ledgewoods. Each weekend I drove her to guitar lessons and even bought a banjo, figuring I might as well try to learn something while I was there. But I could not carry a note in a basket. When I tried to play, the instructor would say, "Jeesh! Tune that thing!"

I thought I had it tuned perfectly.

I also taught Chris and Jeff how to ski and play hockey. In high school, I put them through outdoor survival school—summer and winter. They went to Utah and lived in the snow for a week at a time. When they went skiing, they stayed on the mountain, hiking in on snowshoes and carrying their skis. As our kids got older, I paid for their educations—something my own family had been unable to do for me. By then I was doing very well, so I gave each of my children the best start I could.

I also continued playing hockey, lacing my skates for both the Industrial Hockey League, made up of teams formed by the area's technical companies, and for the Assabet Skating Rink in Acton-Boxboro, a hotbed of hockey. Being part of a team was very important to me. Because of my leg injury, I am not an exceptional player, but when I play, I have a way of forgetting everything else. Some people relax by turning on the television; I played sports, which allowed me to take my mind off things. That was one advantage I had. While on the ice or pitching a game, I did not think about anything except playing.

I took to the ice with the understanding that we were going to win. Even if I got hurt, I would still play. I wanted to contribute. I felt I owed it to my team. I played fair, but if I was hit or something, I would fight back, which is one reason Nancy never came to my games. She thought they were too rough. Also, we often played at two or three in the morning.

During my time in Harvard, I assisted Bob Caldwell, a local environmental engineer, in running the hockey school at the Assabet rink. I had a key to the rink, so whenever my schedule allowed, I opened up the rink at five in the morning and gave free lessons to anyone who showed up. A lot of fathers want to be coaches, but coaches are not out on the ice playing the game. They sit on the bench. A hockey instructor does not sit. He has skates on. When I taught my hockey students, I did it by example, the same way I worked with my engineers. Instead of telling them what to do, I showed them. I love to teach, and I consider sports to be an important part of life.

Students came from all the surrounding towns—Bedford, Harvard, Acton, Boxboro, Concord, Maynard. Some kids came every morning. To teach them how to dive on the ice and jump up without dropping their sticks, I dropped on the ice and did it with them. I taught them to wrap the handle of their hockey sticks with tape so that if they dropped their stick, it was easier to pick up off the ice with their gloves. The tape also prevented the end of the stick from fitting through the holes in the player's face mask, which can really do a job on a player's eye—something I knew first hand. And I taught them what to do if someone ever fell through the ice while playing on a pond.

"Put something in the hole," I told them, "even if the only thing you have available is your legs. That way, they can find their way out." That is what Pop Hartley had done for me.

At Assabet, I also helped start a hockey program for girls. Since we had no other facilities, they had to use the manager's office for their locker room.

"I don't care what the scores are," I told my players at the start of each season. "When you finish this year, you will be better skaters. You will be more skilled." A lot of kids are good skaters but will never be competitive because they do not have that "owning the puck" attitude. You have to fight for the puck, or as I always told my players, "Nobody takes that puck off your stick."

If I found somebody goofing off or not trying, at the end of a session I would pick him as the rabbit. The rabbit got chased by the hounds. The players all started behind the net. After giving the rabbit a head start, I would yell, "Go!" Then the rabbit would have to skate like hell while the remaining guys chased him around. They could check him. They could hit him. They could do whatever they wanted. Nobody wanted to be the rabbit, so it made them hustle.

After practice, Jeff and Chris would often say, "Come on, Dad! We're going to beat you! We're going to beat your ass going around the rink!"

I always skated counterclockwise. Going around the back of the net, you have to do these crossovers, and because of my prior leg injuries, while skating in the clockwise direction I could not cross my bad leg over the other. If Chris or Jeff had said, "Why don't we go the other way?" they could've beat me. But they never realized it, and they never did beat me.

Every morning after skating, I drove to work in Burlington. So that I did not offend everyone by smelling like a locker room, M/A-Com installed a shower next to my office. There is nothing worse than someone opening their hockey bag after the shirts have been in there for a week. The shirts ripen in the bag.

By Land or by Sea

While living in Harvard, I also entered a number of competitive canoe races, including The Great Race, which began at four in the morning on the Charles River in Watertown and ended twenty miles away in Swampscott on the other side of Boston Harbor. The first race began after a bet between two men in a Marblehead bar. Who could complete the distance to the bar from Watertown faster? they wondered. One went by land, the other by sea.[25] Contestants later sported all kinds of contraptions and often competed as teams—in boats, by bike, or on foot. One group ran while wearing trash barrels decorated to look like a six-pack of beer. Another team pushed an antique fire pumper with beer buckets hanging from the sides. Then there was the

Boston Red Sox sportscaster who paddled a boat while sitting up in a bed.

One year I entered the race with Ken Puglia, a microwave engineer I worked with at M/A-Com. If we hit the tide just right coming into Boston, I knew we could paddle right under the North Station rail terminal, which housed the Boston Garden. Rats were everywhere, climbing the piers that held up the station. When Ken saw the rats, he refused to put his paddle in the water, afraid the rats would run up it and climb in the canoe.

"I can't do it," he said, gripping his paddle.

"If you don't paddle, we will be here forever," I said. "And when the tide comes in, we are going to go up with it and meet the rats." If I had thrown a soaked coonskin hat into the canoe, Ken would have been the second man to walk on water.

We were the only team I saw under the station, but it saved time. I would do anything to win.

Another year, I entered the race with Ed McNeely, an inspector for Hughes Aircraft, who had watched the race the previous year and decided it looked like fun. He joined our team in an eight- or ten-man war canoe. After paddling past the East Boston fuel storage tanks, we pulled the canoe out of the water and ran with it across Route 1 near Wonderland, where they once raced greyhounds. We threw the canoe back in the water by Revere Beach, which is open to the ocean, but because we were overloaded and the harbor was choppy, our canoe started taking on water.

"Start bailing!" yelled Ted Morine, a powerful guy I played hockey and softball with. A Tufts graduate and an engineer of geology who happened to be a lot younger than me, Ted was my catcher. Ed and one other guy refused to let go of the gunnels. It turned out they could not swim. So we paddled back to the beach to drop them off, and they finished the race on foot.

Sponsored by Labatt's beer, the race finished on Marblehead Beach, with tables full of all-you-could-drink beer near a row of outhouses. One year while waiting in line for an outhouse, I was in panic mode, when a television reporter came up to me and asked, "What was the toughest part of the race?"

"Waiting for the john," I said.

They put that on TV.

"Was that you?" people called to ask me.

"No," I said. "But it sure looked like me."

Eventually they stopped holding the race because it involved too much drinking.

I also entered the Great Josh Billings RunAground Triathlon. Just north of Stockbridge, in Western Massachusetts, the canoeing portion of the race took place on the Stockbridge Bowl, an artificially impounded 372-acre lake near Tanglewood, which served as the summer home of the Boston Symphony Orchestra. At the time, the course included a 30-mile bike ride, a 6-mile canoe race, and a 6-mile run—a tough race. Ted Morine was my partner in two-man races, and we entered the race together.

After biking, we had to run while carrying our canoes about a quarter of a mile across a parking lot before putting them in the water. As a result of my accident, running hurts, so I never practiced. Even so, Ted and I were running nip-and-tuck with Eric Heiden, who in 1980 won five Olympic gold medals for speedskating, and we finished in the top ten percent of the race. However, later that day I was giving a talk in New York for the International Microwave Power Institute, so as soon as we finished the race, I left without hearing the winners announced and drove two hours to Boston to catch my plane. By the time I made it to the talk, I had trouble getting up on the podium and could not speak. The host had to stand up and apologize for me.

As soon as I got back to Boston, I went to Tufts-New England Medical Center to see what was wrong.

"You couldn't speak because you were so dehydrated," the doctor said. "You push yourself too hard. You could have died."

"I wanted to win," I said. I also felt an obligation to Ted. No one wants to partner with someone who doesn't want to win. It is not fair to your teammate.

The only race I remember my family coming to was on the Nashua River in Harvard. My son Chris, who was about sixteen, and his friend, Andrew Hayward, rented a canoe and decided they were going to show us how youth could beat two old-timers and win a race. Arriving at the race a few minutes early, I rubbed butcher's wax on the outside of my 18.5-foot Jensen Wenonah canoe, to give it a little bit of an edge. Then I threw a cup of water in the bottom of the canoe to act like a level. By watching where it pooled, I could adjust the seats to make sure the canoe was totally balanced.

So many contestants entered the race, they launched us in waves with two minutes between each group. Chris and Andrew had a two-minute head start. They were going like hell, but Ted and I were gaining on them. While Chris and Andrew picked up their paddles in the water, which uses a lot of energy and causes the canoe to move up and down instead of forward, Ted and I were going like pros, doing the J-stroke. Instead of stroking with our arms, we stroked in a circular motion from our waists, slicing our paddles through the water. When we came to a bend in the river, we leaned back to make the bow come up out of the water so that the wind or the current turned the canoe in the right direction. I sat in the bow, and Ted sat in the stern, stroking on opposite sides. After so many strokes, one of us would call out a number—like "Nine!" Then on "Ten!" we would switch sides. That way, we kept right on paddling around the curves. It is all scientific, but kids do not think of the strategy.

When we passed the boys in their canoe, Chris looked awful. Nancy, watching from a bridge, was so upset by how easily we passed them that she drove home—and she was our transportation. When we reached the end of the race, Nancy was not there. She was still angry when I finally made it home.

"You know, Nancy," I tried to explain. "There are two people in a canoe, and I am not going to lose the race when Ted is breaking his butt out there. If we can win, we are going to win. That is what sports are all about, and if they beat me, they will know they beat me."

CHAPTER 10

MOVING INTO MEDICINE

Toward the end of America's involvement in the Vietnam War, I volunteered to help NASA analyze Soviet crop yields with radiometric sensing, which measures electromagnetic energy considered as thermal radiation. In space, radiometric sensing is used to measure the temperature of stars. It can also gauge the health of a crop. A healthy crop has a high moisture content. A sick crop is dry. A perfect absorber is also a perfect emitter. So, you are actually measuring the moisture content of the crop, which acts as the transmitter. A crop that is nice and moist puts out a radiometric signature, or signal. For a given material, emissivity increases proportionately at all frequencies with increasing temperature. Therefore, by measuring the "brightness," or emissivity, of the signature, you can tell the difference between a healthy crop and a sick crop.

In 1979, NASA invited me to consult for them again. So, while still working for M/A-Com, I joined a team to gauge the expected crop yield of corn and wheat in the Soviet Union. The United States used this data in military negotiations. Due to a harsh winter followed by drought, the Soviets were experiencing a severe grain shortage but did not want the world to know that their crops were failing—especially satellite countries like Cuba and Cambodia, which relied on them for wheat. The only sources to buy wheat or corn outside of the Soviet Union were the huge farms in Canada and the United States. In 1972, the United States negotiated a secret wheat-for-peace deal.[26] In exchange for our selling the Soviets 19 million metric tons of wheat and corn on credit at subsidized prices, they agreed not to send troops into Vietnam. However, the Soviets bought more wheat than we intended, causing U.S. food prices to soar.

Working on radiometric sensing for NASA opened the door for me to get into medical research. After reading a couple research papers by MIT professors Alan Barrett and Philip Myer about using radiometers to measure temperature, I started thinking about how this might be used to address medical problems. Every night after dinner, instead of watching television, I relaxed by slipping on a pair of headphones connected to a cassette player and sitting in a dark room listening to medical lectures, which Doc Levine acquired from Harvard Medical School and shared with me. As the doctor described what he was doing in the operating room, such as heart surgery or cancer treatment, I learned medical terminology.

My interest in medicine increased when Kathy Gray, the wife of Bill Gray, a very good friend and microwave engineer at Hughes Aircraft, was diagnosed with late-stage breast cancer. Whenever work brought me to California, I stopped to visit Kathy in the hospital. She died in 1981, and it was tough on Bill and their three kids.

"There's got to be a way to detect this sooner," I said to Bill.

I thought radiometric sensing might be the way.

Breast cancer is among the most feared of all cancers in women. Statistically, one in eight women is likely to develop breast cancer in her lifetime. Even with self-examination and mammograms, the death rate from breast cancer has remained high, primarily because those two methods of detection do not provide an early enough diagnosis to discover and remove the cancer before it metastasizes. Early diagnosis is essential. The size of a tumor at the time of detection is the most dominant key to survival. The larger the tumor, the larger the number of cells it releases. However, if a mass is large enough to be detected by palpation— roughly one centimeter—it has already been in the body for approximately six to eight years.[27][28]

Due to a process called "angiogenesis," a tumor has an apparent higher temperature than the surrounding breast. The body's core temperature averages 37° Celsius (C). A woman's breast, which is considered an extremity like a hand or foot, averages a significantly cooler 34.5°C. However, because the blood flowing to the site of a tumor comes from a person's core, angiogenesis makes a tumor appear larger and warmer than the surrounding tissue. I thought we might use the same technology we used to determine the health of crops to detect tumors. Only instead of measuring the emissivity of crops, I wanted to develop a radiometric sensor capable of determining the depth and temperature of tissue by measuring naturally occurring electromagnetic emissions from the human body.

Because of my work on radiometric sensing, NASA asked me to write a research grant to create a spinoff technology using space technology to create a commercial product that addressed an unmet need. In exchange, they would help me secure a research position at the recently established Eastern Virginia Medical School (EVMS) in Norfolk, near NASA's Langley Research Center. My NASA contact was part of the government's Small Business Innovative Research (SBIR) program, which sets aside a small percentage of money for research from the budgets of various government agencies, including the National Institutes of Health, the Department of Health and Human Services, the U.S. Food and Drug Administration, and the Centers for Disease Control and Prevention. If the National Institutes of Health (NIH) approved the grant, NASA would introduce me to the school.

"Here's this engineer who is working with us," they basically said. "He's got a grant and needs a collaborator."

There is nothing like having a grant. When you have a grant, you have money. Everyone accepts you. So I agreed to consult for NASA, and they introduced me to the medical staff at EVMS. As a result, I became an advisor to the school's Medical Physics Department, which included radiology. However, I agreed to keep the arrangement with NASA confidential until I had data to show for it and won a funded research program. Not even the medical school knew I was consulting for NASA, and I ended up being part of the faculty for close to forty years.

Every six weeks or so, I flew to Norfolk to give a talk or do research, but I never requested a paycheck from NASA. In fact, I received no compensation of any kind from them or the medical school. I covered my own costs and spent more than the grant allowed, often using my own money to pay the engineers who worked with me.

As part of my research, I met with Dr. Judah Folkman, a top cancer researcher for the Harvard Medical School's Boston Children's Hospital and a leading expert on the use of angiogenesis inhibitors. Dr. Folkman agreed that heat preceded metastasis, confirming my theory that angiogenesis makes the tumor appear larger and warmer than the surrounding tissue. Even with a minute tumor, if angiogenesis occurs, it can be detected. I aimed to develop a microwave-based technique to find angiogenesis. That is like finding a pipe in the ground because you can detect the disturbed soil of the trench. When you get a splinter, the area around it becomes red as a result of increased blood flow to the site. As a result of localized inflammation, that increased blood flow is warmer than the surrounding tissue. That is angiogenesis. We did not want to find the splinter. We wanted to find the hot spot.

We used part of the grant to develop a non-invasive radiometer that would see deep into tissue. NASA used a similar radiometer to measure the temperature of targets in space, but to find this hotspot we needed an antenna to focus on localized areas. To make a microwave antenna small enough to use in medical procedures, we increased the frequency, which resulted in a smaller antenna. However, increasing the frequency reduced the depth of detection. Working with Jim Regan, Bob Bielawa, and Bob Williams, we designed our radiometer with a frequency of 4.7 gigahertz. However, because that is the second harmonic frequency (the same frequency at which microwave ovens operate), our radiometer could detect any microwave oven in the hospital.* So we reduced it to 4 gigahertz.

To make our hand-held antenna small enough to place on the breast in multiple places, we made the sensor, or transducer, less

---

* Microwave ovens utilize magnetrons at the lowest source of power. Magnetrons operate at 2.45 GHz and have high 2nd harmonic (4.9 GHz) content. Although the microwave oven is designed to dramatically reduce leakage at the 2nd harmonic, it is easily detected by sensitive radiometric sensing.

than one-inch wide. The antenna itself measured one full inch wide. This allowed the system to see deeper into the breast and enabled us to find tumors as small as two millimeters in diameter, which is prior to metastasis and years before they could be detected by palpitation or a mammogram—by which time the tumor would likely be closer to one centimeter.

The size of a two-drawer filing cabinet, the complete radiometer sat on top of a rolling cabinet which I built in my basement. Radiometers are highly sensitive to interference signals from electrical lines, so rather than plugging our machine into a wall outlet we ran it off of 12-volt car batteries housed in the cabinet. I took no risks, including delivering the radiometer to EVMS. Because the equipment was too large to carry onboard an airplane, Bob Bielawa and I planned to drive it nearly six hundred miles from Boston to Norfolk. But due to the 1979 national gasoline shortage, we were unsure we would make it. Following a revolution that toppled the Iranian monarchy, crude oil production declined worldwide and oil prices to skyrocketed, causing many American drivers to wait in long lines outside gasoline stations.

Before setting out, Bob and I filled several five-gallon fuel containers with gasoline and stowed them in the back of my Chevy station wagon. To prevent someone from trying to steal them, we covered the containers with a blanket. As an extra precaution, we reserved a Hertz rental car halfway along our planned route. If we ran low on fuel, we planned to pick up the rental car, drive it off the lot, syphon the gasoline, and return the rental before continuing our drive.

We made it without needing the rental car. However, while driving back to Boston, we stopped at a roadside rest area and passed several people pushing cars toward the station's gasoline pumps. It is hard to drive by someone pushing a car when you have gallons of gasoline. So we pulled into an empty parking lot before refilling our fuel tank with the gasoline we were carrying.

As Bob later remarked, it was never a question of whether we would make it to Virginia to put the radiometer in place at

EVMS. We would do anything to be successful. On a later trip, Bob, who had a private pilot's license, flew us down in a rented plane.

Radiometric sensing was a big hit for NASA, which used spinoff technology to generate good publicity while helping to justify their space programs. As a result, Edward Sternick, a medical physicist at Tufts-New England Medical Center in Boston (now named the New England Medical Center), asked me to write about how thermography could be used for the early detection of breast cancer, which I did several years later for the *Encyclopedia of Medical Devices and Instrumentation.*[29] This made me somewhat of a guru on radiometric sensing.

Whenever I flew down to Virginia, James Shaeffer, an instructor of radiology at the medical school, picked me up at the Norfolk International Airport and drove me about fifteen minutes to EVMS. Later that same day, someone from NASA drove me to Langley Field. In collaboration with the medical school, I ended up winning thirteen additional SBIR research grants and helped publish numerous technical papers with James Shaeffer and Dr. Anas El-Mahdi, an Egyptian-born medical doctor who headed up EVMS's radiation department. Publishing scientific papers is very important, particularly for a new medical school, and this helped open the door to using microwaves in medicine.

We named our breast cancer detection system OncoScan, after *onco,* the Latin word for *tumor.* Our device used passive, non-ionizing radiometric sensing to detect the difference in temperature between a tumor and its surrounding tissue. OncoScan was not intended as a standalone test, but when used in conjunction with other detection methods, I hoped it would provide a non-invasive, painless, and cost-effective screening tool for the early detection and treatment of breast cancer. Our research also included the use of microwaves to treat tumors, which can be destroyed by heat. The dual-mode transducer, which measured emissivity and could be used with dual radiometers with two widely separated radiometric frequencies, enabled us to see different tissue depths to enhance cancer detection. As a result, in 1980 NASA awarded us a Certificate of Recognition for my brief on the Dual-Mode Microwave Antenna.

Around this time, NASA and EVMS invited me to participate in a televised press conference to discuss how radiometric sensing could be used to help detect breast cancer. When I arrived at the medical school, reporters lined up to ask me questions. Since I am not a medical doctor, I explained that I was only there to answer technical questions and avoided discussing patient data. At the conference, I sat at a table with four medical doctors, including Dr. El-Mahdi and James Shaeffer. A couple of NASA representatives also participated.

The meeting had barely begun when a woman in the audience stood up and asked, "How did the microwaves get into my body?"

Dr. El-Mahdi pointed to me, so I stood and walked up to the podium.

"All objects emit electromagnetic energy," I tried to explain. "They are naturally produced by your body."

"You liar!" the woman screamed. "I've been zapped!"

At that time, many people feared microwave energy emitted by ovens. This later included cell phones. She thought microwaves had somehow gotten into her body. I tried to explain that our passive radiometric breast-cancer screening system did not emit microwaves; it detects them. The radiometer we developed did not just measure temperature. It detected emissivity. The level of emission is based on the temperature of the tumor with respect to the surrounding tissue. The higher the temperature of the tissue, the higher the emissivity, or energy being emitted from it. In fact, warming the area with a hot water bottle or heating pad enhanced detection by increasing emissivity. Two materials—such as pus or a blood vessel—can have the same temperature but emit different levels of emissivity, which we discovered at EVMS. The ability to detect two different materials at the same temperature led to many microwave-based medical products including neonatal and pediatric extravasations, air emboli detection, and the detection of vulnerable plaques in blood vessel walls.

After explaining this, I tried to move on and invite other people to speak, but the woman, a local activist, kept calling me a liar. When security tried to escort her out, her supporters stood up and surrounded her. She became so disruptive, they closed down the conference.

Wow, that was tough, I thought on my way back to the airport. *What a wasted trip and meeting.*

One question I had been asked at the meeting, was whether I had a microwave oven. I admitted I did not. Nancy did not like cooking in them. However, on my way home I stopped at a store and bought one.

"I don't want a microwave," Nancy said when I gave it to her.

"You don't have to cook in it," I explained. "Leave it in the box."

The next time someone asked, I would now be able to say that yes, I owned a microwave oven.

However, because of the perceived microwave hazard, the FDA resisted the use of passive radiometric sensing. They were convinced we were using microwave energy to heat breast tissue—which we were not. The FDA also objected to the name of our device, which they called misleading as it detected both malignant and non-malignant tissue. They used anything for an excuse not to approve a product. So, we used the name "Thermostat," at our meetings instead of OncoScan. I did not want to lose the war by battling for a name.

To convince the FDA to let us begin clinical trials, we first had to overcome its opposition to using microwaves in medicine. I had such a good track record that M/A-Com pretty much gave me a free hand. So in 1985, I began a new company division, Microwave Medical Systems (MMS), to develop medical technology. As I had with other divisions, I eventually hoped to spin the division off as its own M/A-Com company. I submitted my first microwave medical grants to NASA and to the Department of Defense's U.S. Army Medical Research and Development Command. Of great importance to the medical school, these grants resulted in numerous publications.

While we continued working to enhance breast cancer detection, the Army presented us with the need for a single product that could treat injured soldiers by warming refrigerated blood from very low or no flow (0 ml per minute) to a high flow (greater than 500 ml per minute). Blood is typically refrigerated at 4°C, just above freezing. At the time, most hospitals relied on one commercial product designed to warm a low flow of blood and another product to warm a high flow of blood. But on the battlefield, a doctor does not want to say, "Give me a low-flow or a high-flow product" while a guy is bleeding to death. They wanted a single product that could provide everything from 0 to 500 milliliters per minute.

Blood was typically warmed by placing medical tubing in a hot water bath. However, water can freeze and is easily contaminated, whereas microwaves travel at the speed of light and can therefore heat instantaneously. Since the military needed it, I hoped that going after the contract with the Army would convince the FDA to make a faster decision to approve our blood warmer.

For the Army, we developed a microwave blood warmer that did everything requested, but that device also received harsh treatment from the FDA. At the time, the *Technical Manual* for the American Association of Blood Banks (AABB) said that microwave devices damaged red blood cells and therefore should not be used for warming blood. Before getting the FDA to approve our device, it became clear we would have to approach the people who ran the blood banks and get them to change their manual, which would involve another lengthy and expensive research program.

To keep MMS operating while we addressed the perceived microwave hazard issue with the FDA, we needed to develop a medical product that used microwaves without heating either blood or tissue. So in the early 1980s, another M/A-Com engineer, Bill Tice, who lived in Bedford, along with Rick Kelley, Jim Regan, Bob Bielawa, and another very capable engineer, Richard Grabowy, and I designed a sterile docking system that used microwaves to disinfect medical connectors involved in attaching medical tubes, catheters, and syringes in procedures such as kidney dialysis.

To infuse and drain fluids from their bodies, some dialysis patients rely on a soft plastic tube, or catheter, inserted in their abdomen. Four or five times a day, the catheter is connected to a bag containing dialysate fluid, which flows around the digestive organs into the peritoneal cavity. Because the peritoneum is vascular, the fluid absorbs body waste and toxins from the blood. Several hours later, the fluid is emptied into a waste bag and a new bag of fresh fluid streams into the peritoneal cavity. During this process, a plastic connector joins the medical tubing to the catheter. Each time the tubing is changed, a little moisture remains in the connector, which could contaminate the connector with bacteria and lead to peritonitis, a bacterial infection of the lining of the abdominal wall. This can result in a lengthy hospital stay or even death.

The conventional way to disinfect the connector employed ultraviolet energy. However, ultraviolet frequencies do not penetrate plastic and therefore do not address the risk of infection at the connection point, or inner lumen, of the fluid path. Today, most U.S. dialysis patients receive treatment in a medical setting, but at that time, the medical system was moving toward having patients undergo dialysis at home, so we designed a sterile docking system that used microwave emissions to heat and disinfect this connector. The system used a shared antenna to measure the temperature at the point where the heat was applied. The same microwave antenna we used for disinfecting also measured the temperature, which was critical.

To kill bacteria, the transmitter heated the small amount of fluid within the connector for ten seconds. After the radiometer sensed a temperature of 100°C, the boiling point, the device cut the power in half and maintained the temperature to complete the thirty-second sterilization cycle. That way, the system would not reach too high a temperature and deform the plastic, which could compromise the patient's ability to detach the connector from the tubing. Even though we heated the fluid in the connector slightly above the boiling point, the plastic did not get warm to the touch because the fluid—not the plastic—absorbed the microwave energy.

We made the sterilizer portable and easy to operate. The connector included a roller clamp, which the patient could operate with one hand. It automatically put a drop of dialysate fluid into the connector, which boiled during the sterilization process. It also compressed the end of the medical tube to close it down and maintain pressure. And it accurately positioned the connector in the heating cavity, which we coupled to a 20-watt, solid-state microwave source made out of discrete transistors to generate power. We bonded these on the substrate, like inserting a component. The whole system ran on a 12-volt power supply system that we also built as part of the sterilizer so that patients could plug it into their vehicle's cigarette lighter to use while traveling or during a power outage. (A microwave power source for the Thermostat 900 employs a 900-watt source (a magnetron), whereas the sterile docking device requires a solid-state 20-watt source, very little power.)

While designing the sterilizer, I spent countless hours in the dialysis clinics. On a Saturday or Sunday, as long as I did not have a ball game, I often made the rounds with Dr. Gerry Bousquet, a nephrologist who was the head of the dialysis center at St. Joseph's Hospital in Lowell (and also an excellent skier). He later became MMS's medical advisor and served on our board of directors. Dr. Bousquet's patients loved him. He could really make them laugh, like the time he walked into the room of a patient he knew very well. The guy was lying in bed and Dr. Bousquet stuck a thermometer in the man's mouth.

"Now where did I put my rectal thermometer?" Dr. Bousquet looked around, patting his pockets.

The guy yanked the thermometer out of his mouth and made a spitting noise before realizing that Dr. Bousquet was joking. Then they shared a laugh.

While spending time with Dr. Bousquet, I learned that many dialysis patients are also diabetic and some have lost their vision. So we added a tone generator to our device. Having noticed that the blind people who boarded with my grandmother always drank out of tall glasses to hear the tone change as the glass filled with liquid, I ensured the sterilizer made a sound, *Bup, bup, bup, beep!* to imitate the sound of a tall glass filling up when the cycle was complete.

Sterile docking was a good example of the detection and measurement of temperature at the point at which heat is applied. Other applications of sterile docking included reducing the risk of infection in other tunneled, long-term, central venous lines, which are often used in patients with bone marrow transplants, those requiring extended antibiotic treatment or intravenous nutrition, and chronically ill patients (such as those with AIDS) who receive a variety of intravenous medications and fluids. Best of all, the sterile docking device did not involve the microwave heating of blood or tissue. But the FDA would not even let us use the word *sterilizer* unless we could prove that we could kill every possible type of bacteria, not just the four that commonly occurred during dialysis. So, we called it a "disinfection device," which made the FDA feel better, although it was the same product.

Later, our work included developing a device using non-invasive microwave radiometric sensing to provide early detection of air emboli, or air bubbles, in commonly used IV tubing sets. We also used radiometric sensing for early detection of extravasation, leakage from a catheter or IV line into surrounding tissue that can also be life-threatening. I had other ideas for how microwaves could be used in medical devices, but because of the FDA's skepticism and reluctance to approve the use of microwave devices in medicine, getting them approved would be a lengthy battle.

Going into the medical business was much more difficult than developing military products for Hughes and Westinghouse and the other big military contractors. When dealing with the military on a missile program, everyone involved was as eager as we were to be successful. If we had a problem at Hughes, they would send out engineers to work with us on the problem. I always treated the customer like part of the solution. At the outset I would request that the customer had a technical representative involved, particularly during program reviews. But the FDA was not helpful at all. They just kept throwing up one roadblock after another, seeming to look for any excuse to shut us down.

A Great Pilot

Around this time, I decided to learn how to pilot a plane. After flying with Bob Bielawa, I thought this would save time when I visited the Cape. The Friday night traffic was so terrible, I often signed up to pitch an evening softball game in Newton and drove to the Cape at midnight after the traffic had eased. But Nancy did not like me driving down so late after a full day of work, followed by a ballgame. It must have made her worry. I also tended to speed.

"You can't live like this," she'd say. "You can't put in these hours. You don't get enough sleep."

I have never had trouble sleeping. Some people dream while sleeping. I think of projects. I might go to bed with a problem, and in the middle of the night, I wake up with a solution. Then I run to my desk and write it down before going back to bed.

"Don't you ever give your mind a rest?" Nancy would ask.

That is just the way I am. I do not want to waste time.

So together Bob Bielawa and I bought a four-seater, single-engine Piper Archer. There is no greater incentive than owning your own plane. That is how you get committed. A real risk-taker, I would do anything as a challenge. So one day I drove down to the Fitchburg Municipal Airport to sign up for lessons. This old guy, Red, was supposed to be my flight instructor, but when I got there, he said, "You know? I'm getting too old for this, but

I have a young fellow that I have great respect for. He's a great pilot."

I had not yet met him, when this young guy came out of the hangar and said, "Hey, mister, can I wash and wax your plane?"

"How much do you want?" I asked.

"Fifty bucks," he said.

"Go ahead and clean it up," I told him. "Make it look neat. By the way, where do you live?"

"Here."

"Fitchburg or Leominster?"

"Right here. In the hangar."

Turned out, this guy, Chris Cunha, was my instructor. Chris had his helicopter license, his single-engine and multiple-engine licenses, and was a registered mechanic. We had a similar background: When Chris was about sixteen, his mother had remarried a guy who did not want him around, and the guy asked Chris to leave the house.

"This hanger isn't heated," I said, looking inside. "What do you do in the wintertime?"

"I have a cot with a sleeping bag," he said.

Always looking for good technicians, I asked Chris if he wanted a job that would help him afford a better place to live. "Come into M/A-Com on Monday morning," I told him. "Mention my name to Dave Adey, the head of human resources. If he asks any questions, tell him you play hockey."

I often brought in guys from hockey, so whenever I sent someone to personnel, Dave would ask, "I suppose you play hockey?"

"Just say yes," I told Chris. "You'll get a job."

Chris went in, and we hired him. He was a great technician, and we became lifelong friends.

One day Chris and I were at the airport doing "touch and goes," when he asked me to taxi over to a certain spot. I lined up to wait for the go-ahead to take off on the runway. Then he got out of the plane. "You are on your own," he said.

I had done many takeoffs and landings with Chris, but suddenly I was all alone in the pilot's seat. That was kind of terrifying. There is a big difference between taking off and landing. Taking off is not a problem, but you can't stay up there forever. You have to land the plane. Once you get a feel for it, the plane will guide you in so you don't drop too fast and bounce. You can actually feel the air pressure between the plane and the ground. It feels like landing on a cushion. Chris was a good instructor, and my first landing was fine.

Because I could only see out of one eye, Nancy refused to fly with me. Instead, she drove to the Cape and often stayed for weeks at a time. On Friday evenings, I flew down to the Chatham Municipal Airport and Nancy picked me up. Then we spent the weekend down there together. I only took the kids up in the plane when Bob was with me, which made Nancy feel better.

During that time, I became a trustee at Boston's Wentworth Institute of Technology, which ran an aeronautical engineering course. The school wanted to phase out the program due to low student enrollment. It also lacked an airport facility. Wentworth's president, Edward "Ted" Kirkpatrick, a great guy, was known for building parts of an Experimental Aircraft Association biplane and a Steen Skybolt in the basement of his Weston home. Together we met with the faculty of East Coast Aero, a technical school for flight mechanics at Hanscom Field, and realized that instead of letting the faculty go, we could transfer students and faculty to Bedford, and they would be at the airbase with the school. As a result, Wentworth bought the school and moved its aeronautical course to the airfield, which worked very well. Shortly after, the college sold the school to East Coast Aero's faculty. Rather than shutting the school down, we built it up. That is the way mergers should work. Today East Coast Aero is New England's largest flight and mechanic's training school.

Bob and I owned our plane together for several years, but in the mid-eighties, when I went for my physical to renew my pilot's license, the flight surgeon asked me remove my shirt and stepped out of the room. While waiting for him to return, I overheard a loud commotion in the hallway.

"We've had a problem," the nurse said when she returned. "The doctor won't be able to see you."

"Why not?" I asked.

"He collapsed," she said.

I later found out that he had suffered a heart attack and died. So I did not get my exam and let my license drop.

My grandmother, Grace Amanda Walker, and her first husband,
Charles Carr, at about the time of their 1906 wedding.

Grace with two calves on the Carr Homestead.

The Carr Homestead, at the end of
Carr Road in Berlin, Massachusetts.

My father, Lorenzo Carr, and my mother,
Doris Libbey, who married in 1929.

My uncles George and Robert Carr,
after enlisting to serve in World War II.

The farmhouse my grandmother Grace bought on
Province Lake in Parsonsfield, Maine.

Grace and her second husband, Curt Hartley,
known to everyone as Ma and Pop Hartley.

Ma and Pop Hartley (standing behind her) with
(from left to right) Lorenzo, George, Pop, Chet, and Dutch.

I am standing with (from left to right) Frank Clapp,
my sister Shirley Clapp, my brother's wife,
Corinne Peterson, and my brother, Curtis.

Curtis's and my graduation from Tufts University. Standing
(from left to right): our aunt Cora O'Neil, our grandmother
Catherine O'Neil Libbey, Curtis, myself, Shirley, and Frank
with baby Frankie. Kneeling: our parents, Lorenzo and Doris.

Lorenzo with his second wife, Viola Amende,
Doc Levine's nurse.

My 1958 wedding to Nancy Berthold in the living room
of my father's house in Cambridge, Massachusetts.

A 1962 Ferrotec engineering meeting (left to right): myself, Donald Rich, James Regan, Henry Riblet, George Hemple, and Charles "Chuck" Carson. Photo reprinted with permission from the *Microwave Journal*.

162

Ferrotec employees Edward Antoon, Donald Rich, and James Regan, discussing new ferrite material. Photo reprinted with permission from the *Microwave Journal*.

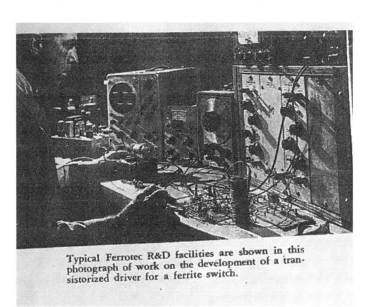

Typical Ferrotec R&D facilities are shown in this photograph of work on the development of a transistorized driver for a ferrite switch.

Ferrotec R&D facilities with an employee developing a transistorized driver for a ferrite switch. Photo reprinted with permission from the *Microwave Journal*.

My best friend, Jim Regan, the finest engineer I have ever
known, who worked with me for nearly fifty years.

Georgie Burton, my long-time secretary and friend.

A portrait of Nancy.

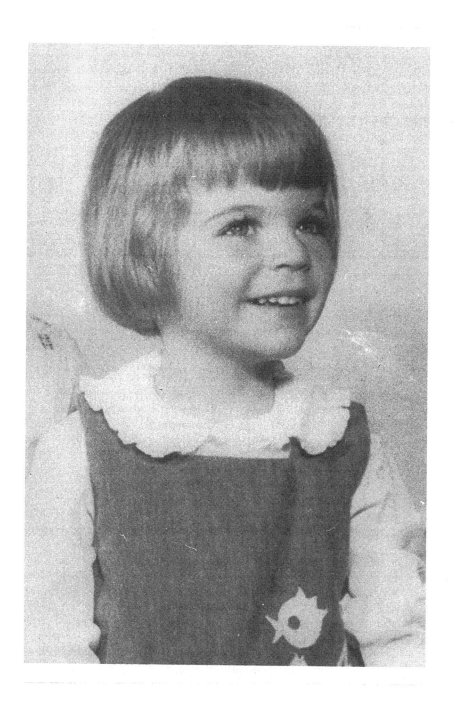

A portrait of Kirsten.

Myself, standing in front of the large rock at the end of
our driveway in Bedford, Massachusetts, with Kirsten, Michael,
Randee, and our St. Bernard (Cynthia and Ted Houston's
house is shown in the background).

Nancy, Jeff, Chris, and myself at the beach
near our Cape Cod house, Sea Broom.

Me, playing fast-pitch softball after
moving to Harvard, Massachusetts.

My hockey teammates, who were all about
twenty years younger than me, for the Acton Bears.
I am seated in the front row on the far right.

The radiometer for the original OncoScan breast cancer detection system developed at M/A-Com. From left to right: John Yates, Harlan Howe, Bob Bielawa, Jim Regan, Georgie Burton, Jimmy Foskin, Thad Litchfield, and myself.

My second wife, Mikelle, and I skiing at Stowe Mountain Resort, Vermont. Photo reprinted with permission.

Myself, standing with the T900 Blood Warmer in the
basement workshop of my house in Woolwich, Maine.
Photo credit, Kelli LK Haines

Me, seated in front of a row of patents in my
basement workshop with the Sterile Docking System.
Photo credit, Kelli LK Haines

170

A recent visit to the Bedford house where
I built an addition after marrying Nancy.

Raymond Roberge and my niece Lawnie Roberge, along with my
daughter, Randee, and myself at the 2022 MTT-S Microwave Pioneer
Awards Ceremony in Denver, Colorado. *Photo credit, LylePhotos.com*

MTT-S President Rashaunda Henderson, awarding me the society's annual Microwave Pioneer Award in recognition of my technical contributions in the field of microwave theory and techniques. *Photo credit, LylePhotos.com*

Age ninety, at home in my office in Woolwich, Maine, overlooking the front garden. *Photo credit, Kelli LK Haines*

CHAPTER 11

AN IDEAL AGENT

Developing medical products while overseeing more than $400 million in sales at M/A-Com's operations in Massachusetts, California, Arizona, and England kept me quite busy. But my life was about to get even busier. In 1985, the Microwave Theory and Techniques Society (MTT-S) selected me as their Distinguished Microwave Lecturer. Part of the Institute of Electrical and Electronics Engineers (IEEE), the MTT-S works to advance microwave theory and its applications around the globe.

While attending Tufts in 1952, I had joined the Institute of Radio Engineers (IRE). One decade later, the IRE merged with the American Institute of Electrical Engineers to form the IEEE, the world's largest technical professional organization, and I have been a member ever since. The same year that the MMT-S selected me as their lecturer, the IEEE made me a Life Fellow, the highest level of engineering, for my contributions to the application of microwave technology in medicine. My selection as a lecturer resulted from my research on radiometric sensing. While running Ferrotec, I had previously lectured in Germany, teaching university students about ferrites. On several occasions, I had also traveled to Israel to advise defense officials on advances in radar-guided missile systems—once resulting in a brief stint in an airport holding cell.

While waiting to meet a M/A-Com sales manager, Ron Kelstrup, at Israel's Ben Guiron Airport, a custom's officer grabbed the slide carousel I had put together for my presentation and dumped it on a table. I put out a hand to stop him, and the young soldier standing next to him hit me with the butt of his Uzi. When the custom's officer began taking apart my slide projector, which had about eight lenses, I put out my hand a second time, and the soldier hit me again.

"You hit me with that gun one more time, and we're going to have a problem," I said.

The guy was careless. Instead of having his Uzi strapped across his chest, he had it dangling down. So, the third time he hit me, I grabbed his gun and threw it on the floor. The last thing I wanted was to have a loaded gun in my hand. Then I whacked him. Next thing I knew, Israeli security guards were all over me.

When Ron arrived at the airport, he could not find me.

"I know Ken got off the plane from Rome," he told a security guard. "What happened to him?"

The guy led Ron to a holding cell, where I was locked up.

"What the hell are you doing down here?" Ron asked me. "Didn't you show them your invitation?"

In my pocket, I had a letter from Moshe Dayan, a national war hero and Israel's minister of defense, inviting me to meet with him.

"I should not need a letter to avoid getting abused," I said.

"Geez." Ron shook his head as the security guard let me out. "How do you get into these things?"

I spent the next day in my hotel room reorganizing my slides and reassembling the lenses for my projector. My presentation went well, but I never could get the projector to focus properly. When I got home, I had to ship it back to the Kodak factory for repairs.

While lecturing for the MTT-S, I spoke at sixty-five universities throughout Europe and Asia in a single year, often giving more than one talk on the same day. However, in India and Japan, I might stay at a single school for a full week and teach an entire course. I mainly lectured about the opportunities of using radiometric sensing in medicine, but I also spoke about weapons systems and commercial products such as underground locators—anything that involved microwaves.

During that time, the United Nations appointed me as a consultant to its International Telecommunications Union in Sao Paulo, Brazil, to assist in building the country's microwave communications systems. While in Brazil, I would lecture for a couple of days at a university discussing antenna sizes and range, while helping their engineers select the best locations for towers and wires to get the least interference.

Unknown to me, the CIA, which gathers foreign intelligence through a network of spies, had been sizing me up. Since my early days working on airplane landing systems at Philco, I had top government security clearance. Because I scheduled my own trips and could go anywhere, the CIA had probably been checking me out for some time. During my time lecturing for the IEEE, the agency contacted me and asked me to gather information for them. As a known lecturer, I was an ideal agent. The CIA also liked that I had a nearly photographic memory and did not need to take notes. After completing a few training sessions, I began receiving assignments.

At work I might get a coded message that said. "Can you be in a particular country on June 3?"

"I don't understand this," my secretary Georgie would say, confused.

"That's okay," I'd tell her. "Let me take care of it."

Then I would schedule a speaking trip to be in the country at that time.

In Taiwan, I once taught a one-week course on ferrites at the National Chung-Shan Institute of Science and Technology where a military officer was assigned to escort me around. Before giving my final lecture, I went out to lunch with him and a dozen guys. A big lazy Susan full of food filled the middle of the table. To eat, you picked out the food with chopsticks. The rotating tray also held drinking glasses and bottles of rice wine, which was significantly stronger and darker than rice wine in Japan.

In Japan, you take a sip, and say, "*Kanpai*," which is like saying, "Cheers!"

So, I picked up my glass, turned to my escort, and said what I believed to be the equivalent word in Chinese, "*Gānbēi!*"

The officer had a big smile on his face and swallowed the entire shot. The rest of us at the table swallowed down our drinks too. Then the officer turned to the person on his right and said the same thing, "*Gānbēi!*" It turned out that what I had really said was "dry cup," or "bottoms up." The Japanese sip wine, but in China, you drink the whole glass. By the time we got around the table, I'd swallowed twelve of these and was quite inebriated, so I could not make it up the stairs to the podium to give my final lecture. A university colleague stood up and apologized for me. The students were all laughing. They knew what had happened.

Upon returning from certain trips, I would give my government contact a rundown of what I had done. It always amazed me how much they knew. For example, while in Taiwan, I liked to walk around. If I walked out the front door of my hotel, a Chinese army vehicle would pull up, get me in the vehicle, and ask where I wanted to go.

"Just across the street," I'd say.

Then they would make a U-turn and drop me off on the other side of the street. I could not even go for a walk.

At one hotel, I tried to dodge them by walking out the back door into the alley. When I got back to Boston, my contact asked, "What were you doing in the alley?"

"You guys really keep an eye on me," I said.

Once, while giving a microwave medical lecture in Italy, I met with a Florence radar manufacturer. Around four o'clock that afternoon, after I had finished up, the people accompanying me offered to drive me back to my hotel. But the area was noted for selling Moroccan leather goods, and I wanted to buy a leather chess board with brass pieces. So I asked to be dropped off at the market and arranged to meet them for dinner back at my hotel.

After buying a good-sized chess set, I hurried through the crowded streets, trying not to be late for dinner. In one hand, I carried the chess set, tied up with string. In the other, my briefcase. At an intersection, I waited with a group of pedestrians for the light to flash *Avanti,* or "go." As soon as it did, I ran around the other people, and a small Italian car struck me and pushed me back into the crowd, knocking down several people. The driver gave me the middle finger followed by several other rude gestures. Then he flicked his hand for me to get out of the way.

In high school, my friend Leo Henebury had taught me that if someone challenges you, you have to act fast and catch your opponent off guard. So, seeing that the driver's door locks were up, I opened the driver's door and whacked him before he could jump out and hit me. When the police arrived, they grabbed both of us and stood us up against a wall. They were pulling out their handcuffs when the people standing around explained how the driver had struck me with his car. Instead of arresting me, the police let me go and offered me a ride.

"That's okay," I said. "My hotel's not very far. But I'm late, so I have to get going."

They neglected to get my name, which was good. Because of my involvement with the CIA, I did not want to attract attention.

When I got back to my hotel, one of the guys I was meeting said, "Did you hear the news? A big fight broke out in the marketplace. Did you see it?"

"No," I said. "It probably happened after I left."

"They arrested a member of the Red Brigades," he said, referring to one of the country's most feared terrorist groups. When I heard that, I wished that I had hit the guy harder.

On a trip to Paris while representing Hughes Aircraft as part of the Roland Missile Program, I got in another fight in the subway at a stop called *L'Enfant*. I was trying to figure out which direction to go when a guy pulled a knife on me and demanded my wallet. I intentionally fumbled and dropped my wallet, but the guy was not too swift. When he bent over to pick it up, I put my knee right into his head. He went down, still holding his knife. Then I stomped on his hand and kicked the knife off the platform onto the tracks.

Named for the top knight of Charlemagne, King of the Franks, the Roland missile was a short-range, surface-to-air tank defense system designed to hit low-flying aircraft. Charlemagne once occupied a territory that now includes France and western Germany. In AD 778, after battling a Muslim army in Northern Spain, the king turned toward home, leaving Roland and a small group of soldiers to guard the pass at the valley of Roncesvalles against an approaching army. They had a hell of a battle, and Roland and his knights were all killed.

M/A-Com developed the seeker head and subsystems for the Roland missile, which was being developed by Germany and France. However, in case of war, the North Atlantic Treaty Organization (NATO) preferred to develop missile systems in more than one country. To have an additional supplier outside the European continent, France was transferring the missile design to the United States.

Wherever I went, the CIA was usually there too, but I never requested compensation. Nor did I ever get paid. That way, no one could track me by following the money. Nancy never knew I was doing work for the CIA. My employees did not know. Even my office assistant, Georgie, and my best friend, Jim Regan, did not know. In all that time, I never let it slip. Everything I did was on the quiet.

My initial commitment to the IEEE lasted one year, but I stretched it to two, traveling to Italy, Taiwan, Japan, Argentina, England, Germany, Holland, Scandinavia, New Zealand, and many other countries. I also traveled to at least as many universities in the United States, once speaking at the University of Arizona at Tucson, Arizona State University in Phoenix, and at Fort Huachuca, a nearby military base, all on the same day. Late that night, as I passed a truck while driving back to Tucson, a tire blew on my rental car. My car rolled over into the ditch, smashing the windshield and pushing in the roof. Thankfully, I was unhurt. After I climbed out, a highway patrol officer stopped to make sure I was okay.

"I'm fine," I said. "But the car's a wreck."

While the officer called a tow truck, we got to talking. "Where are you from?" I asked, recognizing that he did not have a southwestern accent.

"New Hampshire," he said.

"Where?"

"Effingham."

"I was raised on the farm across from Taylor's General Store," I said.

He knew right where it was. Now that we were becoming sort of buddies, I was off the hook. "What do you want to do?" the officer asked after the tow truck pulled my car out of the ditch.

Since I had a plane to catch, I said I would like to drive the car back to Hertz. The tow truck driver got the car running, and I climbed in the mangled car and drove the remaining twenty-five miles to Tucson. I arrived back at the rental company around three in the morning. When I explained to the woman at the off-site rental facility that I had blown a tire, she asked, "Did you put the spare on?"

"Yeah," I said. "The spare is on the car, but if I take the keys out, it won't start."

She walked outside and saw the car, which looked like I had just lost a demolition derby. It was the second Hertz car I had wrecked that year. Previously, after visiting my mother in Florida, I was driving to give an IEEE lecture in Tampa when I spotted a flock of ducks in the road. To avoid hitting them, I intentionally spun the car. One wheel caught the dirt shoulder, and the car went airborne, landing in a canal. Grabbing my suitcase, I pushed open the door and waded through the muck and leaches with my suitcase over my head. A truck driver stopped, spread a plastic mat on the seat of his truck, and gave me a ride to the nearest village, where I called Hertz from a phone booth and explained what had happened. The representative for Hertz asked if I had a way of getting to Sarasota. So I put my head out of the phone booth and asked the driver if he was going in the same direction, which he was. He dropped me off at the Hertz office in Sarasota, where I changed into my suit, rented a new car, and drove the remaining way to Tampa. Although I had missed the pre-lecture dinner, everyone was still there. So I gave my talk.

Following my accident in Arizona, Hertz called M/A-Com to take me off the drivers list. They did not want to rent me any more cars, but Bob Graham, who worked in the finance department and also happened to be my softball catcher, got me off the hook.

"Ken Carr?" he said. "You must be mistaken. He's our technical director." Then he convinced Hertz to leave my name on their drivers list.

Not long after, I was the keynote speaker at a medical conference in Buenos Aires, which I particularly remember because my hotel caught fire. While checking in, I had informed the front desk that I am hearing impaired, but when the fire started, no one came looking for me. Since I do not use my hearing aid while sleeping, I did not hear the alarms. The next morning when I woke up, the power was out. Then I opened my door and saw smoke. I tried turning on the water in my bathroom to soak some towels, but there was no water pressure. At that point, I knew I had to get out. My room was about eleven floors up. I made it down the stairs and out the front door, only to find that the whole hotel had been cordoned off.

"Where are you coming from?" someone asked when I stepped outside. "How did you get here?"

They thought everyone had already evacuated the building. That was a close call.

Starting a New Company

When I first began developing microwave medical devices, I intended to make MMS a new division of M/A-Com. However, due to concerns about liability and the high number of lawsuits in the medical industry, M/A-Com decided not to get into the medical field. Nobody wanted to take on the FDA, but I took it on as a challenge and also as a technical issue that needed to be changed. So in 1985, while lecturing for the IEEE, I gave M/A-Com my notice that I planned to leave the company to run MMS as its own company. Usually when starting a company, I would stay with it for eighteen months. Then the people who worked with me had a choice to either stay with the company or come back to the corporate Tech Center.

"Never take a job based on salary," I told my employees. "Take the job that will get you where you want to be in five years. Set a goal for yourself, and I will help you get where you want to be." Then I would make opportunities available for them. If someone said they wanted to become the engineering manager, I sent them to personnel to get a job description so they could take assignments that would prepare them for the job and meet the qualifications when it became available.

"Where do you want to be? How much education does it take? What do you need?" I always asked people. "I will help you get there."

One engineer, Alejandro "Alex" Chu, came to M/A-Com from MIT's Lincoln Laboratory. Technically competent, Alex had a PhD and worked on proposals. M/A-Com was awarded contracts based on novel engineering concepts and emerging technologies. To stay in program management, Alex wanted more business experience. I encouraged him to attend Harvard Business School's three-month Executive Program for Management Development and authorized M/A-Com to pay for it. The course expanded Alex's credentials, and he now works for the MITRE Corporation, the Federally Funded Research and Development Center in support of the Department of Defense. Because of his technical and business experience, Alex remains very valuable to them.

I also hired Peter Staecker, another capable engineer with a PhD who came from the Lincoln Lab. Because of Peter's involvement with the IEEE, I often gave him time off and justified his travel to attend events such as the International Microwave Symposium, where he often met customers. I did that not to gain favors, but because I wanted my group to be broad in scope and to stay connected to others in the field. Peter later became president of the IEEE.

By adding people to my staff, I expanded the Tech Center to do more research work. Dick DiBona understood me and my desire to excel in development and research. He also recognized the benefit to M/A-Com. From the day Ferrotec merged with Microwave Associates, Dick surrounded me with financial, legal, and business staff to allow me to concentrate on research and development. Dick understood me.

Just as I had after being told I had to leave home at sixteen, I always looked ahead at where I wanted to be in five years and took the jobs and courses—such as in executive leadership or law—most likely to get me there. I believe that in every five years something will occur, good or bad, that you have no control of, and it will change your five-year goal. That is part of following the path: What do you need to know to take the next step?

Sometimes this got me in trouble. I often seemed to make decisions on my own, without depending on other people. That can be a good thing, but it is also a fault, like my not telling Nancy that I intended to leave M/A-Com. To protect my wife from more stress, I had not fully discussed my plans with her. To spin off MMS as its own company, I would have to make the same decision as my team. I could either leave M/A-Com and stay with MMS, or I could stay with M/A-Com and leave MMS.

At that time, I reported directly to Dick DiBona, then president of M/A-Com. So I made a deal to take over MMS and make it my own. The corporation would give me all the patents that applied to medicine and transfer and license them to the new company, along with any medical devices and equipment that we had made. Any engineers I worked with had the choice whether to stay with MMS or to stay with corporate technology. In return, I gave M/A-Com a warrant for stock, making them a part owner of my new company. The handoff was very friendly, and I agreed to stay with M/A-Com for four more years while starting my own company. That would give me time to finish my commitments to Raytheon and Hughes, including developing the seeker head we were working on for the Advanced Medium-Range Air-to-Air Missile (AMRAAM).

In the early eighties, M/A-Com's Corporate Technology Center supplied a winning proposal to Hughes to deliver the components and subsystems for the AMRAAM missile, the weapon system that replaced the Sparrow missile for the F-14 fighter aircraft. Before merging with M/A-Com, Ferrotec had pioneered the use of suspended substrate. Because we excelled at this, we used suspended substrate extensively in the design of the airborne fire control radars.

I also hoped to enroll in medical school. John DiBiaggio, the president of Tufts, invited me for lunch at his house with the dean of admissions to talk about my plans. "Why do you want to start over?" he asked me. "You're considered tops in your present field."

John was not very encouraging. Tufts did not want someone who was approaching sixty to start medical school, potentially take a coveted spot away from a younger student, but after being part of the IEEE lecture series, I decided to spend the rest of my life developing medical applications for microwave technology. I wanted to use my knowledge to improve patient outcome and help more people.

While I could have enrolled in medical school at EVMS, for Nancy's sake I wanted to stay in Harvard. The same year that I decided to leave M/A-Com, I went to NASA and the CIA and informed them that I would no longer be able to consult.

"Was it because you didn't like working on weapons systems?" someone asked.

"No, no," I said. I wanted my military personnel to have the best. But I traveled too much and wanted to spend all of my time at home with Nancy, who was still having a difficult time.

One Saturday, I drove downtown to the general store and to the post office, doing errands, and people were asking, "How's Nancy? Is Nancy okay?"

"She's fine," I said, confused.

Jeff stood in the driveway, waiting for me when I drove home. Before I could ask what was going on, Nancy came out and said something like, "Please don't talk to Jeff."

I made an excuse and walked across the street to see our neighbor, Bill Tilley.

"You didn't know?" Bill said. "The ambulance came to your house yesterday."

I found out that Nancy had passed out. I believe that Jeff called the ambulance, but by the time it arrived, Nancy had recovered and declined treatment. A couple of times I came home and found Nancy collapsed on the floor. Unsure what was wrong, I carried her up to bed.

Cynthia Houston often called or made a point of dropping in to visit, but after our move to Harvard, Nancy had grown quite isolated. I blame myself for that. I wish I had quit work and spent more time at home. I made a lot of mistakes—like not staying involved in church.

I found it so easy to design things, to make things. Those were problems I could solve, but after Kirsten's death, it was so hard not to have closure. One question that has always plagued me is whether there is a life after this one. I've never really had an answer.

I only knew that I wanted to spend the rest of my time taking care of Nancy. But I waited too long.

CHAPTER 12

FLYING HOME

In the fall of 1986, I had just finished lecturing in India at the University of New Delhi and was scheduled to speak in Japan before flying home. But when I arrived at the airport, I discovered that Russia had blocked the airways, postponing and canceling many flights. Around midnight, I sat in an airport terminal, staring at a rotating list of cards for upcoming flights, when my flight was delayed. Knowing I would be late for my lecture, I felt frustrated. Then I had a sudden sense that I needed to go home. I do not know how to explain it, but it felt like a premonition.

Midnight in India is around noon in Boston, so I found a phone, called Georgie, and asked her to cancel my lecture.

"Tell them I have an emergency at home," I said.

What made me say that? I had never canceled a lecture, but from the beginning I had felt bad about the whole trip. Having nearly reached the end of the lecture series, I did not want to be away anymore. I wanted to go home and tell Nancy that I was leaving M/A-Com to spend more time with her. As soon as I got home, I planned to take the weekend off to talk with Nancy about whatever she was going through.

The earliest flight from New Delhi to New York left the next morning. "Help me get on that flight," I asked the agent behind the ticket counter.

The following morning, as I boarded my rearranged flight, the outside temperature reached 100° Fahrenheit. Before being cleared for takeoff, our plane sat on the runway for nearly six hours. Ten hours later, we landed in London, and I continued on to New York, where I caught a connecting flight to Boston.

When I finally arrived home, everything seemed normal. I let Nancy know that I wanted to talk and set up that weekend so we would have time to ourselves. Chris had recently graduated from high school and enlisted in the Navy, and I believe Jeff was spending the weekend at a friend's house. However, I did not mention to Nancy the subject I wanted to discuss. Concerned about bringing up a conversation that I suspected she would find unpleasant, I had to be careful. On Saturday night, I planned to take Nancy out to one of her favorite restaurants, Vincenzo's in Chelmsford, where we both knew everybody. Over dinner, I would explain my decision to reduce my travel and start my own medical company so I could do research and spend more time together. Whatever was going on, I wanted to work this out so we could go on with our lives.

That Friday I drove home from the office around seven o'clock and found a note from Nancy on the kitchen table. She wrote that she had gone up to bed and had fed the rabbits and Tiffany, our Newfoundland, who might need to go out. She also mentioned a couple of dinner options that she had left for me to warm up in the oven. Then Nancy wrote about a personal matter—something so private that out of love and respect, I am unable to share it. However, I suspect Nancy had been struggling with it since Kirsten's death.

After apologizing, she signed her name, *Love, Nancy.*

I took Nancy's note as a breakthrough. Until then, she had been unwilling or unable to discuss the issue with me. You cannot offer a solution if you don't understand the problem. That is true of engineering and of anything else in life. So when I read Nancy's note, I felt that for the second time she had turned my life around, the way she had by walking into my hospital room all those years before. Now that she had broached the problem, we would finally be able to talk. I thought Nancy would come back to me and we would be able to do things together again. You can't know how good I felt, believing we would work this whole thing out.

After reading Nancy's note, I opened our bedroom door to check on her. Nancy had on a little heating blanket. The orange light was lit up, so I left her alone and walked down to my basement shop where I made furniture. Close to midnight, I got into bed very quietly, careful not to wake her.

In the morning, Nancy was still sleeping. So, I made a special breakfast—eggs and a fruit cup and so forth. Then, I carried it up to her on a tray, planning to finally have the discussion that the two of us should have had years before.

Nancy had the sheet pulled over her head, so I set down the tray and pulled back the sheet. Nancy was not breathing. Here I was, hoping that we were going to have this great conversation, and Nancy was gone.

The first call I made was to 911. The second was to Randee, now married and living in New Hampshire.

"I tried to call Mom at about seven last night," Randee said, "but she didn't answer the phone."

Randee must have called right before I got home. I do not know exactly when Nancy died, but she could hear the difference between bird songs. If she had been alive when Randee called, she would have answered the phone.

Some details are difficult to recall—the way I could not recall who had been in the car with me the day Kirsten died. If it is emotional, it sort of leaves me. It is good to let your emotions out, but I have never been able to do that. As a child, I did not cry when my mother killed my rabbits. I did not cry when I was hit by the car. And I never cried when Nancy died. Jeff said he could see it in my eyes, but I could not cry. I felt like I had to hold everything together, particularly for Jeff, who was still in high school.

"It's not fair, Jeff," I told him after he returned home. "But we will make it."

The state medical examiner attributed Nancy's death to dilated cardiomyopathy, a condition in which the heart muscle stretches and becomes thinner, enlarging the inside of the chamber. As a result, the heart weakens and can no longer pump blood efficiently. To get more oxygen, it speeds up, which can lead to heart failure. The condition has several possible causes, including heredity, certain medications, and the overuse of alcohol.

Several months later, I was cleaning out Nancy's things and my friend Dr. Gerry Bousquet went through the bottles of pills in Nancy's dresser drawer.

"What was she doing with this?" he asked, picking up a bottle. "I don't like what I'm seeing in this drawer."

Gerry trashed the bottles.

I knew Nancy took medication, but I never saw what was in the bottles. Just like I never saw her drink. Neither did her best friend, Cynthia Houston. Whatever the official cause, I truly believe that Nancy died of grief over losing Kirsten. She died on October 4, 1986, one week before the twentieth anniversary of Kirsten's death.

At the time, Randee and her husband had a four-month-old daughter. Michael was out west, stocking shelves at a grocery store in Colorado. While in the Air Force, he had married a young woman from the Philippines, but they quickly divorced. His second wife was also Filipina; they had two daughters and moved to Texas with his wife's parents. Nancy had sent Michael money to enroll in college at the University of Texas, but when I went out to give a lecture, I discovered that Michael had never enrolled. Sometime later, his second marriage also ended in divorce. After Nancy's death, I bought Michael a ticket to fly home from where he was living in Colorado and drove him to Gould's clothing store in Acton to buy him a suit for her funeral.

We held Nancy's memorial service at the Congregational church in Harvard. People from town said that the funeral procession to the Shawsheen Cemetery in Bedford was the longest they could remember—265 cars. All the guys I played sports with and all the guys from work showed up, along with several people from Hughes, who flew out from California. They all knew Nancy. We buried her beside Kirsten and her aunt Viola, who had died several years before.

Whether from grief over losing his mother or from the difficulty of his own life, three years later Michael hung himself from a tree. He was thirty-five. I flew his ashes home, and we laid him to rest beside his mother and sister.

The first year after Nancy's death, I went to her gravesite every day. I knew Nancy was not there, but I would apologize for not spending more time with her. I also apologized for leaving her behind the day Kirsten died. And I would say, one more time, that I loved her. I do not know if there is life after this one, but I hope there is. I would like to see Kirsten and Nancy again.

CHAPTER 13

COMMITMENTS

Losing Nancy was hard on all our children, but it was perhaps hardest on our youngest son, Jeff. My own mother had asked me to leave home at sixteen. Jeff lost his mother at nearly the same age. With Chris at the naval training center in Pensacola, Florida, that left just Jeff and me at home. Although I often made breakfast, I was not much of a cook. That was Nancy's specialty. Thankfully, Jeff had a lot of friends whose families frequently invited him over for dinner, and he often spent the night at their houses. Although Chris and Jeff never shared my interest in competitive team sports or woodworking, we got along very well.

After losing Nancy, I stopped lecturing for the IEEE and limited my involvement with NASA to spin-off technology based on my work with Eastern Virginia Medical School. But after giving my notice at M/A-Com, it took me longer than I expected to finish my commitments, including for the AMRAAM missile program. At that time, all advanced fighter aircraft such as the F-14, F-15, F-16, and F-18 used the AMRAAM missile. Hughes Aircraft was responsible for designing the fire-control radar (the radar system on the aircraft) on the F-14, F-15, and F-18. Westinghouse designed the fire-control radar on the F-16. Because of our use of suspended substrate, Ferrotec, and later M/A-Com, worked with both Hughes and Westinghouse on the fire-control radar, which combines with the missile to form the AMRAAM missile system.

In a typical government contract, the organization soliciting bids draws up a Request for Proposals (RFP), which defines the mission and requirements. Contractors—such as Hughes or Raytheon—then submit proposals to the agency. The program office that issued the RFP assembles a source selection team to evaluate the proposals based on the previously defined criteria. Upon narrowing the field of choices, the program office awards the contract and monitors its execution. Components and subsystems are then defined by the winning contractors, who subsequently solicit bids from other subcontractor companies, such as Ferrotec and M/A-Com.

Newer fire-and-forget missiles like AMRAAM are guided by radar systems that lock onto the target. Once a fighter pilot recognizes that he is being tracked, the pilot must determine what kind of tracking technology is being used: optical, which is heat seeking, or microwave? If the missile has an infrared heat-seeking capability like a Sidewinder, which is a supersonic air-to-air missile carried by fighter planes, the pilot heads for a bright spot like the sun or the moon. Then he'll do a quick U-turn so the missile that is tracking him will head for the bright spot. Or he can eject a beacon or a flare to divert the missile. If the plane is being tracked by radar, the pilot takes a dive and heads for the ground, before pulling up. The ground emits so much clutter that the missile sees too many objects and loses sight of its target. A pilot has only a few seconds to make a decision.

During my long relationship with Hughes Aircraft, I worked with the Radar Systems Group, led by Richard "Dick" Jamison, and the Missile Systems Group, led by Ted Wong. Both Dick and Ted reported to Ken Richardson, the president of Hughes.

M/A-Com's Technology Center designed the prototype of the seeker head subsystem for the AMRAAM missile. The seeker head, the missile's major subsystem, defines the target, a crucial function. As technical director, I personally oversaw its construction and insisted on being in on the design work. Since I never wanted to lose my touch on the bench, every Friday I continued working alongside Jim Regan and the other engineers, putting the seeker head together.

At the time, I had just completed my 1985-86 lecture series as the Distinguished Lecturer for the IEEE, so we transferred the manufacture of the seeker head to the newly formed M/A-Com Sub-Assembly Group, which delivered the initial production unit to Hughes to test whether it worked properly when integrated into the missile. But before Hughes completed the testing, M/A-Com's Sub-Assembly Group requested the return of the unit to take additional data.

While walking around M/A-Com's Sub-Assembly Group during a program review, I noticed that the microwave circuit on the unit looked different than I recalled. Having been intimately involved with the seeker head's design, I saw that the circuit board was missing a component, a ferrite circulator, which Hughes engineers had previously determined it needed. Without the circulator, the missile would be vulnerable to crosstalk, or interference, caused by multiple reflections. This would make the missile susceptible to false signals that could trigger an early detonation and cause the missile to miss its target. To solve this problem, M/A-Com's Technology Center had worked with Hughes and added an isolator (a three-port circulator with a third port terminated). Then we wrote a formal engineering change order—a common step when you recognize a required system change during the development phase of a product. However, it appeared that someone in M/A-Com's Sub-Assembly Group had ignored the change order and elected to manufacture the earlier version of the unit, which lacked the circulator.

After discovering the problem, I called Rick Segal, the AMRAAM production manager at Hughes's Manufacturing Division in Tucson, and asked if I could fly out to see him. When I arrived, Rick invited me into his office. However, I requested that we meet outside in the parking lot where we would not be overheard.

"This is serious," he said, catching my concern.

"Very serious," I said. If I was correct, the problem I was about to discuss could present a multi-million-dollar program delay for the AMRAAM missile system and had the potential to affect M/A-Com's profits, employee bonuses, and shareholders' stocks. When the Air Force learned of the mistake, they would have to place the missile production on hold. An error of this magnitude would also be embarrassing and costly to Hughes and to all of the branches of the Armed Services that employed the missile. So, in the scorching, 100-degree parking lot, I told Rick that I believed someone at my company had made a mistake.

Whoever made the change was probably trying to make the unit simpler, which would have reduced the delivery time and allowed M/A-Com to release funding and take an early profit. I am a ferrite guy. I tend to put isolators in everything, which I often got accused of doing unnecessarily. But without the circulator, the missile might not work correctly. When you replace a subsystem, the replacement must occupy the same space and mate with the existing connections. It must fit in the same slot. This requires a whole new layout to accommodate the added component, so you have to change everything to make the subsystems interchangeable.

Rick called a team meeting, and I flew back out to Tucson to explain the problem. I met with Rick's key program people and engineers in a Hughes conference room.

"You all know Ken Carr," Rick Segal said.

"Yeah, we know Ken Carr," they said.

After being introduced, I warned everyone not to write anything down. That is how confidential this was. I did not want the Air Force to find out about the mistake before I had a chance to work out a strategy for how we were going to fix it.

Then I told everyone what I had told Rick. Someone at M/A-Com had made a mistake. We could have argued about who was at fault, but blame causes people to run for cover. Finger pointing only delays implementing the solution. The object was to identify and solve the problem. If you want to be successful, belly up to the bar. Admit your mistake and fix it. We needed the weapons system. The important thing was to act fast, not to point fingers.

Knowing that Hughes had to explain the problem to the Air Force, Rick asked if I would be willing to accompany him to Eglin Air Force Base in Florida and report the error to the commanding military people. Without telling anyone at M/A-Com, I agreed. After I divulged the problem, the Air Force general overseeing the program went into a tirade. "How long is it going to take you to fix this thing?" he demanded.

"Eight months," I said.

"What do you mean eight months?" The general pounded the table.

An eight-month delay could result in the program being canceled. I explained that in order for us to include the missing component in the seeker head, it would take us four months just to change the tooling on the circuit board and machine grooves for the housing.

Then the general calmed down. "You know," he said. "I have to give you credit for coming here and admitting a mistake. Why are you doing this?"

"I could never live with myself if I thought I was involved in a product that did not support my troops well," I said.

Luckily, the Air Force had a pending program delay of its own, so the general gave me six months to redesign the seeker head and fix the problem. "If you can do that," he said, "we will phase it in with another change, and the program will not be further delayed."

I agreed, and we shook hands on it. A handshake is golden. I had given both the Air Force and Hughes my word. By assuming responsibility up front and immediately addressing the solution, I felt confident that we could meet the target date by working together. Otherwise, an unwanted program delay would have certainly occurred.

As soon I got back to M/A-Com, I scheduled a technical review meeting and called my Tech Center together—Jim Regan, Rick Kelley, and all the guys involved in the program. It felt like going into the locker room at halftime. The guys in the Tech Center determined it would take eight months to complete the redesign and implement the solution, but we had just six months.

"I want you guys to work as many hours as needed to get this problem corrected," I said. "It is going to be tough, but we have to get it done."

I authorized any overtime required to add the missing circulator.

We made the changes and completed everything on time, and the AMRAAM missile became a very successful program. Later Ted Wong, the missile's systems manager at Hughes who became the company's vice-president, sent me a letter saying that he was impressed with my integrity. That is why they liked working with me, that and my relationships with the guys I worked with. The customer is part of the solution, not part of the problem. Our ability to work with our customer was very important. I could really count on the team, including the team at Hughes.

That is also probably one of the reasons that Hughes Aircraft invites me to their annual retirement party. I believe that I am the only non-Hughes employee there, but they invite me every year. A lot of people get a contract, but they are not considered part of the team. One year at a Hughes party, I was sitting next to Dick Jamison, who led the Radar Systems Group, and Ken Richardson, the company president.

"I really appreciate being invited," I said to Ken, "because, as you know, I'm not a Hughes employee."

"If you ask any person in this room, they would say you're one of us," he said. "That's why you're here."

Another Start

Ken Richardson, who had graduated from Tufts with a degree in mechanical engineering one year before me, and I became good friends. I later recruited him to serve on the board of directors for Tufts University. When Ken's first wife, Connie, died of cancer he wanted to get remarried to Connie's best friend, but he was worried about his kids, who might not have been in favor of it. On a trip to attend a Tufts board meeting in Boston, he mentioned wanting to talk to me about a personal issue. Ken took me to a restaurant at the Four Seasons Hotel and asked my advice about getting remarried. We talked so long, we were the last people there.

"Your kids should want you to be happy," I told him as the waitstaff put up chairs on the tables around us. "And they should be happy if you are happy. Your being happy is the best thing you can do for them."

Going on with my life after losing the only girl I had ever loved was really hard. When Nancy died, people wrote me letters and mailed me all kinds of books about how to deal with trauma. I read the letters, but I do not recall reading the books or articles. Every situation is different. How could they possibly apply to my situation?

Women would come up to me and say, "My husband passed away umpteen years ago. I know what it's like to be lonely." Some mentioned that they'd left messages for me at my office, which is how I discovered that Georgie, who was very protective of me, had not been giving me their messages.

"You are an easy mark," she said, I suppose because of how lonely I was. "They are not right for you."

Still in mourning, I briefly dated one nice-looking woman, a secretary. Although not really interested in going out, I also did not want to live alone.

About a year after Nancy died, I finished teaching a week-long microwave course at the Georgia Institute of Technology and was scheduled to fly back to Boston from Atlanta. My flight left in the evening, and I did not like to be away from Jeff for too long. So I called the airline and got a standby seat on an earlier flight. After boarding, I sat down in my assigned middle seat. While I organized papers to work on during the flight, a woman threw her knapsack toward the window seat and hit me in the head.

"Excuse me," I grumbled as she tried to get to her seat. "Let me get up."

"I can make it myself," she said, stepping over me.

As soon as she squeezed in, this really flamboyant guy with his shirt unbuttoned walked down the aisle. A gold chain flashed around his neck, and he was laughing loud enough to attract a lot of attention. It turned out he was sitting in the aisle seat on my right. *Oh, great*, I thought. His name was Larry Driscoll, and he happened to be a white-knuckled flyer. Every time the plane creaked, he grabbed the arm rests.

"Relax," I said, explaining the different noises. "I'm an engineer. I also used to fly planes."

"Where're you from?" he asked.

"Cambridge," I said.

He looked surprised. "I teach in Cambridge. What school did you go to?"

"Rindge Tech."

"I'm a teacher at Rindge!" he said.

In 1977, Cambridge High and Latin consolidated with the trade school to form the Cambridge Rindge and Latin School, which is where he taught. After a long talk, Larry asked if I was married.

"No," I explained. "I'm a widower. My wife recently passed away."

Larry suggested that he had a friend, "Mikelle," he would like me to meet and asked for my number: *Yeah, sure*, I thought, assuming he meant a guy. Still, I gave him my business card and accepted a piece of paper on which he'd written a phone number, never intending to call.

About a week later, a woman phoned my office and left a message, which Georgie did not give me. When the woman phoned again, Georgie was away from her desk and the call came through to me. So I picked up the phone.

"Hello," a woman said. "My name is Mikelle. You met a friend of mine on a plane."

Hearing a woman's voice surprised me. I later learned that as soon as Larry had stepped off our plane, he called Mikelle and gave her my number, saying, "I just met the man you are going to marry."

Mikelle was in her mid-forties, divorced, and living in a Belmont apartment with her teenage son. She suggested we meet for a drink. I was completing a proposal and had a lot of work to do. I also had a softball game to pitch that night. However, I agreed to meet her in the rotating restaurant on the top floor of the Hyatt Regency in Cambridge. Then I called her back and warned her that I would have to leave early for my game. If she showed up and I suddenly had to leave, I worried she might think I did not like her.

I arrived at the restaurant first. At five foot two, Mikelle was petite with short brown hair. She was also very attractive, but the whole time we were talking, she kept looking at my mouth. I had recently taken a hockey stick to the head, which broke two of my incisor teeth and resulted in nine stitches between my nose and my upper lip.

After a while, Mikelle blurted, "Are you going to do anything about your teeth?"

"Yes," I said, "but my dentist refuses to fix them until I agree to stop playing hockey."

Although getting a stick in the face was unusual, I did not wear a face mask and occasionally got injured. I once gave a talk at a review meeting for the AMRAAM missile with two black eyes and a broken nose held together by a metal nose clip. I looked like a raccoon. The Air Force guys were impressed, but the folks from M/A-Com were a little annoyed. After the meeting, one of the board members mentioned my appearance to Dick DiBona. "Ken is the best guy we have technically," he said. "But he's playing all of this hockey, and he's going to get himself killed."

Dick happened to be a good hockey player, but he had stopped playing. He offered me a bonus if I would agree to stop playing hockey. "I'm willing to offer you a check equal to your annual salary," he said.

I was being paid well, but I turned down his offer.

"You're kidding." Dick shook his head.

"I just love to compete," I explained. Playing hockey was my way of getting my mind off of things. While chasing the puck, the only thing I thought about was the game. Playing sports was how I survived.

Mikelle and I ended up going out again, and my dentist eventually fixed my teeth. I love dancing—something I missed. Mikelle loved dancing too. So we often went to the Sheraton Inn in

Boxborough and the Parker House in Boston, where they played oldies.

The first time Mikelle came over to the house in Harvard, we had a couple of drinks and she stayed over in Chris's room. After joining the Navy, Chris had left behind a pet snake. Jeff had one too—a nine-foot boa constrictor that weighed fifty pounds. Both snakes stayed in Chris's room, and sometimes they pushed the lids off their cages to roam around the house. In the middle of the night, Jeff's boa constrictor got loose. When Mikelle woke up, the snake's head was right next to hers.

"There's a snake in my room!" Mikelle hollered, practically falling down the stairs.

"Oh, Charlie," I said, making breakfast in the kitchen. "The snake's name is Charlie."

I went up and put him back in his fifty-five-gallon fish tank. Mikelle soon overcame her fright, getting to the point where she regularly handled the snake. She even bathed him in the bathtub.

In many ways, Mikelle was the complete opposite of Nancy. Nancy was quiet and reserved; Mikelle was boisterous and out-spoken. At M/A-Com events, Mikelle quickly mixed with ev-erybody—something Nancy had no longer been able to do after losing Kirsten. Mikelle enjoyed going out, including watching my softball games. She even liked to ski.

After dating for about six months, Mikelle was pushing to get married, so the following Valentine's Day, I took Mikelle and her son skiing in Utah, along with my son Jeff, who was about the same age as Mikelle's son. An old-fashioned guy, I asked Mi-kelle's son to meet me in the hotel lobby one night before dinner. After we sat down, I asked his approval to marry his mother. I hoped it would help us get along. He acted like it was no big deal, but when I knocked on the door of their room with flowers to take Mikelle out to dinner, she was crying. Not wanting his mother to remarry, Mikelle's son had yelled at her. The night started off as a disaster, but when I proposed, Mikelle said yes.

I assumed my children might feel the same way as Mike-lle's son did about our marriage. So I did not ask them. Maybe I should have, but I did not want to be single. Even though Nancy and I had gone through our share of difficulties, we had a great marriage, and I hoped to have another great marriage. I wanted another start. Randee had her family. Chris was in the Navy. And with Jeff about to start college, I did not want to come home to an empty house.

On July 9, 1988, I married Mikelle at a big wedding at the Congregational Church in Harvard. My children and Mikelle's son attended, along with her parents and two brothers, with whom I got along great. Since I was Congregational and Mikelle was Episcopal, a minister and a priest officiated the service, which was attended by a whole entourage of people, including many from Hughes Aircraft. People came from all over—the entire Harvard softball team, the Acton hockey team. And, of course, Larry Driscoll.

The day of our wedding was so hot, I bought a dozen fans to put in the church windows. After, I donated them all to the church. Then we had a big party at the Sheraton Inn in Boxborough. One of the guys I knew from town had a yellow 1953 Cadillac convertible with big fins. With the top folded down and Mikelle and I sitting up on the backseat, he drove us from the church to the reception. It was quite the event. Nobody got out of line, but we had a good time. Mikelle was Scottish, so for our honeymoon we toured Britain and visited her family's ancestral castle in Scotland.

After the wedding, Mikelle and her son moved into my house in Harvard. I fixed an apartment for him in the basement. Did my kids like it? No. There was a lot of conflict. Mikelle and Jeff did not get along. Neither did Jeff and Mikelle's son. One day I came home from work and discovered that the windshield of my Boston Whaler, parked on a trailer in my driveway, had been shot out with a pellet gun. So had the window in the loft above the garage.

"Did you use the pellet gun?" I asked Jeff.

"Dad, I wouldn't do that," he said, suggesting I ask Mikelle's son.

I found him in the basement lying back on his bed. "Did you use the pellet gun?" I asked.

"Yeah, I used your f—ing pellet gun," he said, holding up his hands like it was no big deal. "You have enough money, so you can afford to replace the windows."

Soon after, Jeff went off to college at the University of Maine at Orono, and Mikelle's son joined the Army.

Before our marriage, Mikelle had started a small company that installed telephone systems in hotels, but she and her co-owner did not always get along. When I asked Mikelle if she wanted to keep working, she said no. I helped her sell her half of the business to her partner, and she retired.

A couple of years before, I had custom ordered a Porsche 911. I have always liked sports cars. Back in the early sixties, I raced MGs at Lime Rock Park in Connecticut. Paul Newman, Steve McQueen, and James Garner also happened to race there. I drove down in my own car and took off the headlights and folded in the mirrors before each race. But Paul Newman was in a different class and raced Datsun 240Zs. He drove down with a trailer full of cars and picked which one he wanted to use. I do not think I ever won a race. Because I could not afford to lose my car, I always backed off in a tight spot. I only raced for a couple of years, but I like to drive fast, which is why I drove a Porsche. Mikelle wanted one too. A neighbor, who drove for the Porsche racing team, was selling a Porsche 911 SC special Weissach edition, of which only 468 were ever made. I bought it for Mikelle, who was thrilled.

At the time, I felt very fortunate to have married Mikelle, but some of what my grandmother had said about Nancy was probably true of Mikelle. I think she married me to find a home for her son, and I wanted to find a replacement for Nancy.

In retrospect, I think I married too soon.

CHAPTER 14

OVERCOMING OBSTACLES

While finishing my commitment to M/A-Com, I became involved with "spook work," including a top-secret defense project that my employer did not know about. The project involved
designing a new missile for NATO. On a "need-to-know" basis,
even I did not know the full extent of the missile system I was
helping to develop. I oversaw the design of the key components
and subassemblies, such as the antenna, at Microwave Design
and Manufacturing (MDM), M/A-Com's West Coast antenna facility, which reported to me. Microwave Associates' facility in
Luton, England, which I also oversaw, was to produce other parts
for the system.

Since the program was classified, our Luton facility did not
know who was making the antenna, and our California facility
did not know who they were making the antenna for. To disguise
the project, we made it look like we were developing a radar system for commercial airlines. We also made sure that the program
did not make money. That way, no one at M/A-Com would pay
much attention to it.

Harvey Muhs, a microwave engineer from Hughes Aircraft
who worked on antennas, founded MDM. His key guy was
Charles "Chuck" Watson, a strong technical engineer and world-
class cyclist who often won long-distance bike races. Chuck was
walking muscle, a physical specimen. Both he and Harvey had
previously worked for Hughes' Radar Systems Group. Harvey, a
heavy smoker, developed lung cancer—a real tragedy.

One day at M/A-Com, Larry Gould came up to me and said,
"What are you going to do about Harvey Muhs?"

"What do you mean, 'What am I going to do?'" I asked. "He's
still working."

"You've got to replace him," Larry said.

"When the time is right," I said. "When he can't work or no longer wants to work anymore."

I flew out and talked to Harvey. In fact, I took Harvey and his wife, Joy, out to dinner. As his cancer advanced, he had lost his hair due to chemotherapy. Since I often gave lectures as a member of the faculty at EVMS and was an adviser to Tufts-New England Medical Center, I asked Harvey for a copy of his medical records and brought them to both groups. It turned out few people survived his type of cancer. The doctors at Tufts projected that Harvey had one year to live. The medical staff at EVMS suggested he had just nine months. *Now what am I going to do?* I wondered. When you ask questions, what to do with the information you receive becomes a problem.

Years before, I had been in a similar situation when Nancy's father, Kurt, was diagnosed with glioblastoma, an aggressive brain tumor with no known cure. Because of my medical connections, I knew chemotherapy was not doing him any good and would only make him sicker. After building a wheelchair ramp from his steeply sloped driveway to his front door, I suggested to Nancy that her father would be better off stopping chemotherapy treatment. But when Nancy's mother, Margaret, found out, she got really upset.

"He's not a doctor," she snapped.

She was right. I am not a medical doctor and should not have said anything. That is when I learned to be more careful. But Kurt was Nancy's father, and he was my good friend. I liked Kurt a lot. After talking to the doctors at EVMS and Tufts, I also knew that he would have felt better in his final days if he had stopped chemotherapy. So I suggested that Nancy or her mother talk to a doctor about stopping chemotherapy. Kurt died a few months later, at age seventy-six.

At the time, I was doing medical research and becoming quite knowledgeable about cancer statistics and survival. As I've mentioned before, you cannot provide a solution unless you understand the problem. That is the rule an engineer lives by. So after meeting with the doctors about Harvey Muhs's condition, I flew back to the West Coast and had another dinner with Harvey and Joy. When Harvey asked if I had heard anything about his prognosis, I ducked the question.

"I haven't heard back yet," I said. "But before we meet again, you should talk to your doctor and ask for statistics on the different types of lung cancer." I planted the question, knowing that his type of cancer involved small cells and was very aggressive.

After speaking to his doctor, Harvey knew his cancer was terminal.

A week later, he called me back. "You knew, didn't you?" he asked.

"Yes, I did," I said. "But I made a mistake asking for your records. I'm not an MD, so I could not be the one to tell you."

A number of years after Harvey died, Chuck Watson called me up and said that M/A-Com had decided to sell MDM. In 1986, the same year I lost Nancy, Dick DiBona had suffered a serious stroke and got sidelined. Dick really was the glue that held M/A-Com together. Tom Burke, who had been the company's chief financial officer, became the new president, and Larry Gould became chairman of the board. However, in the fall of 1989, Tom Burke was fatally injured in a car accident, and the board hired Tom Vanderslice as the new CEO. Tom had previously overseen Hewlett-Packard's Massachusetts computer operation, which he downsized by selling off divisions. Now that Tom was coming to M/A-Com, he was about to do the same thing, which did not make him very popular.

When I asked Tom about MDM, he assured me that the facility was not being sold. However, Chuck Watson soon called me back. "A group is in here looking us over," he said. "Are we on the auction block?"

"No," I assured him. "The president of the company promised me."

Then I hurried over to Tom's office to see what was going on. His secretary said he did not have time to see me.

"He has to see me," I said and pulled up a chair outside of his office, knowing that at some point Tom had to come out.

When Tom finally opened his door, I asked if MDM was being sold.

"I don't have to tell you anything," Tom said. "You work for me. Don't forget it. I can do whatever I want."

"You lied to me," I said, explaining that he could not sell MDM because it was a classified area.

Tom, who had only been my boss for a few weeks, asked what they did there, but because he did not have a "need to know," I could not tell him. When I refused, he threatened to fire me for insubordination.

"You don't have to," I said. "I gave my notice four years ago."

The NATO program was so secret that the government had installed a direct telephone line at M/A-Com that even Georgie did not know about. Every building at M/A-Com had its own phone room, like a big closet, that all of the telephone extensions went through. I had a key to the telephone room. To call my government contact, I would step into this room and clip my phone onto the two terminals. "This is Ken Carr," I would say, and the contact would be on the other end. So as soon as I learned that MDM was being sold, I called my contact and said, "I have to inform you that I have lost control of the program."

Soon after, the FBI cordoned off the building and removed the secure phone line. Then the government pulled the missile program from M/A-Com. As far as I know, the program died, but because it was classified, I could not tell anyone what had happened, not even Georgie. A few weeks later, I packed up my office.

Knowing that I was exiting M/A-Com to run MMS, it was not difficult to leave.

Perceived Hazards

As with other companies I had spun off, M/A-Com engineers involved with developing medical products were free to choose whether to join MMS or remain with the Tech Center. They all chose to go with MMS, including Jim Regan, Rick Kelley, Richard Grabowy, and Bob Williams. So did my secretary, Georgie

Burton. Around the same time, Bob Bielawa also left M/A-Com to start his own company, Microwave Support Systems, in Nashua, New Hampshire. However, Bob Bielawa continued working with me as a consultant, without ever requesting compensation. Later, Ken Puglia and Rick Kelley also retired from M/A-Com and consulted for me.

Located halfway between the towns of Harvard and Burlington, MMS operated out of a two-story building on Goldsmith Street in Littleton. Because the building lacked an elevator, we were limited to twenty-five employees. I had previously chosen the location as part of my deal with M/A-Com, so that after putting in a full day of work, I could stop by MMS on my way home to see how things were going. Because I wanted to focus on technical work, I hired Jack Mahoney, a businessman I played softball with, to run the company. As I had with M/A-Com, I served as both the chairman and technical director of MMS.

Given that the medical business was new to me and the FDA was wary of microwave products, M/A-Com's board of directors and the management of Hughes had warned me many times not to go into medicine. While most people had embraced microwave ovens, the emerging cell phone market caused just as much, if not more, controversy. In 1973, Motorola had manufactured the first cell phone, a 2.4-pound Goliath that required a ten-hour charge to talk for thirty minutes. Nearly a decade later, Nokia introduced the first mass-produced cell phone.[30] However, because cell phones use microwave radio frequencies, people feared the phones would give them brain cancer or "cook" their brains.

As a founding member of the IEEE's Health Care Engineering Policy Committee, I became an expert witness for Congress, answering questions and advising various committees and congressional leaders about microwave problems and cell phone safety. Later, in 2010, the Maine Legislature invited me to testify about cell phone safety in response to proposed legislation that would have required cell phones to carry a warning stating that they could cause cancer. In a letter to the editor of a local newspaper, I suggested that if cell phones were printed with warnings, they should say, "Inappropriate use of this cell phone may result in rude public behavior and dangerous driving!"

The legislation failed, but people had the same fear about using microwaves in medicine as they did about cell phones. MMS had successfully used passive radiometric thermography to detect tumors with OncoScan. We used microwaves to eliminate bacteria with our sterile docking system. We also developed the world's first microwave-based, in-line blood warmer, the ThermoStat 900. We were in the process of developing a microwave-based, non-invasive brain temperature monitor, a catheter that employed radiometric sensing to treat life-threatening heart arrhythmias, and a system to destroy blood-borne viruses in the bloodstream. Before marketing these products, we still needed approval from the FDA, which had a history of rejecting medical devices developed by small companies. Unlike larger medical companies with more funding, the perception was that small companies often had to rush a product to market to survive.

While people were probably correct to advise me to stay away from medicine, I remained convinced that I could change people's opinions about the perceived hazards of using microwaves in medicine. I just did not know how difficult it would be.

Because our sterile docking system did not heat blood or tissue, I hoped it would support MMS until the FDA granted us permission to market our blood warmer. Soon after leaving M/A-Com, I signed an exclusive license with a major medical supplier, which operated a nationwide chain of kidney dialysis centers, to market our sterile docking system. Unfortunately, I quickly discovered that the medical industry is not like the military, where everyone is working together toward the same goal. When you sign a marketing agreement with a medical company, they can put you on a shelf and tie you up, while never intending to sell your product. In my opinion, that is what this company did to us.

MMS initially built one hundred units of the sterilizer, intending to use them in clinical trials. After our Littleton facility tested the units to make sure they worked correctly, Jim Regan, Rick Kelley, and I rented a truck and drove the units down to a facility in New Jersey. Before leaving, we asked the company's quality control officer to plug in the machines to ensure they were all functioning and met the requirements. Then we watched while they warmed them up. All of the lights came on, and we listened for the tone generator, *"Bup, bup, bup, beep!"* The machines all passed inspection, and the company signed off on them. However, they later claimed the units did not work properly.

Since the company made disposables for dialysis equipment, and disposables make money, I suspected that they did not want a product in the marketplace that would eliminate disposables. The more disposables the company sold, the more money they made. At that time, the government was spending roughly $20,000 per year per patient on disposables for dialysis equipment, but with a manufacturing cost of only $3,000, our unit would last the lifetime of the patient. Rather than helping the sterile docking device gain acceptance, the company appeared to be trying to keep our product off the market. That way, we could not sell it to someone else. This threatened to put us out of business, so in 1991 we took them to court to void the contract.

To prove our system killed all four types of bacteria that cause peritonitis, we had initially teamed up with Sandra Fessia, a professor of microbiology at the University of Massachusetts at Lowell. However, because students conducted the tests, the company rejected our data. At our own expense, we paid to repeat the tests at Microtest Labs in Springfield. Only later did we discover that this was unnecessary. As long as the process is overseen by a professor, data collected by college students is used in testing all the time.

The trial ended in late 1994 with a settlement in our favor; however, the company appealed the verdict three times. I wanted to keep fighting. In hockey, when some guy elbows you and takes a cheap shot, you fight back. For me, it was drop-the-puck time. But one of my board members, Dick Melick, a founding partner of the Melick and Porter law firm in Boston, said, "Let's get on with life, or we are going to go out of business." For the sake of MMS, we had to move on, so we accepted the settlement.

Rather than making money, the sterilizer ended up costing us money. I learned one thing: Do not develop a product unless it relies on disposables. And definitely do not develop a microwave-based product that eliminates disposables because medical companies are going to get rid of it. Going through this experience with our first business partner was not exactly walking into a friendly house. I believe that is why everyone had warned me not to go into medicine.

After the settlement, we redesigned the sterilizer for the Japanese market (which did not require FDA approval) and sold it to Japan Medical Supply (JMS). In 1999, the FDA finally approved the sterile docking system. The microwave technologies I developed and the related patents were the first microwave-based products ever approved by the FDA for use within the medical community. However, by then the medical industry had greatly reduced its use of continuous ambulatory peritoneal dialysis and continuous cycling peritoneal dialysis, which were done at home, in favor of treating dialysis patients in medical centers. Our sterilizer was never put into use.

Blood Warming

While attempting to market the sterilizer, we were still waiting for the FDA to approve our blood warmer. To pressure the FDA to make a decision, we elected to address a need for the military by working with the Army. I hoped this would give us greater leverage with the FDA and speed along the approval process. In 1988, when I had first flown to Washington to bring the blood warmer before a panel of FDA doctors for approval, they referred me to the *Technical Manual* prepared by the American Association of Blood Banks (AABB), which said, "Microwave devices damage red cells and should not be used for warming blood."[31]

"You will never get a medical product using microwaves approved by the FDA, because microwaves damage blood," a spokesperson for the group said. "Unless you can address the *Technical Manual* and get the AABB to change it, you are never going to get a product approved."

I took that as a challenge. It was a problem that had to be solved.

"If I can get them to change their statement—because it is not true—will I get the device approved?" I asked.

"Yes," he said.

I knew I was right, but I also knew that to succeed, I could not alienate them. So whenever someone at the FDA brought up a concern, I would say, "Gee, I would love to give a lecture about that." Then I would schedule another trip down there to give a talk.

Each time we developed a product, I realized that we could develop it into something else. One example was our early extravasation detection system, a medical device that non-invasively monitored and detected the infiltration of unwanted leakage into tissue surrounding an IV catheter during IV drug administration. We developed this device in collaboration with EVMS. However, it became obvious that before the FDA would approve any microwave-based device for patient use, we would need to convince the AABB to revise its technical manual. So I got in touch with the manual's editor, Dr. Richard Walker, who gave me the safety guidelines about microwave devices damaging red blood cells.

"What would it take to make you change that statement?" I asked.

He gave us the criteria and said, "If you can heat blood components and show that there is no damage, as well as how much of a safety margin you have without causing hemolysis, we will change the manual."

We also developed a catheter that used microwave/radio-frequency heating and cryogenic cooling for myocardial ablation to correct life-threatening heart arrhythmias, so the FDA asked us to also prove that microwaves could be safely used to heat tissue. The FDA drew these hard lines, but I did not fight with them. I love a challenge. *I will put together a team*, I thought. *I will develop a system and be the inventor, but I will get medical doctors to publish the research.* As Harry Truman has been credited with saying, "It is amazing what you can get done if you don't worry about who gets the credit."

In 1990, I became a member of the Board of Overseers for the Tufts College of Engineering, reviewing curriculum to better prepare students to enter the medical physics industry. I also served as a technical advisor to the Medical Physics department of Tufts-New England Medical Center. To prove that microwaves could be safely used to heat blood and tissue, I teamed up with Ray Connolly Jr., a physiologist who directed the Surgical Research laboratory at the Tufts-New England Medical Center; Dr. Steven Schwaitzberg, the head of surgery; and a group of doctors at the medical center. And I gave them the criteria.

"How high can you heat blood before it causes damage?" I asked. "We are going to find that number."

You should not use microwaves to heat blood in bulk, such as in a blood bag, which has a non-uniform shape and depth and cannot be evenly heated. For example, if the blood is in the tubing portion of the bag, which is very small in diameter, it could become very hot while the rest of the blood remains lukewarm. To solve this problem, we designed a small microwave cavity—like a miniature microwave oven—about three inches square and two inches deep, into which we inserted a disposable cartridge similar to a bobbin, wound with a short length of IV tubing. The IV tubing and plastic bobbin are transparent at both the microwave heating and the radiometric sensing frequency. The IV tubing presents a uniform cross-section and uniform heating of the flowing blood. Using radiometric sensing, we could accurately measure the inlet and the outlet blood temperature as well as the temperature of the blood at the point at which the heat is applied. Radiometric sensing also allowed us to measure the flow rate and to detect air emboli.

Responding to a solicited grant to fill an unmet need for the military, we built the fluid and blood warming system with the disposable cartridge for the Army in collaboration with Major Martin Schreiber, MD, the chief of trauma and critical care at the William Beaumont Army Medical Center in El Paso, Texas, and with Major Stephen Bruttig, the deputy director of the U.S. Army Casualty Care Research Program at Letterman Army Institute of Research at the San Francisco Presidio Army base.* The ThermoStat 900 In-line IV Fluid and Blood Warming System could handle blood flow rates from zero to 500 ml per minute, eliminating the need for different blood warmers to accommodate different flow rates. This represented a huge step forward. Previously blood was heated by immersing the tubing in a warm water bath, referred to by doctors as "Pseudomonas Tanks," for the dangerous bacteria the tanks sometimes contained. If a tube leaked, it would suck in water, contaminating the tube and the blood.

With support from an NIH grant and in collaboration with the staff of the Department of Surgery at Tufts-New England Medical Center, we conducted extensive testing of in-line microwave warming of blood and blood components. For our tests, we used baboons, which have a blood system similar to people. With nicknames such as Pat Boone (after the singer), Ray Boone (after the baseball player), and Daniel Boone (after the frontiersman), the animals lived in cages at the Tufts' veterinarian school research lab.

Our tests showed there was no significant change in blood component longevity between samples warmed to 49°C with microwave energy vs. control samples. This resulted in several significant publications, including in the November 1991 edition of the *U.S. Army Medical Research Development Command N-E-W-S*, in which Maj. Bruttig wrote, "Successful testing of the warming device has been conducted with various intravenous fluids, including blood, with an error rate of + or − 0.1 degrees centi-

---

*   The Army defined a solicited request to develop a single blood warmer to meet a specific flow rate: zero to 500 ml per minute. Because the product was needed by the Army, which required FDA approval, I hoped the FDA would approve the blood warmer.

grade... The success of this contract effort has drawn enthusiastic support for the promise of microwave technology in other health care endeavors."

While we were testing the blood warmer, a patient who was bleeding profusely flatlined on the table in the operating room at Brigham and Women's Hospital. Fortunately, the doctor was an experienced trauma surgeon who broke open the man's chest wall and massaged his heart to restore the patient's heartbeat. However, the doctor had to quickly go from a very low flow of blood to a high flow, 500 ml. My T900 IV Fluid and Blood Warmer saved the man's life.

I also developed a second blood warming device: a minimally invasive, portable, intravascular blood warmer.[32] If a soldier is injured on the battlefield or someone is trapped in a vehicle or under a collapsed building and their body temperature drops to 33°C, they will go into shock and die. At that time, the most effective method for re-warming blood involved inserting a catheter into both the femoral artery and femoral vein and connecting the patient to an external heat exchanger—a technique that is technically difficult and often results in considerable blood loss.

To accurately monitor the temperature of the blood during the warming process, I designed a flexible catheter that could be inserted into a patient's blood vessel (the superior or inferior vena cava) with a self-centering microwave antenna. The blood vessels are three-quarters of an inch in diameter. A catheter connected to an external 100-watt transmitter could raise a person's body temperature 3°C in ten minutes. That takes someone right out of shock. A miniature umbrella with non-conductive nylon fingers expands around the tip of the catheter to center the antenna, which is the heat source. Without restricting blood flow, the umbrella also prevents the antenna from touching the blood vessel walls. So if someone is buried in a pile of rubble or in a collapsed building, rescuers can use this device to keep them alive. This same system can be used to feed patients intravenously, keep up their blood volume, and keep their vital signs constant. Because the system does not require a conventional external heat exchanger or IV lines, it eliminates additional blood loss.

For our work making the sterilizer, blood warmers, and other microwave-based medical devices, I wrote and was awarded thirty-nine Small Business Innovation Research (SBIR) grants for MMS and raised more than $13 million. An SBIR grant is intended to develop products that create jobs. I used the money to cover overruns and spent my compensation from the grants to pay for additional research. To address the perceived microwave hazard issue with FDA, I spent an additional $450,000 of my own money to develop the blood warmer. With my medical team, I also published technical papers to educate the medical community and the FDA on novel ways to use microwaves in medical devices.[33] We pulled out all the stops.

In honor of my work, Tufts University gave me its 1991 Distinguished Electrical Engineering Alumnus Award. The following year, just after I turned sixty, the Wentworth Institute of Technology invited me to be its commencement speaker and honored me with its President's Award along with an honorary Doctor of Engineering Technology degree, adding three orange bars to my robe. For years, I had attended every Wentworth graduation and helped institute a program giving honorary bachelor of science degrees to Wentworth students who, fifty years prior, had only earned engineering certificates but were still working in the field. Having twice dropped out of graduate school—first because of my job obligations at Philco and second because of my accident—I questioned whether I had truly earned the right to use the title of doctor.

"You are being given all of the rights and privileges of the degree," the provost, George Balich, said. "I don't know many people with PhDs who have done as much as you have."

He convinced me that I had more than earned it.

That summer, on August 12, 1992, Richard Walker wrote me a letter stating that the AABB had modified its *Technical Manual* to state that controlled microwave devices were now allowed for heating blood under the organization's standards "as long as the heating is in-line, the blood is not warmed above 38°C, and a warming system is in place with a visible thermometer."[34] Later, we successfully convinced the AABB to remove the 38°C limit and increase it to 42°C. Eventually, they removed the temperature limit altogether, instead stating that "When blood is warmed, it must be done so as not to cause hemolysis." As a result of our work, the subsequent edition of the AABB's *Technical Manual* included this change.

With so much controversy over microwaves and people calling me a liar, screaming that they had been zapped and their brains were being cooked, I could now hold up the letter from the AABB and say that I could, without a doubt, prove that microwaves do not damage blood. It is excess heat that damages blood. Suddenly, people's perceptions had turned from microwaves being a hazard to being a way to address unmet needs. This signified another huge breakthrough. Through radiometric sensing, we were solving problems that could not be solved any other way.

On February 24, 1994, the FDA granted MMS permission to market our IV Fluid and Blood Warmer, ThermoStat 900. The administration's approval opened the door of medicine to many microwave-based products, such as our myocardial ablation catheter and the early extravasation detection monitor. Because I did not intend for MMS to create its own sales force, we relied on companies that liked our products and wanted to go into business with us by licensing our products. To market the blood warmer, we needed a company that already had a sales force.

At the time, I was chairman for the Scientific Review Committee for the University of Pennsylvania. They put me in touch with Tim Lenihan, an engineer and former student at the university who worked for Arrow International, a medical supply company in Reading, Pennsylvania. Tim introduced me to Ray Neag, the company's sales manager and one of its founders, and I signed an agreement with Arrow to market the blood warmer. However, Arrow's salespeople were accustomed to carrying around briefcases with needles and catheters and did not want to roll a 70-pound gorilla of a machine around the hallways. They did not even drive trucks or vans. I would never keep a company in a contract that was not best for everybody. It is not good for the company, and it is not good for the product. It is a situation in which nobody wins. So we let Arrow out of the contract.

Two years later, I met with Jack McGinley, the executive vice president of Baxter Healthcare Corporation, in Deerfield, Illinois. Jack happened to be a Canadian hockey player, and we became good friends. After our meeting, I signed a contract to produce the fluid and blood warmer for Baxter. The market leaders in the anesthesiology field, Baxter owned the majority of the blood warming units being used by hospitals, including catheters and equipment for collecting and storing blood. Our system met every single performance specification, and their representatives were absolutely amazed.

Larry Williams, the director of Baxter's Anesthesia Consulting Group, praised the quality of our team and the innovation of our product line. "It has been some time since I experienced the excitement I have for this venture," he said during a presentation to Baxter's management. "We will set the stage and help prepare the programs and services that will be needed to launch the ThermoStat 900 to our territory and regional managers nationwide. Expectations are high!"

Baxter planned to work with us on all of our anesthesia products, including the early extravasation monitor, the air emboli detection system, and IV site monitors—our entire product line. We were in the big time. *We made it!* I thought, ready to pop the champagne. *We should have a celebration!*

One year before, the Massachusetts Technology Collaborative recognized MMS with an SBIR Award for "exemplary performance in the development and commercialization of technology through the Federal Small Business Innovation Program." For our contributions in critical patient care, the following year the U.S. Army Medical Research and Material Command selected MMS as an Army Success Story, "Creating Tomorrow's History." And in 1999, we received the prestigious Tibbets Award as a "model of excellence" from the Small Business Administration and the National Institutes of Health.

Now one of the biggest medical companies in the world planned to buy all our products. I thought that we were off and running. Instead, we went through a period of nothing but problems.

CHAPTER 15

PROBLEMS

After receiving FDA approval to market the blood warmer, MMS moved to a one-story, 20,000-square-foot facility on School Street in Acton and ramped up production. Our initial agreement with Baxter Healthcare required us to build thirty systems a month, but they quickly increased the number to fifty.

Okay, I thought. *Fifty systems per month. We'll expand.* We built more benches, installed new equipment, and hired more employees.

Richard Grabowy, who had a master's degree in software engineering and had formerly worked with a medical company, was the engineering manager for the blood warmer. Rick Kelley, a mechanical engineer responsible for the overall design of the ThermoStat 900 and its disposables, oversaw production. Jim Regan and Bob Williams were responsible for the microwave component design. The guys did a great job. Every unit was within spec and MMS shipped them on time. Unfortunately, after we shipped the first few lots—roughly 160 systems—Baxter canceled our contract. It had nothing to do with our work. To decrease their liability, Baxter's board of directors had decided to get out of the anesthesiology business. The blood warming units used by hospitals relied on disposable blood bags, but if someone mishandled a bag and it burst, Baxter got sued because they had the deepest pockets. Baxter Healthcare owned the blood warming equipment, but once the patent protection lapsed, they were no longer supplying the disposable.

When our contract ended, MMS went from producing fifty units a month to zero. Hoping to reimburse our vendors for the more than $1 million we owed them, I sent Jack McGinley a notice asking Baxter to pay us. The numbers the company had given us were a rolling forecast, which meant they were not obliged to pay. However, Jack called the division manager and instructed him to send the money. After our previous fiasco with the large dialysis supplier, I was relieved. I liked Baxter and enjoyed working with Jack McGinley. Whenever I went to Chicago, we went out for lunch and talked about hockey.

The financial settlement with Baxter allowed me to pay off our suppliers, but after investing so much money in the blood warmer, MMS was broke.

At the time, I had just recovered from my fourth eye surgery and been diagnosed with Sympathetic Ophthalmia, a rare condition brought on by eye surgery or trauma in which the immune system attacks both eyes. Two decades after reinjuring my eye while playing hockey, I had slipped while building a stone wall behind my house and hit my head against the protruding rocks, breaking my glasses and fracturing my eye socket. Once again, Mass Eye and Ear reconstructed my left eye.

After each accident, the damage to my eye had worsened. Now, my eye doctor informed me that I had an 85 percent chance of going completely blind. When Dick Melick, one of MMS's board members, heard about my diagnosis, he packed an overnight bag, walked into Mass Eye and Ear, and told the medical staff that he wanted to give me one of his eyes. It was impossible, the doctors explained. They could not transplant an eye.

After Dick left the hospital, a couple doctors called me. "We had an amazing visit today," one said. "A person, someone who is not even related to you, came in and offered to donate one of his eyes to you."

Dick never told me what he had done. He and his wife, Susan, had recently retired to Florida. After arriving for our board meetings, Dick usually took a hotel limo back to the airport, but after our next board meeting, I offered to drive him to the airport. On the way, we had a very long talk.

"Dick," I said. "I got a call from a couple of doctors at Mass Eye and Ear. I am aware of what you offered to do for me, and I want to thank you."

"Why should I have two eyes and you have none?" he asked. "Anyway, there's no need to thank me. They could not take my eye."

"It is what you intended to do," I said. "I do not know if I would have been prepared to give up an eye for you."

"That's the difference between you and everyone else," Dick replied. "Everyone else would have said, 'I would've done it for you too.'"

"I can't say that," I admitted, knowing how hard it is to see out of only one eye. "That is a tough question."

"You realize that I am the first one to arrive for your board meetings?" Dick asked. "I do that intentionally to talk to different employees—engineers, machinists, secretaries. I sit down and impose myself on them to see how the company is doing. Your employees not only respect you, they would walk the plank for you. If they have any problem in life, they know that you will be there for them. That is what keeps them here. They will be here for their entire lives."

Regrettably, that was not the case. Having lost the contract with Baxter and facing the possibility of going blind, I had to restructure the company. In 1999, I called together my employees—more than one hundred people—and announced that I was downsizing Microwave Medical Systems. Here I had thought we had finally made it, and instead I had to let all of the production people go, including many who had just joined the company.

I blamed myself. Most of MMS's investors were medical doctors, board members, and friends—including Dick Melick and Dr. Gerry Bousquet. Many had contributed between $50,000 and $100,000, and I felt personally responsible for letting them down. Rather than ducking my duty, I called my board members and investors together and explained that I was folding the company. They assured me it was not my fault. We remained friends, but it was very distressing.

The day we closed our Acton facility, MMS's employees used their own cars to move our equipment into a one-room storefront in Ayer, one town over from Harvard. Kevin Hardin, a friend who designed kitchens, leased us the space, which had a large storage area with just enough room for our benches and lab tools. This allowed my technical staff to continue their research, but we had to abandon our entire production capacity.

Because Baxter was getting out of the business, it ordered their entire blood product inventory, including the T900 blood warmer, to be destroyed. However, a friend who was a Baxter sales manager arranged to have the blood warmers loaded on a trailer truck and driven off the property. Then we picked them up and stored them in a nearby storage rental unit.

When MMS closed, I lost roughly $1.5 million in personal loans to the company, plus money I had invested. Whenever I received a check from NIH for grant work, I never paid myself. I invested everything back in MMS.

Although not required, I paid each employee two weeks' severance pay from my own pocket. Then I resigned from the board of directors, which took over management of MMS. Gerald Gaudette, a board member who owned Gaudette Insurance Agency in Worcester, stepped up as the CEO. This made it possible for me to bid on the patents and intellectual property and buy back the company. The most important objective was keeping the core technical team together, which is why I temporarily relocated the company in Ayer, near many of my staff members' homes.

Jim Regan, Bob Williams, and Ken Puglia, who had all been with me since Ferrotec, continued working with me on an as-needed basis, as did Rick Kelley, from M/A-Com, and several other members of my technical team. My secretary, Georgie Burton, also stayed with me, but because our new office facility lacked a ladies' room, she preferred working from home.

In 2001, I formed Meridian Medical Systems, named after the longitudinal lines that pass through the north and south poles. The highest point of the day, *meridian* can also express the highest period of attainment—a zenith. To me, this represented seeking a new level of achievement. It also removed the controversial word *microwave* from our name, while allowing me to keep

MMS's logo on our equipment. Massachusetts law required at least two shareholders to form a company, so I gave Mikelle a 1 percent share of the new MMS, hoping we would truly reach a new level of achievement.

Around this same time, I sold Sea Broom. Mikelle had remodeled the house, but because I built it for Nancy, Mikelle came to dislike it for the same reason she disliked our house in Harvard. During a visit to Maine to attend the wedding of my canoeing buddy Ted Morine's son, Mikelle and I both liked the area. So I walked into a Bath real estate office and mentioned our interest in moving. The owner pointed us toward some land for sale in nearby Woolwich. Mikelle and I walked around the property, which overlooked the Kennebec River, and one week later, I put down the money to buy nearly eight acres. Then I drew up plans to build a house. The exterior resembled a traditional colonial. However, the interior had the same layout as Sea Broom, with soaring ceilings, a massive, center-chimney brick fireplace, and a balcony with windows overlooking the water. I built cabinets for the new house in my basement woodworking shop, but having turned seventy, I hired a contractor to build the house.

After moving, I built a three-bay timber frame garage with rough-sawn pine harvested from the trees I had planted half a century before at my grandmother's farm. Unfortunately, while working on the garage, I slipped on an icy stone path behind the house and broke my right leg. Unable to crawl back up the hill to the house, I packed my leg with snow and waited for Mikelle to come looking for me, which she did around dinnertime. Mikelle called an ambulance, and the paramedics carried me up the embankment on a sheet of canvas. Later that winter, I finished roofing the garage—in a cast. The following summer, Mikelle planted a garden, which I made sure included Nancy's peonies and waving plumes of sea broom.

While living in Maine, I drove back and forth to Ayer twice a week to run Meridian Medical Systems. Because the drive was two and a half hours each way, I often slept on a cot in my new office, working down there four days a week. Soon after the company moved, Jim Regan, who had once helped haul me through the window of Airtron, was diagnosed with prostate cancer. He never complained.

"How was your bone scan?" I asked one day.

"Oh, it came out fine," Jim said.

Well, that was not true. It was a disaster. I intended for MMS's location in Ayer to be temporary, but wanting Jim to remain close to his home in Waltham and close to the cancer center, I kept the business in Ayer so he could keep working, while praying his health would improve. Jim worked up until two weeks before his death. His wife, Marie, asked me to give the eulogy at his funeral, which I did. Jim was my best friend.

Shortly after Jim's passing, Bob Williams retired, and Rick Kelley moved to Nashua, New Hampshire, where Bob Bielawa operated his microwave component company. Bob and I had remained close since our days at M/A-Com, so I relocated MMS to the old mill on Chestnut Street that held his company, and we shared a facility, which included private offices, lab and test space, a machine shop, and a large conference room. The mill was a three-hour drive from my house in Maine, so I often stayed overnight at a motel while working.

Both Rick Kelley and Ken Puglia had previously worked with Bob, who was skilled in the use of MMIC technology. Bob's staff included microwave engineer Joe Sylvia as well as Ted Grosch, a microwave instructor on the faculty of the University of Massachusetts. Bob had his staff, I had mine, and everybody knew each other. It was a natural blend. With the additional technical staff and the improved facilities, we were up and running.

Managing the Farm

Soon after Mikelle and I moved to Maine, my son Chris called from Utah, where he had moved after leaving the Navy. Like Jeff, Chris was an extreme skier. He also worked on the slopes as a photographer. While studying pottery and ceramics at the University of Utah, Chris learned to speak fluent Navajo. Now married with a son, Chris wanted to move back east. To help his family, I invited them live at my grandmother's farmhouse.

Ma Hartley had died of heart failure in 1981, three years after Pop. My uncle George had also passed away. In a will drawn up by herself, my grandmother left her property to her three surviving sons: my father, Chet, and Dutch. As a memorial to Robert, Ma wanted to keep the farmhouse and campground in the family, but when the will went to probate court, my father and uncles could not figure out how to divide up the farm. At the time, I was starting Microwave Medical Systems and needed the money for the company, but my father called me and said, "You have to buy it. We can't leave the farm to anyone else in the family."

I seemed to be the only person all three of them could agree on. Chet and Dutch also called, asking me to buy the property. To ensure they got a fair deal, I asked my uncles to each have the farmhouse and campground appraised and bought the property for 10 percent more than the highest appraised value. I also paid the overdue taxes and bills. Then I wrote my father and my uncles checks for their share of the estate, and my father moved into the farmhouse. Chet, who really liked the place, later joined him. I made Chet the manager and bought the campground a truck for him to drive. However, because Chet and his wife were having marital difficulties, my uncle asked me to hold onto his portion of the money and use it to pay his salary, which I did—plus interest and social security. Unfortunately, this caused a rift between me and Chet's son, Richie, who had spent a lot of time on the farm with me when we were growing up.

After Chet died in 1989, my uncle Dutch and his wife, Betty, moved into the farmhouse with my father. He, Dutch, and Betty all loved to play cribbage and lived there together until Dutch died a couple of years later. By that time, my father's health was also declining. I hired a camper, Joseph Schmidt—who went by "Smitty"—to live at the campground as the caretaker year-round. I gave him two camps—numbers three and four (the first is now the Carr Library). Smitty loved the place. However, he had a severe form of arthritis, ankylosing spondylitis, that caused his head to face the ground whenever he was sitting, so he could only look at you sideways. After meeting with Dr. Clement Sledge at Brigham and Women's Hospital in Jamaica Plain, I offered to pay for a surgery that would allow Smitty to look forward, rather than down. But Smitty would not let me pay for it and never got the surgery.

Once a week, I drove to the farmhouse to see my father and talk with the campers, many of whose families I had known since childhood. We never advertised. We never went looking for campers. Many of the people camping there today are the fourth generations of families who originally camped there. We have about forty cabins and fifty sites, plus the recreation hall. The structure of each cabin is owned by a family, but the campground owns the land, leasing to campers from May through November. It is a beautiful spot.

The local hardware store, Ring's, had two tables at the end of the counter where regulars stopped by every morning for eggs and coffee. One morning, while talking to the owner about wanting to provide a good breakfast for my father, who now lived alone, a guy sitting nearby said, "I go by the Hartley place every day." I arranged for the café to make my father a good breakfast every morning, and the man dropped it off.

After falling and breaking his hip, my father was scheduled to undergo an operation at Goodall Hospital in nearby Sanford. The surgery itself was pretty straightforward, but because of his age and weight, my father knew he had a 50/50 chance of making it through the surgery. I explained the risks and tried to convince him to go to Mass General, which had a more practiced team of doctors, but my father wanted to stay in Maine.

"They have good doctors here too," he insisted.

Not wanting to be bedridden, my father went ahead with the surgery but never came out of the anesthesia. He died on February 18, 1994, two days after his eighty-sixth birthday. Because I had allowed our father to undergo surgery without talking it over with the family, my brother Curtis blamed me for our father's death. But our father was of sound mind, and he had made the decision himself. Our mother had died in Miami two years before.

By this time, Smitty had also passed away. So when Chris decided to move back east with his family, I hired him to manage the campground, honoring Ma's request to keep it in the family. I also bought Chris a professional kiln to help him start a pottery business. However, after a couple of years, when managing the campground did not work out, Chris and his family moved to a nearby house, which I bought for them.

Connie Benzing's estate and golf course, which adjoined the campground, were now owned by Dave and Carol Porter. I hired Dave to manage the campground, and we became friends. They even held a "Ma Hartley Night" for the people in town who remembered my grandmother. I stood up and told stories about how Ma loved to dance, how she would offer people mints so they would lean in close and she could smell their breath to see if they had been drinking, and how—because of the years her own children had spent in foster care—she donated all the proceeds from the campground's dances and beano and bingo nights to the St. Charles Children's Home in Rochester. As far as I know, I am the only one Ma talked to about sending the money to the children's home.

I made sure to discuss Pop Hartley as well, particularly his time in the Navy. Then, after I sat down, other people got up and told stories. It was a great evening.

Paddling Home

Throughout life, one thing that kept me going was sports, particularly playing hockey. During one scrimmage in Tyngsborough when I was almost sixty years old, I ran into a friend, Kevin Wholey, the procurement manager for Raytheon's Missile Systems Group. The Tyngsborough ice arena, Skate 3, was close to Nashua and had three rinks. Kevin was there to watch his son play for the University of Massachusetts at Lowell.

"What're you doing here, Ken?" Kevin asked when I leaned my hockey bag and sticks against the wall to watch the game being played. "Picking up your kid?"

"No," I said. "I'm skating."

"Which rink?"

"This one."

"Nah," Kevin replied. "You must be mistaken. You can't be playing on this one. The University of Massachusetts team is skating in this rink."

"Yeah," I said. "We're scrimmaging them."

He looked at me in disbelief. "These kids are going to kill you."

I laughed. I was sixty and skating against twenty-year-old kids, but the young guys were gentlemen compared to the old guys playing in the Old Timers League who thought they should have been in the pros.

I skated and taught hockey until my early seventies. For most of that time, I also skied. One of my last times on the slopes, I was skiing in Utah with Bill Gray and his second wife, Kay. But because I can only see out of one eye, I misjudged a change in the slope and hit the snow with a face plant, breaking my collar bone and two ribs.

"In fact," said the hospital radiologist who reviewed my X-rays, "it looks like in the past you've broken every rib."

"Oh, yes," I said. "Some more than once."

"What do you do to break so many ribs?" the doctor asked.

"Hockey," I said.

I did not want to be the defenseman who let a goal get past me on the ice. Not exactly known for being careful, I stepped in front of slap shots. In addition to being hit by the car, I broke my right leg nine different times—playing softball, skiing, and hiking. Never once did I break my leg playing hockey. However, after Mikelle and I moved to Maine, I stopped playing both hockey and softball. I no longer had time to drive to the games. When I retired, my hockey team, the Assabet Bears screwed a hockey puck to the blade of my stick and gave it to me for my birthday. "That way nobody can ever say they took the puck off your stick," they said.

On weekends, I often kayaked up the Kennebec River to Richmond or downstream to Bath. In the beginning, Mikelle went with me in a two-person kayak. We watched seals sunning themselves on the rocks or osprey soaring overhead. Sometimes we stopped for lunch at a little café before paddling home. In spite of the difficulties we had been through, things were pretty good.

At our shared facility in Nashua, my MMS team was working alongside Bob Bielawa's team. The NIH had awarded me several Small Business Innovation Research grants that I successfully completed in collaboration with EVMS. And we had made significant progress developing new microwave-based medical devices including a myocardial ablation catheter, a newborn brain temperature monitor, and a monitor to detect neonatal and pediatric extravasations. I hoped these would solve unmet medical needs and improve patient outcomes. However, the biggest challenge still lay ahead.

CHAPTER 16

NEW DEVELOPMENTS

Several years after moving to Woolwich, I received a phone call from the State Department's Bureau of Educational and Cultural Affairs. Friends from Bath, Pete Zimowski and his wife, Jackie, had volunteered to host a foreign exchange student through the Future Leaders Exchange (FLEX) program and listed me as a reference. At the end of the call, I inquired how to become part of the program.

"What are your questions?" the woman asked.

"Well, I live in the boonies and have no kids at home," I said. "Would I represent a good host family?"

It turned out that living in a city and having children at home were not requirements for the program, so I asked to be considered as a host family. A sixteen-year-old Ukrainian student, Yuliya Salata, was scheduled to fly into Washington in a few days, but at the last minute, her host family had backed out. I offered to host her. Then, realizing that I should ask my wife, I put the lady on hold and tracked down Mikelle.

"What do you think about taking in a high school student?" I asked.

"We're too old to be taking in high school students," she said.

"It's only for one year," I reasoned. "We are not adopting her."

So Mikelle agreed.

Years before, we had sponsored a six-year-old girl, Lora Beth, by making a monthly donation to a program that helped children in America. Her family lived in the rural coal mining country of West Virginia. Since Mikelle's family was from South Carolina, we drove down to visit. The family was very nice—but boy, the poverty. They lived by the railroad tracks in a house so small I drove by it three times, looking for the number. Although neat and comfortable, the house looked like a place someone working on the railroad might use to store equipment. If you put your hand out the window, the train would've hit it. Lora Beth's father, Keith, had black lung disease from working in the mines and could barely talk; Keith's wife, Ginny, had lost a leg from diabetes. When we took them out to dinner, Ginny had to order for her husband, who could not read the menu.

Sometime later, Ginny called me up. "I hate to ask," she said. "But do you think you could loan us money to move to another house?"

Without expecting anything back, I sent them a check for the amount requested—a few thousand dollars, not a lot. Years later, Ginny called back, really excited.

"We have good news," she gushed. "We've got the money saved up. We can pay back the loan."

"No-no-no-no," Mikelle said, listening in.

But I interrupted her. "That would be terrific!" I replied, knowing how hard the family must have worked to save up that money.

They were so proud of being able to repay us. They had probably been saving for years. So we accepted their check. After, I assured Mikelle that we would find a way to repay them, and when Lora Beth enrolled in college to become a nurse, we used the money to buy her supplies, including a computer. Today, she works in the nursing field. In fact, we were invited to Lora Beth's wedding and were asked to sit with her family. The ceremony took place in a small Baptist church, built with donations and labor by the congregation. However, the members did not have enough money to finish the bathrooms. Before leaving, I asked how much they needed and wrote them a check. Being in a position to help felt good.

By signing up to host a foreign student, Mikelle and I were once again in a position to help. However, we never could have anticipated how important Yuliya would become to us—or we to her. As part of the FLEX program, Yuliya was one of just twelve students chosen to study in the United States that year from more than two thousand applicants. Petite and shy with brown hair and blue eyes, she spoke fluent English. In Ukraine, her family lived in a one-room apartment that they rearranged into a bedroom at night. When Yuliya arrived and saw that she had her own room with a bathroom and shower, she asked, "This is mine?"

Except to eat, she did not come out of her room for two days.

While living with us, Yuliya attended Morse High School across the river in Bath. As a high school senior, she played soccer, worked hard, and excelled academically. Mikelle and I both liked her. We also enjoyed spending time with the Zimowski's exchange student, Tina Odilavadze, a concert pianist whom I tutored in math. Just before Christmas, we drove both girls to Boston for a weekend to show them all America had to offer. While Mikelle rested at the hotel, I intentionally took the girls for a walk on Boylston Street, across from the Boston Commons to the historic M. Steinert and Sons Steinway piano showroom. Through the window I saw a grand piano. *I've got to get Tina on this thing*, I thought.

"Wait a moment while I talk to the manager," I told the girls and asked a saleslady if I could speak to the manager.

"Is there a problem?" she asked.

"No," I said. "I have a favor to ask."

An older woman came over, and I explained that I was accompanying two young ladies who were standing outside. "One is a recognized concert pianist from the Republic of Georgia," I said. "Would it be possible for her to play a piece on a piano?"

After the girls came in, the manager led Tina to a nice upright piano. However, I pointed across the showroom floor to a concert grand piano. "That one."

The manager raised her eyebrows. Without sheet music, Tina sat down and played several classical pieces. A crowd gathered around, trying to name the music.

Tina wowed them all.

As we were leaving the manager said, "You can bring her in anytime."

While walking back to our hotel to meet Mikelle for dinner, I asked the girls if they had noticed the price tag on the piano.

"Yes," Tina said, "ninety-two thousand dollars."

"In America you can buy a piano like that," I told them. "But you have to want it, and you have to earn it."

After Mikelle joined us, we walked to a nearby Italian restaurant, Limoncello, on North Street for dinner. I happened to know the owner, Maurizio "Mo" Badolato, an Italian immigrant who previously worked as a waiter at a nearby restaurant on the Common that I used to frequent with Dick Melick. After winning $1 million in a lottery, Mo had opened his own restaurant. "Only in America," he told Yuliya and Tina, stopping by our table.

To give the girls a real taste of the city, we stayed at Boston's historic Parker House Hotel. Built in 1855 with elegant dark oak walls and burnished bronze fixtures, it is the country's longest continuously operating hotel. Early the following morning, I went downstairs to Parker's, the hotel's famous restaurant, and introduced myself to the hostess.

"You must be from Eastern Europe," I said, noticing that the young woman spoke with a slight accent.

Surprised, she replied that she came from Lithuania.

"In that case, you must speak Russian," I said, knowing the Soviet government had forbidden people in the countries it occupied from speaking their local languages. "And you probably live in Walpole."

"How did you know?" she asked, flabbergasted.

I named a couple of former Ferrotec colleagues—Ramonas Kalvaitis and Al Kriskunas—who were also Lithuanian and lived in Walpole, which had a large Lithuanian community. Then I told her about Tina and Yuliya, who also spoke Russian, and asked whether she would speak Russian to them when Mikelle brought the girls down for breakfast, which she did. I directed them to table number 40—the same table where in the summer of 1953 John F. Kennedy proposed to Jackie Bouvier. Yuliya sat in Kennedy's seat, and Tina sat across from her in the seat once occupied by Jackie. They had a great time.

During the school year, Yuliya worked in Bath as a receptionist for the Realtor who sold us the land for our house. I sometimes packed sandwiches and drove across the bridge to eat lunch with Yuliya in the waterfront park, overlooking the Kennebec River.

At the end of the school year, I asked Yuliya whether she would like to attend college here. She enthusiastically agreed, but had to first fly home and complete a series of exams to graduate from high school. That summer, Mikelle and I flew to Ukraine for a week to meet Yuliya's mother, Iryna, stepfather, Sergey, and younger brother, Ivan. During our visit, we stayed at her family's small apartment in Merefa, near the northeast city of Kharkiv. In preparation for our visit, they had totally remodeled the bathroom with a new sink and shower. To accommodate us, Iryna moved into the apartment next door with a friend. Sergey and Ivan stayed with their grandparents, Alla and Yuriy, in the country.

While in Ukraine, I taught at Yuliya's high school, Merefa 6. The teachers and students all spoke English, but the pupils were so shy that on my first day, they would not speak in English. When I asked where the restroom was, they pointed through the window toward a row of cement outhouses. Each contained two cement pads that you straddled to squat over a hole in the ground. One thing I knew from growing up at the farm was that in winter kids did not dillydally in an unheated outhouse. Tragically, in the spring of 2022, Russian forces totally destroyed the school. Ukrainian soldiers had used the school as barracks, and the Russians, who had invaded the country three months before, wiped it out.

Toward the end of our visit, I asked Yuliya's family if we could host her for four more years so she could attend college in the United States. Because of my relationship at the Wentworth Institute of Technology, I paid for Yuliya to enroll at the college to study engineering. The next year, Yuliya transferred to the University of New Hampshire to major in International Affairs and minor in French. To help with the cost, she became a resident assistant. As I had with my own children, I bought Yuliya a pair of ice skates and gave her skating lessons. While supervising the school's ice rink for the UNH athletics department, Yuliya met another student, Matthew Borowski. Two years after her graduation, they married in Conway, New Hampshire, near where I used to ski. Iryna attended the wedding, but since Sergey's visa had been denied, I walked Yuliya down the aisle while a friend held a laptop so her family in Ukraine could watch the ceremony online.

After traveling around Asia to recruit top students to American universities, Yuliya worked her way through Lesley University in Cambridge and earned a master's degree in education. Then she formed a preschool in nearby Medford. Mikelle and I helped with the documentation so Yuliya's mother, father, brother, and grandparents could join her in Massachusetts, where they all live today. In fact, Ivan, briefly lived with me in Woolwich, while attending school just up the road.

Advanced Cardiac Therapeutics

Meanwhile, I continued developing medical products. On March 1, 2007, while still president and technical director of Meridian Medical Systems, I co-founded Advanced Cardiac Therapeutics (ACT), an independent company founded entirely on MMS's patents (of which I was the sole inventor) and intellectual property to develop microwave-based integrated catheter tips.

Back in the seventies, the radiometer we built for OncoScan was as big as a two-drawer file cabinet. Twenty years later, for our in-line blood warmer, we successfully reduced the radiometer to the size of a deck of cards. The next step was to make a radiometer small enough to introduce a catheter into a blood vessel, which took two years and $250,000. MIT's Rad Lab had revolutionized warfare by developing radar systems small enough to fit on aircraft. We took an entire radar system and made it small enough to fit on the tip of a catheter—something that had never been done before.

We were the first to place a dual-frequency antenna, a passive diplexer, and a radiometer on a catheter. The same diameter as the shaft of a wooden Q-tip, the catheter was less than 10-millimeters long and 2.5-millimeters in diameter. Only the transmitter was located externally. The MMIC chip, which was the radiometer, allowed us to measure the temperature of blood or tissue at the exact point at which heat or cold is applied.[*]

Until that time, no MMIC chips existed for microwave frequencies. They were made at lower frequencies, but this radiometer, which we developed in the mid-eighties, was so unique, we kept it as a trade secret, the way Gillette famously protected the composition of the grinding stones on which it sharpened razor blades and Coca-Cola protected its formula. The radiometer included three chips, one with a filter, but because the technology for the radiometer was already known, we could only patent the changes we made to its design. So instead of patenting the design (which would have required us to publicly describe the design features that made the radiometer unique, potentially enabling another company to manufacture it without our knowledge), we protected it as a trade secret.

We initially designed the Integrated Catheter Tip for use in cardiac ablation surgery, in which a doctor threads a long, flexible catheter through the blood vessels to the heart to treat various arrhythmias, including atrial fibrillation. If left untreated, "A-fib" significantly increases the risk of stroke and other cardiac complications. To block abnormal electrical signals to the heart and restore a normal heart rhythm, a doctor applies heat or cold to a small amount of tissue. The goal is to damage the tissue without scarring or damaging the blood vessels.

If you really want to understand a problem and learn how the surgeon addresses the issue, you have to witness it. So I pulled on a gown and mask to attend surgeries at Mass General and

---

[*]   To both apply heat and measure temperature, the radiometer chip necessitated a dual-mode, or dual-frequency, antenna, or transducer. Normally, the transmitter (or heating) frequency is at a lower frequency, and the radiometer (or receiver), is at a higher frequency. The radiometer actually requires three MMIC chips. To reduce cross talk, we split the functions without putting too much gain on one chip. Otherwise, the circuit became unstable, the same way you get feedback from a microphone while someone is talking when the output signal flows into the input. The same thing happens with MMIC chips if they have too much gain on a single chip.

Brigham and Women's Hospital. As I previously had with dialysis patients, I wanted to see what people were going through. During open-heart surgery, a doctor would tape a long line across a patient's back, all the way up their side and under their arm around to their chest. After carefully cutting through the tape into the patient's skin, the doctor performed the surgery. Using the ablation catheter, which doctors put right up through the groin or the shoulder, replaced the need for this surgery. Instead of open-heart surgery, which required a lengthy stay in the hospital followed by a long recovery, cardiac ablation became an overnight procedure.

Catheters used for cardiac ablation surgery typically measure 110 centimeters long, with an external transmitter on one end. The transmitter (microwave, radio frequency, or ultrasound) or cryogenic cooling source, is external to the patient and is coupled through the catheter to the dual-frequency antenna. The transmitter and receiver operate at different frequencies. The dual-mode transducer transmits the first frequency and receives the second frequency. The antenna transmits the heating frequency. It also receives the return signal, which we amplify so doctors can measure temperature, pressure, and contact. They can see also the formation of bubbles, which are dangerous. Without having this ability, an electrophysiologist is blind to what is happening. It is strictly by the seat of their pants.

In addition to the microwave components, the catheter includes an irrigation cooling path and EKG contacts. The tubing for the cooling path is inside the catheter, and the tip of the catheter (which includes the MMIC chip radiometer) is inside the patient. To prevent the transmitter from damaging the receiver (which is the radiometer), the transmitter and receiver are separated by a diplexer. To cool the surface, the tip of the catheter sprays water at the abrasion site like a showerhead, and the antenna surrounds the tip like a helix.

Before MMS developed radiometric sensing using a shared antenna, doctors relied on conventional temperature sensors such as thermocouples (formed by combining two wires of different metals that operate like a thermostat and generate a voltage, which is a function of temperature). However, because thermocouples disturb the antenna pattern, they were remote and could not measure temperature at the point at which energy was applied. To gauge the temperature of the heat applied during myocardial ablation, doctors wore a stethoscope and listened for a popping noise—the sound of blood boiling inside the patient's blood vessels—which meant that the amount of heat was too hot and caused damage. Sometimes, the noise was audible without a stethoscope and people in the room could hear the blood boiling. We eliminated that possibility by measuring the temperature at the ablation site. However, because we did not yet have FDA approval, the procedure was only allowed under specific conditions when the benefits to the patient exceeded the risks.

Our work on cardiac ablation was done with the support of an NIH grant in collaboration with Dr. Paul Wang and the staff of the Department of Surgery at Tufts-New England Medical Center. As I had formerly promised the American Association of Blood Banks and the FDA, MMS agreed to only develop microwave products in which temperature (hot or cold) was measured at the point at which energy is applied.

To measure temperature or tissue differences in emissivity, we used radiometric sensing on all MMS products. Various tissues may be the same temperature but have different emissivities. An air bubble, for example, has no emissivity and looks quite different from blood or tissue, which has very high emissivity. Just as when I was measuring the health of Soviet crops, the expression we use in blackbody theory (which explains how a surface absorbs energy) is that a perfect absorber is a perfect emitter.

We included the radiometric sensors on catheters used to ablate cardiac and prostate tissues, for the intravascular warming of blood, for detecting vulnerable plaque in the arteries, for measuring intravascular blood flow, and for detecting air emboli. Because all of the products developed by ACT were based solely on my patents, I received 30 percent of the shares of the new company. My co-founder, Tim Lenihan, had transferred to Europe to head Arrow's new European facility. He later left Arrow to start his own catheter manufacturing company, Contract Medical International (CMI), in Dresden, Germany. Tim hired Peter Van der Sluis as the CEO of ACT, which had its own employees and operated out of CMI's facility. Many of ACT's management team also came from CMI.

Under our license agreement with ACT, MMS would continue developing the catheter and ablation markets and be reimbursed for our time, with the understanding that MMS would own and license the patents to ACT. In return, when the catheters were sent to market, MMS would receive royalties based on the sale price from ACT. Since all ACT's products were based on my inventions, I acted as a consultant and managed the patent portfolios for both ACT and MMS. I provided the microwave technology ability, and Tim Lenihan provided the catheter-making ability.

Before approaching the FDA for approval for the myocardial ablation catheter, ACT received the CE Mark (European approval). This included a clinical trial in Belgium, where, on February 28, 2011, a hospital in Bruges held the first-in-man ablation study. Because of the risks, the trial for the catheter only included people who were not expected to survive. They used it on a man who was going to die from a heart arrhythmia—and it worked. The man was so grateful to be alive the next morning, the doctors told us he was crying. Because of our product, he lived.

To make it easier to approach the FDA for approval of the integrated catheter, Peter Van der Sluis set up ACT as a Delaware Company with an office in Laguna Beach, California. ACT's employees remained in Germany. However, as a small company the cost of conducting a clinical trial was very prohibitive. Because the device had not yet been approved by the FDA, ACT was required to support all of the costs for the trial, which was not covered by insurance. This included paying the doctors involved in the trial, covering the hospital's medical costs, and providing free equipment. In the case of the myocardial ablation catheter, this involved supplying roughly twelve thousand catheters per test site, which would cost millions of dollars. So we could not afford to pursue it. Normally big companies pay for the funding. Often, a venture capital group steps in and takes over a smaller company, which in a way is what happened to us. The FDA did not approve our myocardial ablation catheter until after one of the world's largest medical companies acquired the patent.

Technical Backup

After losing Jim Regan, I began looking to hire a technical consultant to take Jim's place. Bill Gray, my longtime friend who worked at Hughes, recommended Robert Allison, a microwave engineer familiar with radar systems, who had software experience. After Allison took an early retirement from Hughes Aircraft's Radar Systems Group, I contracted him to consult for MMS. A Californian, he frequently flew to the East Coast and stayed in Woolwich with Mikelle and me, and we became friends.

MMS paid Allison to provide technical backup on projects for ACT. His contract subjected him to a consulting agreement that encompassed strict confidentiality requirements, including a provision that all further developments of the catheter technology would remain the property of MMS and be licensed to ACT. The company's Field of Use involved microwave and radio frequency (RF) sensing for the ablation of heart tissue, while MMS retained all rights outside of ACT's Field of Use. Allison and I were the microwave people who (along with the other members of my team) made the antenna, the radiometer, and the diplexer for the Integrated Catheter Tip, which was ACT's only product.*

Our development of the catheter technology continued from 2007 to 2010. However, on three separate occasions ACT vio-

---

* When you have a patent, you can find many applications for the technology, with various licenses for each separate use. Each agreement has a license fee. If the company you license is successful, you obtain a royalty. When you license a patent, you can restrict its Field of Use, which limits what the licensee is allowed to do with it. The same technology for the myocardial ablation catheter could be used to treat a number of other conditions that also required ablation, including heating tissue to treat benign prostrate hyperplasia (an enlarged prostate) and for renal denervation to treat hypertension but were not included in ACT's Field of Use.

lated the terms of the MMS license agreement, including contracting another company to assemble the catheter tip, which involved the microwave radiometer chips. To build the radiometer, ACT bypassed us and shared our trade secrets with another company. I only found out about the violation because ACT used an electronic assembly house run by several guys I had previously worked with at M/A-Com, and one of the engineers called me up. "Hey," he said. "Nice to be working with you again."

I said, "What?"

Rather than canceling our agreement or taking ACT to court—which does not do anyone any good—after each violation I offered them a reasonable settlement. In each case the license agreement was revised. As a result, ACT added a royalty provision to their MMS license agreement and paid us compensation. I did not want to terminate the license agreement and put ACT out of business.

Brain Temperature Monitor

While working on cardiac ablation, I developed a non-invasive radiometric sensing system to monitor the brain temperature of newborns. During birth, a lack of oxygenated blood flow to the brain can cause newborn death or brain damage, including lifelong difficulties such as cerebral palsy, clinically referred to as hypoxic-ischemic encephalopathy, or HIE. One way to reduce the damage caused by this condition in full-term infants is to induce mild, therapeutic hypothermia by carefully lowering a baby's body temperature to between 32.5°C and 33°C and maintaining this temperature for up to seventy-two hours before slowly warming the baby back up.

Through my work with Dr. Tom Bass at the Eastern Virginia Medical School and Dr. Dorothea Jenkins at the Medical University of South Carolina, I helped develop a hypothermia-based system to reduce incidence of HIE. Since this cooling procedure targets the brain, MMS made an antenna contoured to fit the curvature of an infant's head. But first, I needed the right dimensions.

"What size is a baby's head?" I asked Dr. Bass, walking by a row of hospital cribs.

He offered to get X-rays, but I walked over to a crib and measured a baby's head between my thumb and pinky. "Four and a half inches," I said.

"How do you know that?" Dr. Bass asked.

"Slightly larger than a softball," I said.

My contribution to this system included the Dual-mode Intracranial Temperature Sensor, which involved two different radiometric frequencies, one that was shallow and one that allowed you to see deeper. Accurately measuring a newborn's brain temperature through the skull required a dual-mode transducer, which I had developed and patented.[35] Compared to conventional techniques, this is a more reliable indicator of brain temperature. To develop the technology, I wrote a grant to the NIH's Children's Health Care division and served as the principal investigator.

Viral Inactivation

I also continued to develop a non-invasive, microwave viral inactivation system to destroy blood-borne viruses in the bloodstream. This was the next step for the ThermoStat 900 blood warmer.

It turns out that viruses are more susceptible to temperature than is blood. Research conducted at the New York Blood Center proved that exposing blood to a high temperature for a short duration of time was effective in destroying some of the world's deadliest blood-borne viruses—including HIV, hepatitis, and Ebola—while maintaining the activity and protein structure of the blood.

Measuring temperature at a remote site would not work. The temperature of blood must be measured at the point it is heated as it flows through IV tubing. Prior to the development of MMS's In-Line Microwave Fluid and Blood Warmer, there was no way to elevate the temperature of blood to the required range—75°C to 85°C—for the short time required to destroy blood-borne viruses.

The key to heating blood is radiometric sensing. The same antenna that heats the blood also measures the temperature. As long as you precisely heat the blood for a short duration of time—five or six milliseconds—as it flows through a short length of plastic IV tubing at a rate of 200 milliliters per minute, the blood is not damaged. Microwaves see the fluid inside the plastic tubing, which is transparent at both the heating frequency and the microwave radiometric sensing frequency, not the temperature of the tubing. As a result, microwaves instantly heat and sense the temperature of the blood as it passes through the tube.

Working with Dr. Chris Stowell, the head of blood services at the Massachusetts General Hospital Blood Transfusion Service, and Dr. Robert Finberg at the Dana Farber Cancer Institute in Boston, I successfully demonstrated the destruction of blood-borne viruses in the laboratory using short duration, high-temperature microwave heating of stored and bagged blood.[36][37]

I filed the patent for the viral inactivation system back in 1997, but it was on the back burner. At the time, I had just settled MMS's three-year lawsuit with the dialysis supplier for our sterilizer, and MMS had lost its manufacturing agreement for the IV-inline fluid and blood warmer with Baxter. We just went from one problem to the next.

Later, I got so involved with developing the myocardial ablation catheter and forming ACT, I just did not have the time to develop and market these products.

CHAPTER 17

BETRAYED

A couple of years before turning eighty, I decided to step down as president of MMS to focus on research and continue working as the company's technical advisor. To ensure the technology and products I developed would be brought to market to improve patient outcomes, I wanted to bring someone new into the company who could manage it far into the future. Ideally, I hoped to find a marketing manager familiar with catheters, so that after completing the design for the myocardial ablation catheter, I could work on renal denervation and other applications.

I had previously offered the job to Mike Rogge, the marketing manager of Baxter's Anesthesia Products Division, but after downsizing Microwave Medical Systems, I could not afford to hire him. At the time, roughly a decade later, Mike was the marketing manager for Atricure Inc., a global leader in cryogenic ablation that specialized in atrial fibrillation treatment solutions. Since Mike was no longer available, I considered Sean Carroll, a West Point graduate with significant marketing and contract experience with catheters. Sean's father is my good friend, Dr. Ronald Carroll, an oncologist from New Harbor, Maine. Along with another good friend, Dr. George Roth, a well-known neurosurgeon who retired to Woolwich, we often met with our wives for a monthly breakfast and discussed my medical products. However, my youngest son, Jeff, asked me to consider him for the position.

After graduating from the University of Maine with a degree in political science, Jeff had briefly sold textbooks. I encouraged him to sell medical products. At the time, my work involved developing the sterile docking system for Japan Medical Supply (JMS), which sold dialysis equipment and support products, such as needles. So, I wrote a letter to Dr. Hajime Kimura, the president and CEO of JMS. A Chicago radiologist, Dr. Kimura had helped test OncoScan. His father-in-law, the former president of JMS, had founded the company. Following his father-in-law's death, Dr. Kimura returned to Japan to run JMS, which owned a hospital with the largest dialysis center in Hiroshima. After receiving my letter, Dr. Kimura arranged to meet me in San Francisco for dinner.

"I have a favor to ask," I said when we got together. "I would like to have you consider hiring my son, Jeff."

"Fair enough," Dr. Kimura said, just like that. "He's hired."

"But you have never met him," I said.

He quickly replied, "The apple never falls far from the tree."

I was pleased. Jeff is very personable. He is good with sales and was a good-looking kid. JMS put Jeff in its San Francisco sales office. Whenever I flew out to visit, I took Jeff skiing. His boss, Hiroshi Kamigouchi, the head of sales for JMS in North America, also skied very well, and the three of us often skied together in Utah. When Hiroshi died suddenly at a young age, I flew out to support Hiroshi's family. By then Jeff was engaged to a young woman he had met in college. In the late 1990s, he informed me that he planned to leave JMS and move back to the East Coast. So, wanting to honor Japanese customs, I flew to San Francisco to meet with Dr. Kimura and asked to have my son back to work for me.

"I am honored you asked," Dr. Kimura said.

Jeff soon moved back to Massachusetts and joined Microwave Medical Systems as the sales manager. However, about a year later, he left MMS to join a start-up Boston tea company. Jeff later sold products for a medical company that developed pregnancy and malaria test kits. The job required significant travel, including to Africa. By then Jeff was married and had two young daughters. His family lived just north of Portland, Maine. Because their house was on a busy street, I worried my granddaughters might run into the road. After everything Nancy and I had gone through after Kirsten's death, I knew that if anything happened to one of the kids, that would be the end of everything. So I gave Jeff money to help him buy a house in a secluded neighborhood on the coast and built him several pieces of furniture, including a twelve-foot desk with bookcases for my granddaughters.

Every year for Thanksgiving and Christmas, Mikelle and I invited our children and their families to Woolwich for a big dinner. Nearly two dozen people filled our home, including Yuliya's family and Larry Driscoll, who had introduced me to Mikelle. Mikelle loved big gatherings and did all the cooking—including two Thanksgiving turkeys—while I rearranged the living room furniture and set up folding tables so we could all sit together.

Wanting to spend more time with his family, Jeff asked whether I would consider hiring him to market products for Meridian Medical Systems. At the time, Mikelle was encouraging me to retire. Over the years, she and Jeff had grown very close. Because of Jeff's previous departure from the company, I had misgivings, but many fathers would like to think that their sons will follow in their footsteps. So in September 2010, I hired Jeff as MMS's sales manager. Soon after, I made him president of the company.

Having my youngest son run my company made me proud. Neither Randee nor Chris had any experience in or wanted a career developing and marketing medical products. Meanwhile, I remained the technical director and CEO of MMS and continued interfacing with ACT on all legal and patent issues as well as on MMS technology. At the time, I was fully funding MMS and paid Jeff's salary while never drawing any personal compensation from the company. Everything I made through grants and contracts, I invested back into MMS. Since 2001, I had also kept the company going by loaning it more than a million dollars. However, to support Jeff and work with him on contracts and licensing, I decided not to apply for additional grants to fund further research and product development.

As part of Jeff's agreement to work for MMS, I gifted him a 24 percent interest in MMS. Three months later, on New Year's Day 2011, I gave him an additional 25 percent. Mikelle retained her 1 percent share. After Jeff joined the company, he suggested I sell Robert Allison shares of MMS and give him a position on the management board. Since I planned to retire, I hoped that Allison, who I considered a good friend, would provide the technical support Jeff would need to keep the company going. So the following August, I arranged to sell Allison a 15 percent interest in MMS, which watered down the company's stock. But as CEO and chairman of the management board, I remained the largest shareholder with a 42.5 percent interest in the company.

At the time, I was developing the Cool Cable, a smaller, more flexible Integrated Catheter Tip designed to treat hypertension (renal denervation). To help reduce blood pressure, this minimally invasive procedure involves ablating the nerves located in the renal arteries. It is fairly simple to reach the heart by inserting a catheter through the groin and manipulating it through the blood vessels, which are larger and reasonably straight. Inserting a catheter into the renal arteries, which are smaller in diameter and bend sharply, is difficult. I needed to design a smaller-diameter catheter flexible enough to thread through these arteries without damaging the vessel walls.*

A smaller diameter cable absorbs more electromagnetic energy, making it "lossy." This heats the coaxial cable inside the catheter, which becomes too hot to touch. Because the cable may touch blood vessel walls, this could be dangerous. To cool the cable, I enlarged the hole in the hollow center conductor by lowering the impedance of the cable, which allowed a coolant to flow through the center conductor.**

---

* The dual-mode frequency antenna on the catheter tip couples to the RF or microwave transmitter, which remains outside the body and produces heat for the ablation. The antenna allows a second frequency, which is the receiver or radiometer frequency. The MMIC receiver is so small, it is totally integrated into the catheter tip, as is the diplexer, which separates the transmitter frequency from the receiver frequency. The use of a common antenna to both transmit heating (hyperthermia) or cooling (hypothermia) and to receive radiometric sensing allowed doctors to measure temperature at the exact point where heat or cold is applied, fulfilling the promise I had made to the FDA to always measure temperature at the point at which heating or cooling is applied.

** A lower impedance cable will provide a larger diameter center conductor for a given outer conductor diameter.

Before surgery, the electrophysiologist could select the proper treatment and catheter for use with either a gaseous or liquid coolant. If using a gaseous refrigerant (which cannot be released into the blood flow surrounding the catheter), the coolant could be returned to the source through the dielectric material separating the center conductor from the outer conductor of the cable. If using a liquid (which can be released into the blood flow), the coolant provided irrigation, cooling the tissue between the antenna and the blood vessel.* The key was the flexible, hollow center conductor, which allowed the coolant to flow through the cable. The first small-diameter catheter to transmit microwave energy for tissue ablation while using radiometric sensing to measure temperature, this was a significant development. In April 2012 I filed a provisional patent application for the "Heating/Sensing Catheter Apparatus For Minimally Invasive Applications," which was finalized as a nonprovisional application (also known as a utility patent) on December 10, 2012, with myself as the sole inventor and applicant.

At the time, Covidien, a Massachusetts global health care products company, was developing a rigid, needle-like catheter capable of using elevated temperatures (hyperthermia) to destroy cancerous tissue by inserting the rigid catheter into a tumor. To reduce the temperature of the catheter as it enters the skin and passes through bodily tissues, one of Covidien's affiliates wanted to include the Cool Cable concept in its cancer treatment line. My relationship with Covidien's president, Richard Meelia, went back to when he founded the company. But after my experience working with Baxter Healthcare, I wanted to avoid licensing all of MMS's technology to a single company. I enjoyed working with the people at Baxter, but unless you plan to merge, it is risky dealing with one company on multiple products. If they pull the plug, you lose everything. Instead, I intended to license the Cool Cable patent to different companies for different Fields of Use. So I allowed Jeff to negotiate a restricted Field-of-Use

---

* The myocardial ablation catheter could also use the Cool Cable, but did not require it.

license with Covidien, while reserving the right to make the final decisions.

Unfortunately, Jeff's and my relationship began to dissolve. MMS had several FDA approved products ready to bring to the market, including the Thermostat 900 In-Line IV Fluid and Blood Warmer; the Early Extravasation Detection IV Site Monitor (for both pediatric and adult applications); an Air Emboli Detection System; a device that measured the flow rate and volume of infused liquids in IV tubing; the PDM-3 Sterile Docking System; and the Viral Inactivation System. We had worked hard to get the FDA to validate and approve our products, but I could not afford to continue as MMS's sole investor. Bringing funds into the company was very important. To help people, you have to be successful. I wanted to find new customers for products the FDA had already cleared, but Jeff seemed more focused on marketing products that were not yet FDA approved, such as the brain temperature monitor.

I also had difficulties with Robert Allison regarding poor workmanship related to mistakes on a radiometer-based unit for the brain temperature monitoring system. In one instance, Allison put a connector in wrong and installed a radiometer circuit board upside down, so the unit did not work correctly. In another instance, a component was missing, which meant the unit could not have been tested as required. Having built my reputation on maintaining the highest quality workmanship, mistakes like this were embarrassing.

When I went to the Air Force command about problems with the AMRAAM missile, I wanted to fix the mistake I uncovered even though I knew it could cause a program delay. I could not have lived with myself knowing that American troops were being supplied defective weapons. I felt the same way about developing medical devices. We were developing the brain temperature units for patient trials at Eastern Virginia Medical School and the Medical School of South Carolina (MUSC). People would make decisions based on the clinical data from those tests, and the information was of paramount importance for saving lives and improving patient outcomes, such as reducing cerebral palsy. As a result, I informed Allison that he could no longer ship products directly to customers from his home without having them inspected by Rick Kelley, who oversaw the product design file, including quality control and production.

During this same time, we also discovered a serious flaw in the newborn brain temperature system. Instead of measuring actual brain temperature, the system measured the temperature beneath the skin's surface. It also did not accurately measure the surface temperature. To address these problems, I called for a February 5, 2013, MMS management meeting at my home in Woolwich. However, rather than attending my meeting, Jeff and Robert Allison met at MMS's facility in Nashua and asked Rick Kelley to participate in a telephone call with Volcano Capital, a New York venture capital firm interested in partnering with MMS to develop and market our brain temperature monitor by forming a new company, Brain Temp Inc. As the manager and principal investigator of the NIH Small Business Innovative Research Grant program for the brain temperature monitoring system, I expected to be included in the meeting. The grant, which I had written, is awarded to the principal investigator, not the company. So, Rick, who was working with me to resolve the technical issues on the system, called me, quite upset.

"What do you want me to do?" Rick asked. "I am not going to the meeting without you."

"Let's not work against each other," I said. "Support Jeff."

I did not want to lose Rick's influence. At this point, my company was totally breaking up. I kept trying to get everyone to work together, but the ongoing conflict between Jeff and Robert Allison and me was splitting MMS into two teams—Jeff's team vs. my team.

During a February 12, 2013, conference call with Ned Brewer, MMS's corporate counsel, Jeff and I agreed that we could no longer work together. I gave Jeff two options. He could either resign from MMS and I would pay his salary through April, or he could present me with a phase-out/buy-out plan in which I would retire from all corporate governance of MMS, including as CEO, while continuing to consult for the company and retaining my ownership interest in it. However, I wanted an advisory role to consult and continue doing research, which I loved.

Terminated

On March 1, 2013, MMS and Volcano (operating through a new company named GRAT) formed Brain Temp Inc. (BTI) to develop and market the brain temperature monitor.* The BTI board consisted of Terry Wall (who formed Volcano Capital after the $990 million sale of his previous company, Vital Signs Inc., to General Electric in 2008); my son Jeff (with Robert Allison acting as his appointed observer); and a third director who I believe was associated with one of Volcano's family of companies.

This was a tremendous opportunity for Jeff, and I hoped he would leave MMS to manage BTI, formed using five patents on which I was the sole inventor. Later that same month, Mikelle asked me to meet her and Jeff for lunch at a favorite Bath restaurant to discuss his phase-out plan. I went, expecting that Jeff would accept one of the two previously discussed options. Instead, he spoke about wanting to include a nonexclusive, limited Field-Of-Use license for the Cool Cable technology as part of a contract he was negotiating with Covidien.

I owned the patent for the Cool Cable technologies, which I had not assigned to MMS.** The patent was very important to

---

* Forming BTI was a joint effort, with my patents and Volcano's money. Because MMS contributed the patents, it owned slightly less than 50 percent of the new company. Volcano, which supplied the funding to finish developing the system, owned the remaining 50 percent, with a third company holding the remaining small, but deciding, share.

** In November 2012, my patent attorney, who I had worked with for more than twenty years, asked whether I wanted to assign the Cool Cable patent to MMS. I responded that I was intentionally not assigning the patent to MMS because of the difficulties I was having with Jeff and Robert Allison. The following month, my patent attorney retired and transferred his duties to another lawyer at the same firm. On April 4, 2013, before filing the International Application (PCT), this new patent attorney questioned whether I wanted to file the PCT application in the me. However, believing that Jeff would soon present me with a phase-out plan, I allowed him to negotiate a limited Field-Of-Use license with Covidien for the cable technology, while personally maintaining the Cool Cable patent and protecting the trade secrets for the radiometer.

In April, Jeff requested that I expand the MMS Board of Managers to include Robert Allison. Knowing it would be necessary to add a new member once I resigned, I agreed on the condition that Jeff deliver the agreed upon phase-out plan, including a repayment schedule for the money MMS owed me. After the April deadline passed without a phase-out plan, in late May I hired a Boston law firm with a well-known mediator, Dr. Barrie Greiff, a psychiatrist and faculty member of the Harvard Business School.* Still hoping to work out an agreement, I suggested that MMS pay me $5,000 per month for the remainder of my life—well aware that I would not live long enough to collect the money I had invested, or I would have to outlast Methuselah. But Jeff did not attend a single meeting.

Only later did I discover that on or about the same day that I retained a mediator, Jeff signed a consulting agreement with John McCarthy, an engineer involved with ACT.** As CEO of MMS, I oversaw the preparation and signing of consulting contracts, but Jeff contracted McCarthy without my knowledge,

---

name of MMS. I responded, "My decision NOT to assign the patent to MMS was intentional."

*   Although not a lawyer, Barrie consulted for Gordon Katz, a Boston lawyer with the firm Holland & Knight, a very prestigious company known for mediating disputes with Fortune 500 companies and the breakup of large family businesses. I retained the law firm until September 26, 2013.

**   Previously, in November 2012, John McCarthy had attended an MMS program review via Skype on Robert Allison's computer and was observed by Bob Bielawa, who insisted Allison turn off his computer because our discussion included company trade secrets. Also in 2012, ACT's management team violated the ACT/MMS license agreement by filing five patents, to which Robert Allison later added his name as a co-inventor in 2014. At the time, I oversaw MMS's patent portfolio and required Allison to file patents through me, but because ACT's management team filed through a different patent firm, I was not aware of what they were doing.

suggesting that he was organizing his own team, no longer needing Rick Kelley, Bob Bielawa, or—for that matter—me.

In early June, I received an email arranging a meeting of the MMS management board to discuss the structure of the company. I looked forward to attending, believing that Jeff would finally present me with a phase-out plan. On June 10, 2013, Jeff, Robert Allison, and I met by phone. Also attending were Ned Brewer, who had been MMS's counsel and secretary of the board from shortly after I founded the company, and a law firm that I believe MMS engaged on Jeff's behalf. As the CEO, I should have been the one to call meetings, but Jeff called the meeting with no agenda and without my having any legal representation. The lawyer, who I believe Jeff hired, informed me that Jeff and Allison were exercising their rights as majority owners, and that, effective immediately, I was terminated.[*]

In effect, so was my team—Bob Bielawa, Rick Kelley, and Ken Puglia—who had been with me for more than forty years. While they did not receive formal termination notices, MMS no longer used them as consultants. These guys developed and made all of MMS's products. Without them, I knew MMS would fail.

Ned Brewer resigned immediately. He later told me that in forty-plus years of law, he had never witnessed a sadder spectacle than what had transpired that day. Soon after, Mikelle moved out of our house, indicating that she would come back after Jeff and I got things squared away. A friend and I helped Mikelle move into a three-story house across the river, and I rebuilt the kitchen cabinets in her new home, hoping there was a chance we could get back together.

Prior to my termination, Rick Kelley, Bob Bielawa, and I had repaired and redesigned the dual-mode transducer for the brain temperature monitor. Bob was so skilled at putting chips down, he helped fix the problems without asking for one dime of compensation. Although we had completed the NIH program, I spent my own money to make sure the system worked correctly.[**]

---

[*]   This also caused me to lose my consulting agreement with ACT.

[**]   The measurement of brain temperature is determined by measuring surface

However, I failed to get the units back to EVMS and MUSC. Instead of shipping the two units to the hospitals to complete the patient trials, I believe they were shipped to the Volcano/BTI facility in Colorado. So, I never found out if we solved the problems. We completed the requirements for the NIH grant, but did not have data to get the system approved by the FDA.

To keep my engineering team together, on August 28, 2013, I formed a new company, Applied ThermoLogic (ATL). At the time, I was working with Mike Rogge of Atricure and Frank Lattanzio at EVMS to make a cryogenic ablation catheter, which involves cryogenic cooling rather than microwave or RF heating. Mike was negotiating the costs, and Atricure was offering to pay for the research to complete the design of the cable, which I hoped to make smaller and more flexible than the current myocardial ablation catheter. In return, Atricure would enter a license and development agreement based on cryogenic ablation and microwave radiometric sensing, which would allow us to combine the techniques for cryogenic ablation with microwave radiometric sensing for the first time.[*]

I had previously explained to Jeff why I was forming ATL, including my intention to continue working with my patent firm to assign the Cool Cable patent to my new company. However, my patent attorney had retired, turning the details over to anoth-

---

tissue temperature together with the measurement of shallow (or subcutaneous) tissue temperature and projecting deeper target brain temperature. The accuracy of temperature measurement depends on the match of the antennas when in contact with the tissue. The match of the antennas, in turn, is seriously impacted by trapped air bubbles between the surface of the tissue and the surface of the antenna. These ongoing patient trials involve full-term newborns, which limits the size of the patient's head. The proposed fix was to minimize the formation of trapped air bubbles, which we accomplished by rounding the smaller antenna located in the septum of the larger antenna and allowing the dome-shaped antenna to protrude into the tissue. We applied a similar approach to the larger (or subcutaneous) temperature antenna. If needed, the larger antenna could include a thin pillow filled with a liquid or powder to prevent the formation of air bubbles.

[*]   Instead of heating tissue (hyperthermia) and measuring the increase in temperature, you could cool tissue (hypothermia) and measure the reduction in temperature.

er lawyer. So, instead of transferring the Cool Cable patent to Applied ThermoLogic, on January 14, 2014, MMS expanded ACT's license agreement to include cryogenic ablation for myocardial tissue. As a result, I was forced to end my work with Atricure and Eastern Virginia Medical School, which removed me from the faculty the following June after being erroneously informed that I had retired and was "no longer active."

On May 2, 2014, MMS filed a complaint in the Superior Court of the State of Maine, naming both Applied ThermoLogic and me as co-defendants. The suit alleged that I had breached my fiduciary responsibility to the company by competing with MMS. It also contained a cease-and-desist order, preventing me from continuing my work on the Cool Cable ablation program and from further developing an accurate brain temperature monitoring system.[*]

Bidding Blind

At the age of eighty-two, most people do not expect to be handed their first lawsuit, let alone one initiated by their child. But when Jeff caused the company I founded to sue me, it started a lengthy battle in the Maine state court and the United States federal bankruptcy court, as well as courts in Massachusetts and Delaware. Despite my nearly four decades of medical inventions and patents, the bankruptcy court appeared to view a son suing his father as a family squabble. I saw it as the obstruction of medical breakthroughs. Private equity funds likely saw it as an opportunity to snatch millions of dollars at stake.

A modern trend has been for institutional investors to control medical research and development, which has resulted in a focus on exit strategies—how much money a business owner can make by selling a company to investors. By 2013, the catheter-based electrophysiology field had ballooned into a $3 billion market, with fledgling companies reaping $90 million or more in upfront payments by merging with larger medical device companies.[38]

---

[*]   The case was later transferred to the Maine Business and Consumer Court.

After MMS sued me, naming ATL as a co-defendant, I retained a law firm and filed a countersuit against Jeff and Robert Allison to prove that I had done nothing wrong and to protect my lifetime of hard work while saving MMS from financial ruin. In 2015, one week before Jeff was scheduled to give a deposition, his lawyer disclosed that MMS was in financial trouble and might be forced to file for Chapter 11 bankruptcy. However, in exchange for dropping my deposition of Jeff, I was presented with the opportunity to fund MMS. I offered $250,000 to save the company while allowing Jeff and Allison to keep most of their MMS stock.* After agreeing to cancel the scheduled deposition, I never received a response to my offer. On September 25, 2015, MMS filed for bankruptcy. The following month, Mikelle filed for divorce, which a judge finalized on November 5, significantly reducing my personal assets.

The bankruptcy proceedings stalled at the hands of a judge who thought time would heal a "family squabble," far underestimating the value of the underlying technology in a billion-dollar catheter industry. During this time, I lost most of my remaining hearing and could only hear 15 percent of what was being said. When I turned up the volume on the hearing device the court provided, it whistled so loudly, I had to take it off. Even so, my lawyers kept me informed of what was going on, and I attended every court session.**

On March 25, 2016, the U.S. Bankruptcy Court in Portland auctioned off MMS's assets. To my knowledge, the sale was only advertised in a local newspaper, where interested investors were unlikely to see it. The day of the auction, I sat in front of a speaker phone at the end of a twenty or thirty-foot conference table in

---

* Their percent of interest would be reduced to ensure that control of the company returned to me.

** My doctors at Mass Eye and Ear suggested a cochlear implant, but since it came with a high risk and I can only hear out of one ear, they didn't want to take a chance. So they tried an interim fix, and later I underwent an emergency stapedectomy to bypass the small bones in my middle ear with a wire, which partially restored my hearing.

an upper room at Jeff's lawyer's Portland, Maine, office. Jeff sat at the other end of the table, arms crossed, not saying a word to me. The only other bidder besides myself was Coral Sand Beach, a limited liability corporation formed for the bid about three months before by Volcano—the same company with which Jeff had signed the contract to form Brain Temp Inc., where he occupied a seat on the board of directors.

Despite knowing I had zero chance of winning, I satisfied the court that I had the financial ability to participate in the auction. Without having been given a list of what assets were being auctioned off, I was bidding blind. I submitted the opening bid, roughly $180,000—all the cash I could muster after my divorce settlement. Coral Sand Beach participated by phone and placed the winning bid: $250,000—approximately the same amount I'd offered to save the company the year before, while letting Jeff and Robert Allison keep most of their stock.

The auction included 124 patents; license agreements with ACT, Covidien, and Volcano; MMS's roughly 50-percent share of Brain Temp Inc.; MMS's two percent share of royalties on the sale price of the ablation catheters; the radiometer trade secrets and ownership of the MMIC radiometer chips, which were used on all MMS products; and the patent for the Cool Cable—even though ownership was still in dispute. With research grants, I had raised nearly $14 million to develop these products in addition to investing my own money, and the bankruptcy court bundled them all together. The MMIC chip designs alone were worth more than the final bid price. Although I was the single largest creditor, I received nothing from the sale.

After it was over, I took the elevator down to the first floor and walked outside the courthouse, where Yuliya was waiting.

"Are you going to be okay?" she asked, having driven nearly two hours from Medford so I would not be alone following the asset sale.

"Yuliya," I said. "I just lost my life."

After getting something to eat with Yuliya, I drove home to an empty house.

Some people think that because I do not readily show my emotions, nothing bothers me, that I somehow do not feel these things. But that is not true. The problem is, you cannot change things. You have to accept the cards you have been dealt. So, just like when my mother sat me down at the table and told me I had three years to leave home, or after my accident when the doctors told me I would never walk without braces, I made a decision to move on.

Rather than suing MMS, I steered my fight against the professionals who I believed had improperly guided my son into bankruptcy. In 2017, while still a defendant in the lawsuit MMS filed against me, I turned to Delaware Chancery Court and filed a class action lawsuit against one of the world's biggest venture capital firms, New Enterprise Associates (NEA), which in 2014 had become the controlling shareholder in ACT.[*] The court-approved settlement reflected a value of more than $350 million on ACT, based on its use of my company's technology—despite the venture capital firm selling a warrant that locked it up and exploited its intellectual property for just $25 million.

In January 2019 Medtronic, Inc., one of the world's largest medical device manufacturers, acquired ACT (renamed EPIX Therapeutics, Inc.), in the neighborhood of $335 million. I received nothing from the sale. Using my patented design for the Integrated Catheter Tip, I believe that Medtronic now makes our system for heart ablation treatment. When Medtronic bought ACT, they bought MMS's intellectual property, including the patents and trade secrets as well as my designs for the MMIC chips for the microwave radiometer. When Volcano (as Coral Sand Beach) acquired MMS's assets, it obtained the license agreements with ACT, Covidien, and Brain Temp Inc.[**] I lost every-

---

[*]   As part of a sale of three portfolio companies, NEA sold ACT to the same buyer without negotiating three separate deals at fair market value, as fiduciary duties require. The court approved a $9 million settlement payment by NEA to a small class of early shareholders, including me, who were deprived of the value diverted to the purchase of the other portfolio companies.

[**]   The license agreement with ACT included a royalty-bearing provision of 2 percent net catheter selling price (estimated to have a worth of $2 million).

thing. I could have founded an entire research company. That was my legacy.

Friends tell me, "No matter what happens to you, you are very consistent. You just keep going. How can you do that when you've been hurt so badly?"

I have always been like that. Regardless of what happens, I make up my mind to keep going and get on with my life.

Prior to the bankruptcy sale, my lawyer suggested I see a counselor to rule out any health problems, including dementia, which Mikelle had suggested in an email to Robert Allison that I was beginning to show signs of. I met with a specialist on aging and chronic disease who assured me that my cognitive abilities were just fine and gave me a clean bill of health. She then asked how I was doing emotionally.

"Was this the worst time in your life?" she asked.

"No," I said. "I had an accident where my legs were crushed between the bumpers of two cars. I lost my six-year-old daughter, which eventually resulted in the death of my wife, Nancy. While playing hockey and softball and skiing, I have suffered a lot of injuries. I have experienced both physical pain and emotional pain, and I have learned that emotional pain is far more difficult for me to handle than physical pain. But I have endured with a positive attitude because I intend to get on with life and continue my research."

Only, now that I am older, it takes longer for me to recover.

Mediation

Late one February evening, two days before a court mediated settlement hearing with Jeff, I was driving home after giving a lecture at the Wentworth Institute of Technology in Boston. Not wanting to go home to an empty house, I stopped at the Broad Arrow Tavern in Freeport for French onion soup and crab cakes. While waiting to be served, I sat at a small table, when a girl who looked about ten approached me and said hello.

"Hello," I said, thinking she had wandered up to the wrong table. "How are you?"

Then I saw Jeff's wife standing in the doorway. Surprised, I realized that the young lady before me must be my youngest granddaughter, who I had not seen since she was two. After beckoning my daughter-in-law over, I discovered that my older granddaughter was waiting in the car with Jeff. When I asked to see her, Jeff's wife said that my son did not want to see me, but she walked outside and brought in my other granddaughter. Both girls were doing well in school and were excellent skiers. I only wished I could have been their ski instructor—or at least have had the chance to ski with them. We had about two minutes together. But it was an unexpected opportunity, and I was glad to meet them.

On February 14, 2019—one day before my eighty-seventh birthday—Jeff and I sat with our lawyers in separate rooms at the Portland District Courthouse to work out the details of the court-arranged settlement. The mediation hearing began at eight o'clock in the morning and continued past seven that evening. All day, Judge Andrew Horton walked back and forth between our two rooms until we finally agreed on a settlement in which Jeff gave up his share of MMS, and I regained ownership of the company, which now had no assets, only liabilities.

As part of the settlement, I was required to repay MMS's creditors $141,000, for the period after bringing Jeff on, but I could now bring claims on the company's behalf. Two months later, the class action lawsuit was settled in Delaware, and the judge awarded me a bonus for my exemplary behavior in the courtroom. The following July, I settled with Robert Allison for the return of his MMS stock, plus a cash settlement that he paid to me in compensation for 6 percent of the founders' shares in ACT, which I had given him as an incentive to provide the technical support to MMS on the ACT myocardial ablation program.

As a condition of the mediation settlement with Jeff and Robert Allison, I also received access to MMS's files, including emails that had vanished from my personal computer and backup drive from the date I hired Jeff to the date I was fired. With the help of a forensic computer specialist I had previously retrieved a May 24, 2012, email from Mikelle to Robert Allison in which my wife described how depressed she was about the company and seemed to blame me for delays with signing a license agreement with Covidien for the renal denervation cable. Mikelle then asked Allison to help bring more money into the company, writing, "We need to move Ken out of MMS' way … carefully and with love." She then asked Allison for his ideas on how to do that, beyond what she indicated he had already discussed with Jeff. Before signing her name, Mikelle assured Allison that she would delete her email after sending it.

I was upset and embarrassed. Mikelle's email, which included the above ellipsis, was written more than a year before my termination. Adding "with love" did not erase her actions. Her words felt like a betrayal. At the time Mikelle sent her email, we had been married for twenty-four years.

When the settlement hearing was over, Judge Horton asked me, "Would you like to see your son?"

"Yes, your Honor," I said. "I would like to talk with him."

After my lawyers left the courtroom, Judge Horton walked down the hall to escort Jeff into the courtroom. While waiting, I thought about what I wanted to say. When giving a talk, the only thing you have to remember is your opening sentence. You need to have an opening comment to keep your thought process going. I prepared what I was going to say to Jeff: "It takes time for a wound to heal."

After the judge led Jeff into the room, he stood there, apparently waiting for the judge to leave through the chamber doors. As soon as the two of us were left alone, I held out my hand, ready to say what I had planned, but my son turned his back on me and walked out of the courtroom without saying a word. He would not even shake my hand. That really upset me. In hockey, you do not win every game, but even when you are out there beating up on each other, as soon as the game is over, you line up and shake your opponents' hands.

I hoped that over the years Jeff and I could patch things up. That is what I meant by "It takes time for a wound to heal."

I hoped Jeff would say, "It does. Maybe we should work on it."

But I never had a chance to say what I intended. Other than communicating indirectly through lawyers, Jeff has not spoken to me since the day I was fired, and as of this writing, I have not seen my granddaughters since that chance meeting in Freeport. I can't undo what has happened, but I do not like being unable to see my grandchildren. I'd like to have a positive impact on them. If I could see them, I would agree not to talk about the lawsuit or the business. But, in view of my son's actions, I doubt that I will ever see them again.

Going through this legal stuff was a nightmare. During the years of litigation, much of my research and many of the medical devices I developed were destroyed. This included the system for OncoScan, the T900 Blood Warmer, data from clinical research trials, and drawings for all of our devices. The data from OncoScan would have improved the chances of early detection of breast cancer and saved lives and improved patient outcomes. That was my initial goal for getting into medical work, keeping the promise I had made to Kathy Gray. I also lost data on more than one thousand patients, data which proved my system provided earlier cancer detection than any other method yet available.

Although I regained ownership of both MMS and ATL in the settlement, I wasted a lot of time and money on lawsuits—roughly $2 million to pay several teams of lawyers in three separate states. I have accepted the fact that I have lost a fortune, but more importantly, I lost the patents, data, and trade secrets (including the MMIC chip radiometers, which are now being made by someone else). I also lost my reputation, which was badly damaged with my colleagues. I lost the opportunity to financially reward members of my team who had stuck with me for decades. I lost relationships within my family. And I lost nearly a decade of my life—years in which I could have been doing research to develop other lifesaving products. During those years of litigation, I could not raise money or continue my work. Instead, I spent all my time and money in court.

Some years before, I had taken Jeff and one of his buddies skiing in Utah. At the end of the day, I drove the three of us down Little Cottonwood Canyon, outside Salt Lake City. Jeff sat beside me in the passenger seat of our rental car as a long line of cars snaked down the mountain ahead of us. When I pressed my foot on the brake, I felt a sickening thud as the brake pedal went all the way to the floor. I had lost the breaks. If I hit another car, I feared we would both break through the guardrail and plunge hundreds of feet over the side of the mountain.

"Jump in the back," I told Jeff, pulling into the opposite lane.

With everyone leaving the mountain, I had a clean lane. As we passed car after car, I looked for the back of a bus or a big truck with significant mass and strong enough brakes to stop both vehicles if I slammed into it. Finally, I saw one. Just before hitting it, I shifted into the lowest gear. I thought the engine was going to come right up through the hood of the car, but the car slowed enough for me to pull back into the correct lane without hitting the truck, and no one was hurt.

"Dad," Jeff said after it was over, "if we had gone over the rail, you wouldn't have survived."

"I know," I said. "But you might have. That is why I had you climb in back, so the seat would cushion your fall."

What I do not understand, looking back these few years later, is how Jeff could sit across from me in his lawyer's conference room during the MMS asset auction and watch his own father being destroyed. What was going through his mind? My son's actions caused me to question his motives. However, it turned out that joining Brain Temp Inc. was indeed a tremendous opportunity for Jeff. In March 2023, he became CEO of "Brain-Temp," a newly formed Pennsylvania company now advertising "the world's first and only non-invasive and continuous brain temperature monitoring system" for neonates.

With my technical, business, and legal education; my decades of experience founding and running companies; and my knowledge about patents and technology, it would seem logical to ask, "How did you let this happen?"

That is a hard question to answer. I did not fully realize what was going on until 2019 when I received more than 200,000 MMS emails and other documents as part of the court settlement. Perhaps more importantly, I always tried to take care of the people I worked with, retaining people at M/A-Com and paying employees when I had to downsize MMS. Given my experience, I never suspected that my son Jeff would do something like this to his own father.

So, when people ask how I let this happen, the only thing I can say is, "He is my son."

CHAPTER 18

PASSING THE PUCK

Although I have lost contact with some family members and now live alone, I have tried very hard to get on with my life. One way is through volunteering. In 2014, I became an IEEE STEM (Science, Technology, Engineering, & Mathematics) Ambassador working with the Maine Mathematics and Science Alliance to support teachers in the classroom. Some of my best days have been spent igniting the curiosity of young people. Although I do not necessarily expect the students I speak with to become microwave engineers, I hope to make them curious and get them excited about technology.

"Curiosity is a lifetime teacher," I tell every class. "It is the key to understanding and unlocking the potential that exists in all we do. You never stop learning. You have to ask questions and try to understand the problem. When you do that, you can apply what you learn to other things."

Some students assume that everything has already been invented, which is not true. And everything that has been invented can be improved. Most patents improve a concept that already exists. In fact, when we send technology to China for manufacturing, they make the improvements and they get the technology. When production goes offshore, technology follows—a concern I shared in my 1992 commencement speech at the Wentworth Institute of Technology.

Need creates inventions. When developing products for the medical industry, I focused on meeting unmet needs. Since doctors performing heart ablation could not measure temperature, that unmet need became the driving force, the same way the United States invented synthetic rubber during the Second World War. Growing up, we had to pull over and patch a flat tire on the side of the road so often we carried all the supplies with us. But when the Japanese conquered Malaysia and the Philippines, which provided our rubber, we needed a new supply. So we made artificial rubber. Then we reinforced it to take a greater impact. Because we had to innovate, we came up with a better product. It is amazing what you can do if you focus on an unmet need. That is what patents are all about.

As a STEM ambassador, I drove to fifth- and sixth-grade classrooms all over the state, helping young people become interested in engineering, the same way my Sunday school teacher, Bill Linvill, had once helped me.

Standing in front of a room full of kids, I got the conversation going by inviting them to ask questions. "Hey guys," I would say. Boys, girls, long hair, short hair—I called everyone "guys," just like when I taught hockey. "You can ask any question. Even if I don't know the answer, we can discuss it."

You learn more by discussing a problem and trying to come up with answers than by having someone tell you the answer. Discussing the problem excited their curiosity. So I always began by giving them a problem to solve.

"I'm George Washington. The year is 1776, and I want you to build me a lighthouse on the rocky coast of Portland, Maine. There is no electricity. The lightbulb has not yet been invented. And because you can't let ships get too close to the rocks, you have to build a beacon that shines two miles out to sea."

Those were the starting points.

"Why not use a candle?"

"A candle burns down, flickers, and is not reliable," I said, explaining that the best source of light would be whale oil, which preceded kerosene lanterns. Then I described the use of a reflector and a Fresnel lens, which focused the beam of light. "The lens has to turn around the light to scan it. The glass reflects the light forward in phase, like an antenna."

When they began to understand this, microwaves made more sense, because an antenna operates the same way. During the discussion, I continually provided additional clues and information. By the time I finished talking about the size of the part of the structure that turned (which weighed 1,800 pounds) and how it floated on mercury (a liquid metal that does not freeze), they had heard an entire lecture. This included explaining the way a hydraulic jack works, the mechanics of eighteenth-century clocks, and why you do not see the beam from a lighthouse unless it revolves or reflects off something (the same reason I once had to wobulate the antenna for the Mercury space capsule). If I started out by giving them the answers, they would not realize the problems they had just solved. Every step of the way, I taught them something.

Once, when I invited a group of students in Auburn to ask questions, a boy in the back of the room raised his hand. "Are all engineers nerds?" he asked.

"No," I said. "I skied and played hockey and played fast-pitch softball, and I was a ski and hockey instructor. Some of my former hockey players made it to the NHL and other professional clubs—Bob Sweeney, of the Boston Bruins; Tom Barrasso, who was drafted by the Buffalo Sabers but spent his career with the Pittsburg Penguins; and Mark Flanagan, of the Atlanta Flames, now the Calgary Flames."

"You're kidding!" he said.

Having played sports turned out to be a big advantage. Kids liked to find out that I was a regular guy—the way Nancy had commented all those years before when she visited me in my hospital room.

As I had with my engineers, I encouraged students to think and plan ahead for their careers. "Where do you want to be five years from now?" I asked. "What courses or experiences do you need in order to do that? Don't take jobs that don't get you to your goals. Think ahead so you will be ready, but keep in mind that when you graduate from high school, it is not a landing. It is a takeoff. How far and how high you go is totally up to you."

I used my own life experiences to illustrate what I told them. "Don't figure out where you are going to be in your lifetime. Take increments and satisfy goals for those increments. The situation may change based on things that are out of your control, such as my being told I had to leave home at sixteen, or my getting hit by a car."

In 2015, I joined the board for Maine's Dearborn Foundation, a nonprofit that awards scholarships to help outstanding high school students pursue jobs in engineering and precision machining. My long-term friend and accountant, Joe Keaney, invited me to participate on the technical review board. Joe and two of his three brothers were diagnosed with amyotrophic lateral sclerosis (ALS), which causes progressive muscle weakness and has no cure. Having founded the Auburn/Lewiston Boys & Girls Club, Joe had always been very active. However, his medication made him too drowsy to drive long distances. Every few months I picked him up in Portland and drove us one hour north to Fryeburg for the foundation's board meetings—me, the guy with one eye. I also asked Joe to schedule his weekly off-site accounting meetings on Wednesdays.

"I will drive you," I told him. "While you are with a client, I will find somewhere quiet to sit and do my work."

Every Wednesday I drove Joe to his appointments. Whenever in Portland for other occasions, I would call Joe and ask, "What are you doing?" Then I'd pick him up and drive him to the Portland Harbor Hotel for lunch.

Late the following September, I went to pick up Joe at his office for lunch. His condition had not yet deteriorated to the point of needing a wheelchair, so I was surprised and deeply saddened when Joe's assistant told me that he had died suddenly the night before. Joe was sixty-three. At his funeral, Joe's wife, Peggy Ann, thanked me for driving him to appointments.

"That is what friends do," I told Peggy, sharing how Dick Melick had once offered to donate an eye to me.

It takes work to cultivate deep friendships. It takes commitment, and the older I get, the more I appreciate having real friends. Like the cartoonist Charles Schulz wrote in his comic strip *Charlie Brown*, "As we grow up, we realize it is less important to have lots of friends and more important to have real ones."

Well into my eighties, I continued lecturing at the Went-worth Institute of Technology, where I served as a trustee for four decades. I gave special classes to the newly formed biomedical engineering school on legal issues, patents and contracts, how to conduct design reviews, and how to work with the FDA. When conducting design reviews, it is important not to embarrass any-body. Question them and almost lead them into giving you the answer you want to hear. When you discuss a problem, rather than tell somebody that they are wrong, focus on everyone learn-ing. I also gave lectures to executives through the Harvard Busi-ness School's leadership course. The school would bring in a guy with a success story and a guy who had ended up with a bad deal. Occasionally the guy with the bad deal was me. Without naming a company, I would talk about a time I ended up in court.

"I came out of the space and military industry," I told them. "Compared to the military, the medical industry is far more dif-ficult to work with. When I worked with Hughes Aircraft or Westinghouse, we all wanted whatever missile or fire control ra-dar we were developing to work perfectly. So it never occurred to me that people in the medical industry would sign a contract simply because they wanted you to fail."

To be successful, I realized that every product should involve disposables. The sterilizer fell into that category. Because we were curing a problem, we were eliminating disposables, but that was not received well by the medical industry.

At the end of class, the other lecturer and I opened the floor for discussion. The guy with the success story got few, if any, questions. Students did not want to hear another success story. Everyone knows what that is about. They wanted to hear about the problems I faced, so I got most of the questions. The students were all trying to critique what I had done wrong so they could discuss what they would have done differently. I did not mind explaining what I did wrong, such as asking the pipe company for the sizes of the pipes they used and burying a two-inch pipe ten feet deep. I made an impossible target, and I made a mistake.

Then I involved the customer, Columbia Gas, and the electro-magnetics laboratory at Ohio State University in the solution.

While volunteering and lecturing, I also continued my research, which led to several new patents. Because other companies now own the rights to my previous patents, I found new approaches to solve the same problems, such as developing a radiometric-based system to measure newborn brain temperature through the tympanic membrane in the eardrum. Because infants' ear canals are so small, this system uses a 27 gigahertz MMIC radiometric sensor within the ear canal. To protect the infant's eardrum, which is the thickness of a sheet of printer paper, I developed a side-looking dielectric rod antenna with a smooth ceramic tip cushioned by a foam ball. The probe fits into the base of the newborn's ear canal (in close proximity to the base of the tympanic membrane) and uses millimeter frequencies to measure temperature at the base of the eardrum near the carotid artery. Because there is less material in the way, this method is more accurate than measuring temperature through the skull, and it solves the problem of how to measure actual brain temperature, the target tissue.*

I hope to find a way to include the probe for the new brain temperature patent in the ongoing NIH clinical trials. Since my previous system measured the tissue temperature beneath the skin's surface (rather than brain temperature), I believe this to be the first and only system to non-invasively and passively measure newborn brain temperature at the target tissue.**

To prove my new system worked, in 2017, I applied for a collaboration agreement with Mass Eye and Ear, which wanted to team up with two programs. The first program they chose

---

*   The previous microwave detection did not allow an accurate measurement of surface temperature and the sufficiently accurate measurement of temperature at shallow depth we were unable to predict the actual temperature at depth (brain tissue). I was never given the test results of the redesign.

**   The object is to drop the temperature of the brain, not the core temperature of the baby. Because of inflammation, brain temperature can be much higher than core or rectal temperature. To ensure that the patient is not undertreated, the object is to measure brain temperature.

involved MIT. Then, here I was, this eighty-five-year-old guy seeking to be the second collaborator. They liked talking to me, but it took three separate meetings to convince them I could do the job. At the final meeting, I met with Dr. Michael McKenna, his intern, Dr. Nick Dewyer, and four other medical doctors.

"You are interested in this research but are concerned about my age, which you are hesitant to ask," I said. "I'm eighty-five, and I feel good. I can complete this program. But should something happen to me, I have younger people who work with me who can complete the program."

It was true. The other people were younger than me. However, I did not tell them that the guys I had in mind were all retired, and they did not ask.

I stepped out of the conference room while they caucused. When they called me back in, they said, "We are going to support you and your program."

That felt good. I knew I still had it in me, and I wanted to continue helping people. Dr. McKenna's intern, Dr. Dewyer, oversaw the two-year project, which we completed. Because Mass Eye and Ear lacks a neonatal unit, we carried out the work with newborn patients at the adjoining Mass General Hospital (MGH), which is affiliated with Harvard Medical School. MGH provided patients and medical staff for the clinical trials, and I provided the funds for product development and carried out the research through Applied ThermoLogic. The system is now in NIH-funded clinical trials, being tested in states across the country.

Following the increase of severe hepatitis cases in children during the COVID-19 pandemic, I also began considering new ways to use my microwave in-line blood warmer to eliminate blood-borne viruses in the bloodstream. My original system destroyed blood-borne viruses in stored and collected blood. My new system treats blood drawn directly from a patient, a treatment similar to the process for kidney dialysis in which an artificial kidney filters toxins from the blood and sends clean blood back into the patient. However, instead of flowing through a filter, a patient's blood flows through a set of four disposable in-line cartridges.

Linked together by a plastic manifold, each T-shaped cartridge is inserted into a separate three-inch-square microwave heating chamber with an antenna and radiometer that operate like a miniature microwave oven. At a rate of 200 milliliters per minute, blood flows through an IV tube into the first cartridge, which uniformly warms the blood from the body's normal temperature of 37°C to the target temperature for killing viruses, 75°C. The blood then flows through a short length of IV tubing to a second cartridge in a "dwell chamber," which maintains the target temperature of 75° to 80°C for 0.006 seconds, just long enough to kill viruses without damaging blood. Next, the blood flows through the third cartridge in a "rapid cooling" chamber, which quickly chills the blood to 49°C and continues to cool it to less than 30°C. Finally, the blood passes through the cartridge in the fourth chamber, which reheats the blood to 37°C before sending the virus-free blood back into the patient. Because the blood continuously flows through a dialysis-like machine, it gets treated over and over again.

Applying high temperature to blood for a short duration—the same amount of time it takes for a bumblebee to flap its wings once—results in a high level of virus inactivation, destroying HIV, Ebola, and other blood-borne viruses with little, if any, damage to the blood components. The key is short microwave exposure times using microwave heating and radiometric temperature control. A recent article in the *New York Times* announced that, "The only vaccine against HIV still being tested in late-stage clinical trials has proved ineffective."[39] *What now?* the headline asked.

The problems with vaccines is that they can produce mutations that can be more dangerous than the original disease. A vaccine reduces or controls the spread of a virus but is not a cure. My approach is to find a cure. There is nothing like heat to destroy viruses, which are more sensitive to temperature than blood is. The problem with generating heat is, how can you be confident that you are raising it to the right temperature? The only way to do that is to measure temperature at the point where you apply energy. I am putting together a team to address that issue.

On August 16, 2022, at the age of ninety, I was issued a patent for eliminating blood-borne viruses in the blood system. However, because I lost access to the MMIC radiometer chips, I used a microwave integrated circuit and discrete components to build the radiometer.*

I also spent more than $100,000 to recover the patent for the Cool Cable, which I hope to finish developing. However, because the patent was abandoned, others may be using my design for the cable without my knowledge.

The question is what to do with these new patents and technology? I once dreamed of forming a legacy trust so that my personal wealth and research would continue helping others. It is a disgrace that so many of my inventions ended up in litigation, especially the way in which it took place. I could have accomplished so much more, but going to court and going through all these trials took so much strength out of me.

In November 2019, while driving home from my annual checkup at Mass Eye and Ear, I did not feel well. On the way down, my friend Dave Porter had met me in Portsmouth, where I left my decade-old Cadillac, and drove me to my appointment. On the return trip, I picked up my car and drove the remaining two hours home in the dark. Unable to see the road, I pulled up behind an eighteen-wheeler and followed its taillights up the interstate until I recognized my exit.

After arriving home, I felt better, but my blood pressure measured quite high. Later that week, I had trouble speaking and called my friend Dr. George Roth, a retired neurosurgeon. Recognizing the signs of a stroke, he called an ambulance, which drove me to the hospital. George met me there.

---

*   When Jeff included Applied ThermoLogic as a co-defendant and filed the cease-and-desist order, he basically eliminated my ability to obtain funding. But even though I could not find a marketing partner, he could not stop me from funding my own research.

Over the next several hours, I lost my voice, my vision, and my memory. With George, my cardiologist looked over my scans and said I had the arteries of a teenager. He blamed my stroke on stress, linked to the litigation, and warned me to avoid even stressful conversations. After a week, the hospital transferred me to a rehabilitation center in Portland. For two weeks, they put me through all kinds of exercises before sending me home, where I received more therapy.

My daughter, Randee, flew up from Florida and stayed with me. During the previous decade of litigation with Jeff, my daughter and I had become distant, but she stayed for two weeks. We have been in close touch ever since. More than anything, the stroke probably brought us back together. Thankfully, I completely recovered and have returned to all the activities I enjoy, including driving.

On a recent fall weekend, Yuliya invited me down for her daughter Victoria's sixth birthday. She and her husband, Matthew, also have a younger daughter, Charlotte. I drove down to Medford on Saturday afternoon, arriving in time for a big dinner with Yuliya's parents, Sergey and Iryna, living nearby. Yuliya's brother, Ivan, a senior at Wentworth, joined us.

After staying overnight, I said goodbye and drove half an hour west to the Shawsheen Cemetery in Bedford. I miss Nancy so much; I go there quite often. As I stood facing her grave, I read each name carved on the stone: Nancy, Kirsten, Viola, Michael, and my father, Lorenzo. My name is carved on the stone as well, requiring only the year of my death.

As I often did when visiting Nancy's grave, I bought two bouquets from a nearby flower shop—one of red roses and one of white, along with a glass and a bottle of water. Kneeling in the cemetery, I dug a hole with my hands and set the glass in the ground. After arranging the flowers and filling the glass with water, I stood by Nancy's grave and quietly sang,

There's a tree in the meadow
With a stream drifting by,

And carved upon that tree I see
'I love you till I die . . .'
By that tree in the meadow
My thoughts always lie.
And where're you go, you'll always know
I love you till I die.

Every time I visit the cemetery, I sing that song. Nancy was the most beautiful person I ever met—beautiful inside as well as outside. I had married my best friend. When visiting her grave, I stand there for a while, just talking. I apologize to Nancy for some of the decisions I made, such as not taking into account how fragile she was. When Kirsten died, it was more than Nancy could cope with. I apologize for different things—like for doing a terrible job at raising our children. I also apologize for leaving her behind the day Kirsten died and I followed the ambulance to the hospital in my car. I apologize over and over again, wishing I had done more to help her. Each time before leaving I say, "I sure hope I see you again."

I very much hope to see both Nancy and Kirsten again. I wish I could say "I love you" one more time.

On a previous visit I had spoken with the cemetery manager about replacing a bush beside Nancy's grave. Trimmed to a stalk, its trunk was so big around, it looked like a pineapple. So I brought him a new one. The manager agreed to plant it for me. Then he said, "You don't remember me?"

"No." I shook my head.

"Dennis Freeman," he said with a smile. "I was one of your hockey students. You taught me how to play."

When I taught hockey, Dennis was a young boy. Now he was a middle-aged man. It is always a pleasure to meet people who remember you for what you did, and Dennis did a nice job planting the bush I brought him.

After leaving the cemetery, I drove through the neighborhood where I used to take our children trick-or-treating. Then I pulled around a corner and parked the car on Ledgewood Drive, beside our old home. It brought back so many memories. When Nancy and I packed up our family and moved from Bedford to Harvard, we left behind most of our furniture—including pieces I had made. After losing Kirsten, taking it with us was just too painful. All those years later, the house looked the same, with a single dormer facing the street, Nancy's flower gardens out front, and the two-car garage I built onto the back of the house to expand it for our growing family. The clapboards were even stained the same soft gray.

A young couple happened to be in the yard with their four children. The father was carrying a half-sheet of plywood across the lawn, so I stepped out of my car and introduced myself.

"I hope you don't mind me stopping by," I said. "I lived in this house years ago."

The guy, Mike, was really pleasant. He and his wife were both lawyers. As we walked around the outside of house, I told him how I had moved there right before my accident and built the addition while wearing leg braces.

"Are you a contractor?" Mike asked.

"No." I shook my head. "I just like to build things. By the way, if you try to dig up the garage floor, you are going to have a problem with the rebars." Then I described how I had reinforced the floor with steel rods. I also explained why the den floor is higher than the floors in the adjacent rooms of the house. "When I converted the single-car garage into a den, I had the cement poured through the window. It came out so fast I could not keep up, and the cement set before I could spread it. So I had the truck come back and pour more cement to level it off. As a result, the flagstone floor came out three inches higher than I expected. That's why there is a little step up into the study."

"You did it all by yourself?" he asked.

I nodded. "The neighbors thought I was building a runway."

While we stood there talking, I mentioned that I had started the Bedford hockey program, and Mike said he was thinking of building a small rink behind the house.

"Do you play hockey?" I asked.

"No," he admitted. "But I want to learn."

I took that as a good sign. "Where do you work?"

"Hanscom Air Force Base."

I said I once helped with the Bedford Santa Claus Program out there. "Do you, by any chance, know Matthew Borowski?" I asked.

"Matthew and his wife, Yuliya?" Mike's face lit up, and he started talking about Yuliya's family. He knew her kids and everything. "I'm Matthew's commanding officer."

"I am the one who hosted Yuliya when she came over from Ukraine," I said.

Talk about a small world. Before I left, Mike photographed me in front of the house.

Then I drove like hell to get home by four o'clock to call Cynthia Houston, Nancy's best friend. Over the previous months, I had phoned old friends and neighbors, along with the Bedford Police Department and the hospital, trying to piece together details from the day Kirsten died. I had not seen Cynthia since Nancy's funeral. Her husband, Ted, had recently passed away, but through their son Douglas, I discovered that Cynthia lived in an assisted living facility in New Hampshire. I arrived home just in time to dial her number. Now ninety-three, Cynthia remained very sharp. To open the conversation, I broke the ice by asking Cynthia how she liked her facility.

"I hate it," she said.

"How's the food?"

"Terrible."

After catching up, I asked Cynthia if she remembered the day Kirsten died. "Who called the police? Who called the ambulance?"

I believed that Cynthia had called the ambulance after the paperboy found Kirsten lying by the large boulder at the end of our driveway. Cynthia said, no, the paperboy found Kirsten near a rock by the end of her classmate Jackie Healey's driveway, with whom she had gone to play. The paperboy banged on their door.

"There's a little girl on the ground at the end of your driveway," he told Jackie's mother. "I can't get her to wake up."

Mrs. Healey, who was a nurse, ran outside and called an ambulance, Cynthia explained. Then she must have called Nancy.

"Who was in the car with me when I followed the ambulance to the hospital?" I asked. "Was Nancy with you, or was she in the car with me?"

"Nancy was with you," Cynthia said. "She went off with you in the car when you drove to the hospital."

Boy, was I glad to hear that. All these years, whenever I visited the cemetery, I had apologized to Nancy, believing that I had jumped in the car and driven off without her. What a relief to know we had driven off together.

CHAPTER 19

THE END OF THE ROAD

On the wall of my study hangs a print of a painting by a well-known Woolwich artist, John Gable, who happens to be a good friend. The painting, titled "The End of the Road," depicts an old Chevy rack-body truck like the one I rebuilt to deliver drums of range oil to my grandmother's campground. Now old and abandoned, the truck in the painting is rusting away in a farmyard beside several 55-gallon kerosene drums. Having seen better days, it has lost its left headlamp, the way I have lost sight in my left eye. It is also at the end of the road. Now old and abandoned, I am rusting away like that truck.

Am I happy? No, I am not. The events of the last few years have been difficult, but fortunately I am surrounded by friends. I have had an interesting career, which I intend to continue. The end of the road is near, but I am not finished.

As an engineer, my greatest accomplishments were finding solutions and building a team. Many of the people I worked with are now gone—Jim Regan, Bill Gray, Dick DiBona, Art Blaisdell, Marion Hines, Ted Wong, Dick Jamison, Dick Melick, and Peter Rizi (a ferrite guy on the faculty of the University of Massachusetts who I worked with when I was their technical advisor). Many of the other people I worked with at Ferrotec, M/A-Com, and Hughes Aircraft are also gone. It is inevitable. People pass on. Everybody comes to the end of the road eventually. I sincerely hope there is a happy ending to all of this, but before I get there, I want to see a couple more projects to completion.

Until the summer of 2022, after I turned ninety, Bob Bielawa and I shared a test laboratory in Nashua where we did research. Although no permanent employees still worked in the office, we brought in technical people as needed. Bob and I continue to frequently meet in southern New Hampshire, where we moved our storage facility and where I own an independent-living apartment. I love research and am still actively involved in research and development.

By working with Dr. Bass and Jim Shaeffer of EVMS, I really thought I could reduce the number of infants diagnosed each year with cerebral palsy—not to develop a cure, but to prevent cerebral palsy from occurring. That is why I focused my research on creating medical products that would improve patient outcome. Developing medical devices is not just about saving a patient's life; it is about improving their life.

In January 2014, *Down East* magazine published an article, "Newborn Hope," about my work to measure brain temperature. Soon after, I drove to Bath for a haircut and a former classmate of Yuliya's from Morse High School stopped by my chair. "I want to thank you," she said.

"What did I do?" I asked.

The young woman, whose name was Heather, explained that she had recently given birth. "They had to rush my newborn to Maine Med," she said.

"I know the problem, and I am glad," I replied, gathering that the medical staff needed to cool her baby down to prevent brain damage. "Because you are thanking me, I know the outcome was good."

At that time, hospitals in Bangor and Portland both had systems to cool babies down, but they were measuring rectal temperature, which is less accurate than brain temperature. After driving home, I wrote Heather a note, thanking her for her comments. Because few people know who invents a medical device, it is unusual to get recognition. However, the greatest compliment to someone involved in medical research is to have a patient, or in my case, the parent of a patient, say, "Thank you." There is nothing more gratifying.

Several years ago, I attended the IEEE's International Microwave Symposium banquet in Boston, near where I once taught classes for the Army Reserves. While sitting with a group of friends, two engineers whose wives successfully underwent myocardial ablation to treat heart arrhythmias came up to our table

and thanked me for my work. Although the doctors performing the procedures could not have used my catheter, which had
not yet been approved, the men were well aware of my work.
The guys at my table—Alex Chu (who worked with me at M/A-
Com), Edward Niehenke (the Senior Advisory Engineer I worked
with at Westinghouse), Richard Sparks (an engineer from the
early days of Ferrotec), Richard Snyder (who ran his own microwave filter company), and Peter Staecker (who worked with me
at M/A-COM and later became president of the IEEE)—raised
their glasses to give me a toast. Later, they decided to nominate
me for the MTT-S's Microwave Pioneer Award, which recognizes
an individual for a career of meritorious achievement and outstanding technical contribution in the field of microwave theory
and techniques.

I won. After all I had been through, I was pleased, knowing
I could finish my career on a positive note. On June 22, 2022,
I stood in front of a room full of about five hundred engineers
and their guests at the MTT-S Awards Banquet at the Colorado
Convention Center in Denver to receive my award, which reads,
"In Recognition for Pioneering Developments and Commercialization of Microwave Devices for the Detection and Treatment
of Medical Conditions." It was quite an honor to be recognized
by my colleagues, some of whom had been in the audience years
before when I presented my IEEE Distinguished Lecture series.
One even came up to me later in the hotel and thanked me for
teaching him to play hockey.

During my acceptance speech, I mentioned that it was the
seventieth anniversary of my membership in the IEEE. "All the
way back in 1952, I joined the IRE, the Institute of Radio Engineers, which later became the IEEE," I said.

Elsie Vega, the event program manager, stood up and asked
if there was anyone else in attendance who had been a member of the IEEE for seventy years or more. Not a single person
raised their hand. It made me realize how many of my friends and
colleagues were no longer there. Some—like Bob Bielawa, Rick
Kelley, and Georgie Burton—were unable to attend. Some—in-

cluding Richard Sparks, one of the sponsors who nominated me for the award—had recently passed away. Others—like Harlan Howe—were no longer able to travel. The fact that so many people I worked with were no longer living or able to attend made me sad. But when I looked over the audience, I was proud to see Randee sitting beside my brother's daughter Lawnie and her husband, Raymond.

"Over the years, I have had the good fortune to work with the finest technical people, some of whom worked with me for more than fifty years," I said, giving my acceptance speech without notes. Because of my difficulty seeing, I had practiced my talk with Randee beforehand.

The first person I mentioned was my best friend, Jim Regan, one of the most exceptional engineers I have ever known. Then I named a number of other people who had been on my team over the years—Harlan Howe, Marion Hines, Peter Staecker, Alex Chu, Art Blaisdell, Bob Bielawa, and many others. I also mentioned the technical staffs and prime contractors, such as Bill Gray, Dick Jamison, and Ted Wong of Hughes Aircraft, and Tom Van Rankin and Ed Niehenke of Westinghouse. And I thanked the IEEE and the MTT-S for their support, along with that of my friends and family.

After I returned home, Alex Chu, who was unable to attend the conference, called to congratulate me. We had a long talk. The award recognized my work for commercializing products, but I felt that I had failed. "My inventions are commercialized now," I admitted. "But I was not the one to commercialize them."

"Ken," Alex said, "there is a line by a Spanish poet, Antonio Machado, which translates into English as, 'Traveler, there is no road; You make the path as you walk.'[40]

"You made the path," Alex said, "and we followed."

What a wonderful message to receive at the end of the road. In the nomination letter, Alex credited me with single-handedly overcoming the FDA's deep-seated resistance to using microwaves in medicine. They had their reasons for saying that microwaves could not be used to heat blood and tissue. It was up to me to prove otherwise, and I did. The key is using radiometric sensing. It is excessive heat, not microwaves, that damages blood components and tissue. Using microwave radiometry, we addressed that by precisely measuring and monitoring temperature at the point where heat is applied.*

When I first began developing and testing medical devices, the medical community did not accept the use of microwaves for patient care. Even after I convinced the FDA and the American Association of Blood Banks that microwave-based medical products are safe, doctors and hospital medical review boards needed assistance in explaining this to patients. Measuring temperature with microwaves is passive, I explained. Patients were not being radiated. After we convinced the doctors it was safe, they got the approval of patients, but doctors were always telling us to take the word "microwaves" off our products. When patients heard the word *antennas* and realized that microwaves would be involved, they were afraid of being "zapped." So we substituted the word *transducer* for *antenna*. Whenever I visited a hospital for a clinical trial, I also assisted the doctor in writing a brief to put into a patient's treatment procedure. Patients were not about to listen to some microwave engineer, but they listened to the doctors. And the doctors believed in us.

Passive microwave radiometric sensing provides the ability to non-invasively measure and monitor temperature. It is the significant and unique component of all medical products based on microwave technology. Microwaves can be used to generate heat, to measure temperature, and to measure motion. Combining these capabilities with proprietary solutions allowed us to develop products that are unique in their ability to not only mea-

---

* Conventional sensors, such as transistors and thermocouples, perturb the microwave path and cannot be used to sense the temperature of blood and tissue at the point that energy is applied. Only radiometric sensing allows you to use a shared aperture to design an antenna that can be used at both frequencies. When they are located together on one antenna, one is transmitting and one is receiving. The transmitter is ablating the tissue and the receiver is telling you the temperature, as well as when a bubble is forming or when a catheter is making proper contact before you start applying heat. It gives the doctor total control.

sure and monitor temperature, but to heat blood, fluid, or tissue to a specific temperature, and to maintain that temperature at a specific level. Using that technology and approach, I was able to write and win thirty-nine NIH and SBIR research applications, while also contributing to more than one hundred journal articles and technical papers, demonstrating that microwaves could safely meet unmet medical needs.

By promising to always measure temperature at the point where heat or cold is applied, my team and I—including the medical doctors we worked with—convinced the FDA and the AABB that microwaves when properly controlled will not damage blood or tissues. Had I not been able to achieve their approval, there would not be a medical product capability based on microwave technology today. In fact, the IEEE recently launched the *IEEE Journal of Electromagnetics, RF and Microwaves in Medicine and Biology,* a new publication focused on microwaves in medicine—the topic I spoke about in 1985-1986 as the Distinguished Microwave Guest Lecturer for the IEEE.

The products I designed were developed by a team of individuals from many disciplines of engineering—electrical, microwave, mechanical, software—all working together toward a common goal. I am truly honored to have worked with so many talented and wonderful colleagues. I could not have asked for a better team, particularly when working to resolve the concerns of the FDA and the AABB about using microwaves to heat blood and tissue.

I look at life as a long road. There were a lot of incidents and problems along the way, but to receive the Microwave Pioneer Award and the kind words of my colleagues made the journey worthwhile. The important thing is to take the life you are given and do the best you can with it. Over the years I have had a lot of tragedy. I have also been fortunate to have such wonderful friends. Bill Linvill, who convinced me to apply to college. Jim Regan, my right-hand-man. Dick Melick, who offered me an eye. I have shared this journey with so many good people. Consulting for NASA, lecturing for the IEEE, working with the Wentworth

Institute of Technology, Tufts University, and Eastern Virginia Medical School—they have all been great. I am proud of the products I developed with a wonderful and gifted team of engineers and medical doctors.

I am now the sole owner of MMS and Applied ThermoLogic. The Viral Inactivation System is really important, but I do not believe that I have much time left. How long can a person expect to last? At ninety-one, I am too old to find new investors. With only one functioning eye and ear, no one is going to invest in me, but it is a shame to let these patents go away unnoticed. I would love to find a little start-up microwave company and give to it the rights to this technology. If I thought someone would put them to good use, I would assign the patents. Otherwise, I will freely assign the rights to the research hospitals that have collaborated with me on the development of these products so they can do something with them. This includes OncoScan and my other products. Although my patents are now in the public domain, if someone wants to work on them, I will gladly provide the support.

However, because medical companies lack microwave capabilities, I am assembling a technical team to support them. Most of us are retired. We are basically a team of old guys with great attitudes, but we will be available as consultants to assist medical companies (which need microwave capabilities) and microwave companies (which need medical product capabilities) interested in developing these products. I created Applied ThermoLogic to consult and support MMS. As my health has begun to deteriorate, I am appointing Bob Bielawa as the new president to carry the company forward and complete its mission. Bob has the experience of running his own company and has been with me since my early days at M/A-Com. Most importantly, I trust him. Although the rest of the team would be paid consultants, I do not expect any compensation. As I did while consulting for NASA and EVMS, I will not charge anyone for my time. I will just be available to help. Despite all I have been through, I hope to continue using my experience and knowledge to create technologies and find business partners to advance medical progress and improve patient outcome.

My friends and colleagues, particularly at Hughes and M/A-Com, all warned me not to get involved in a business that depended on developing microwave medical products. They thought I would fail. Do I regret doing it? No, I do not. To tell you the truth, I do not think I would have gone into medicine if I were doing it for money. But money is not what drives me. What drives me is using my abilities to create products that are helpful to mankind. I like developing products to improve patient outcome. I can see no better way to do that than by using radiometric temperature sensing to eradicate blood-borne viruses in the bloodstream.

Throughout my seven-decade career, whether working on missile systems to protect our country or on medical devices to improve patient's lives, I did my best to make the world a better place. I would like to say, "I did that."

That would be enough.

ACKNOWLEDGMENTS

The most important thing you can say to someone is "Thank you." Although many people who joined me on this journey are now gone, I would like to thank Bill Linvill, the teacher who influenced my life more than anyone else. Thank you for seeing my potential and encouraging me to go to college.

I would also like to thank the doctors, nurses, and staff at Longwood Hospital for putting up with me while I was in traction recovering from my accident. I don't think they had patients quite like me.

To Jim Regan, who joined me at Airtron in 1957 and remained with me through nine companies, thank you for being so dependable. When I called for volunteers during the Cuban Missile Crisis, yours was the first hand to go up, and I miss our morning coffee at the bench. There are people who come into your life and change it altogether. You were one of those people.

To my team, especially to Bob Bielawa, Rick Kelley, and Ken Puglia, thank you for your friendship, fine workmanship, and support. Bob, you are not only a good engineer, but whenever I needed someone, you were first in line. Thank you for our long conversations and for leading the team to complete my wishes. And to Georgie Burton, thank you for typing my dictated letters. You made everything I wrote look great.

I am also grateful to the people who worked with me at the Tech Center and for Dick DiBona for helping me keep the group at M/A-Com together. Harlan Howe, when our wives first met at the hospital, we were competitors, but together we made a great team. Alex Chu, thank you for being a real friend for many years.

Dick Melick, you were not only a Microwave Medical Systems board member, you walked into the hospital with your overnight bag, ready to donate an eye. Even though it wasn't possible, I am honored that you were willing to do that for me. I am also grateful for the support of the other MMS board members, including Dr. Gerry Bousquet. Thank you for being a friend I could talk to.

To Edward C. Niehenke and the team of individuals who nominated me for the 2022 MTT-S Microwave Career Award, thank you for recognizing my contributions to microwave engineering.

I am also grateful to the doctors and medical schools that supported my work especially those at EVMS, Tufts-New England Medical Center, and Mass Eye and Ear. And to my good friends Dr. George Roth and Dr. Ron Carrol, whom I met when I moved to Maine, thank you for being a sounding board for my ideas. When you are in the room, George, you bring the conversation to a whole new level.

John Gable, thank you for allowing me to use your watercolor "The End of the Road," for the cover of my book. When I first saw it, about twenty years ago, I looked at the truck and thought, *That's me.* I've thought about writing this book for about a decade, but your painting provided the inspiration to tell my story.

To my daughter Randee, thank you for taking care of me after my stroke, for staying with me, and for helping me with my recent move. And to my niece, Lawnie, thank you for your diligent genealogical research on the Carr family and for sharing your memories and photographs.

Most of all I would like to thank the most important person in my life, Nancy. The song says it all.

PERSONAL NOTE

I met Ken about ten years ago at a Super Bowl party hosted by our mutual friends Pete and Jackie Zimowski in Bath, Maine. At the time, my husband, Dana, and I had recently lost our seven-year-old daughter, Ruth, to complications from cerebral palsy. When Ken mentioned he was developing a system to help reduce the occurrence of cerebral palsy in newborns, I wondered, *What if it could have helped our daughter live a longer, fuller life?*

As a contributing writer for *Down East* magazine, I asked Ken if I could interview him for a story. Not long after, I parked in Ken's Woolwich driveway and knocked on his door, pen and paper in hand. At the height of his career, Ken was ready to launch not only the newborn brain temperature monitoring system, but a whole host of microwave medical devices designed to improve patients' lives. Ken's professional achievements and his descriptions of the time in which he'd grown up captured my interest. As Ken and I sat in his basement workshop, with its walls lined by plaques for his many patents, he vividly shared about growing up in Cambridge, marrying Nancy, and the tragic death of their daughter, Kirsten. "Someone should write a book," I thought.

Seven years after *Down East* published my essay, "Newborn Hope," Ken contacted me through a friend and asked if I would help him do just that. On summer break from teaching English, I agreed to spend a few months helping Ken write his experiences.

"I do not think you can do it that quickly," he said.

Once a week, typically on Thursday afternoons, Ken and I sat at the corner of his kitchen table overlooking the Kennebec, typically sharing a slice of cheesecake that he had bought just for the occasion. As summer turned to fall and fall to winter, we talked about the events, people, and discoveries that shaped his life and helped him introduce microwaves to medicine. Throughout, Ken patiently answered my questions and sketched numerous drawings of radar systems, medical devices, and their components to help me understand his work. Two years and many slices of cheesecake later, this book is the result of those conversations. While the words are Ken's, I developed the historical context for Ken's experiences and shaped those experiences into chapters.

I would like to add my personal thanks to Sarah Fraser who accurately transcribed hundreds of pages of recorded interviews from Ken's and my conversations; to Elaine Starner, who expertly edited the first draft of Ken's manuscript while providing valuable feedback; to Chris Berge of Berge Design for designing the cover; and to Greg Sharp and the team at Sea-Hill Press for skillfully bringing Ken's book to print. Additional thanks go to Jan Iler, secretary of the Parsonsfield-Porter Historical Society; Bill Taylor, president of the Effingham Historical Society; and to the Kittery harbormaster, Cambridge Historical Society, and Ken's former colleagues and their families who provided valuable details for the book. And thank you to my family for providing a listening ear to Ken's stories and for covering all of the bases at home while I was in my shed writing.

I would also like to thank Ken for trusting me with his story and for introducing me to the memorable cast of characters who inhabit the pages of this book. Of these, I find Ken to be the foremost. A man of seemingly unlimited energy, extraordinary vision, and unstoppable determination, Ken is rightly counted among the Greatest Generation of Engineers. Thank you, Ken, for including me on your journey and for sharing your memories, wit, and wisdom with me.

–Meadow Rue Merrill

BOOKS CONTRIBUTED TO

Encyclopedia of Medical Devices and Instrumentation, published by John Wiley & Sons, New York, 1988.

Microwave Engineering Passive Circuits, Peter A. Rizzi, Prentice Hall, Englewood Cliffs, New Jersey, 1988.

New Frontiers in Medical Device Technology, Edited by Arye Rosen, PhD., and Harel D. Rosen, M.D., John Wiley & Sons Inc., New York, New York, 1995.

Stripline Circuit Design, Harlan Howe Jr., Artech House, Dedham, Massachusetts, 1974.

AWARDS

1978: IR-100 Award for the TERRASCAN Underground Utility Locator

1980: NASA Certificate of Recognition for brief entitled "Dual Mode Microwave Antenna"

1983: NASA Certificate of Recognition for creative development of a scientific contribution determined to be of significant value in the advancement of NASA's Aerospace Technology Program

1985-1986: IEEE Distinguished Microwave Guest Lecturer, lecturing at sixty-five universities in the United States and abroad

1987: Elevated to IEEE Life Fellow

1989: IEEE/MTT-S International Application Award for the application of microwave technology in the detection and treatment of cancer

1991: Tufts University Third Annual Distinguished Electrical Engineering Alumnus Award

1992: Wentworth Institute of Technology President's Award

1995: Massachusetts Technology Collaborative SBIR Award for exemplary performance in the development and commercialization of technology through the Federal SBIR Program

1996: U.S. Army Medical Research and Materiel Command Success Story Award for contributions in critical patient care, presented in their publication entitled *Creating Tomorrow's History*

1999: Prestigious Fourth Annual Tibbetts Award for "unique contributions as an SBIR Model of Excellence" from the U.S. Small Business Administration and the National Institutes of Health

2022: Microwave Pioneer Award of the IEEE Microwave Theory and Techniques Society recognizing a career of meritorious achievement and outstanding technical contributions in the field of microwave theory and techniques "for pioneering developments and commercialization of medical devices for the detection and treatment of medical conditions"

PATENTS

Note: This is a list of the U.S. patents and doesn't include non-U.S. patents.

Non-Medical:

Patent No.	Patent Description	Inventor(s)	Issue Date
3,289,111	Ferrite Device Utilizing the Shorted Turn Effect, with Electromagnet Winding Inside Waveguide and Adjacent to Ferrite Material	KL Carr	11/29/1966
3,289,115	Reciprocal Stripline Ferrite Phase Shifter Having a Folded Center Conductor	KL Carr	11/29/1966
3,295,074	Y-Junction Stripline Switchable Circulator Contained Within a Hollow Low Magnetic Permeability Cylindrical Tube	KL Carr	12/27/1966
3,355,679	Impedance Matched Stripline Ferrite Y-Circulator Having Increased Ground Plane Spacing at the Junction of the Center Conductors	KL Carr	11/28/1967
3,534,296	Tandem Connected Circulators	KL Carr	10/13/1970
3,673,518	Stub-Tuned Circulator	KL Carr	6/27/1972
3,806,837	Plug-In High Power Waveguide Circulator	KL Carr S Segal	4/23/1974
4,686,498	Coaxial Connector Millimeter	KL Carr	8/11/1987

Medical:

Patent No.	Patent Description	Inventor(s)	Issue Date
4,346,716	Microwave Detection System	KL Carr	8/31/1982
4,557,272	Microwave Endoscope Detection and Treatment System	KL Carr	12/10/1985
4,614,514	Microwave Sterilizer	KL Carr J Regan	9/30/1986

4,647,281	Infiltration Detection Apparatus	KL Carr	3/3/1987
4,715,727	Non-Invasive Temperature Monitor	KL Carr	12/29/1987
4,774,961	Multiple Antennae Breast Screening System	KL Carr	10/4/1988
4,815,479	Hyperthermia Treatment Method and Apparatus	KL Carr	3/28/1989
5,073,167	In-Line Microwave Warming Apparatus	KL Carr R Grabowy	12/17/1991
5,198,776	Microwave System for Detecting Gaseous Emboli	KL Carr	3/30/1993
5,334,141	Extravasation Detection System and Apparatus	KL Carr J Regan	8/2/1994
5,364,336	Therapeutic Probe for Radiating Microwave and Ionizing Radiation	KL Carr	11/15/1994
5,531,662	Dual Mode Microwave/Ionizing Probe	KL Carr	7/2/1996
5,616,268	Microwave Blood Thawing with Feedback Control	KL Carr	4/1/1997
5,661,110	Microwave Detection Apparatus for Locating Cancerous Tumors, Particularly Breast Tumors	KL Carr	9/2/1997
5,683,381	In-Line Microwave Warming Apparatus	KL Carr R Grabowy	11/4/1997
5,683,382	Microwave Antenna Catheter	T Lenihan KL Carr	11/4/1997
5,690,614	Microwave Apparatus for Warming Low Rate Infusates	KL Carr	11/25/1997
5,779,635	Microwave Detection Apparatus for Locating Cancerous Tumors, Particularly Breast Tumors	KL Carr	7/14/1998

5,782,897	Microwave Heating Apparatus for Rapid Tissue Fixation	KL Carr	7/21/1998
5,919,218	Cartridge for In-Line Microwave Warming Apparatus	KL Carr	7/6/1999
5,983,124	Microwave Detection of Tumors, Particularly Breast Tumors	KL Carr	11/9/1999
6,146,359	Apparatus for Controlled Warming Low Flow Rate Infusates	KL Carr J Regan	11/14/2000
6,210,367	Intracorporeal Microwave Warming Method And Apparatus	KL Carr	8/4/1999
6,424,869 B1	Dual Mode Transurethral Microwave Warming Apparatus	KL Carr J Regan	1/3/2000
6,496,738	Dual Frequency Microwave Heating Apparatus	KL Carr	2/6/2001
6,587,732	Heat Treatment for Viral Inactivation	KL Carr	12/1/1997
6,932,776	Method and Apparatus for Detecting and Treating Vulnerable Plaque	KL Carr	6/2/2003
7,197,356	U.S. Continuation-in-Part Application for Microwave Detection Apparatus	KL Carr	5/18/2004
7,263,398	Method and Apparatus for Measuring Intravascular Blood Flow	KL Carr	6/25/2003
7,699,841	Microwave Apparatus for Controlled Tissue Ablation	KL Carr	3/16/2006
7,734,330	Method and Apparatus for Detecting and Treating Vulnerable Plaque	KL Carr	3/23/2005
7,699,841	Controlled Tissue Ablation	KL Carr R Allison	3/16/2006
7,734,330	Detecting and Treating Vulnerable Plaques	KL Carr	3/23/2005

7,769,469	Integrated Heating/Sensing Catheter Apparatus For Minimally Invasive Applications	KL Carr R Allison	6/26/2006
7,933,660	Detecting and Treating Vulnerable Plaques	KL Carr	3/30/2005
7,989,741	In Line Warming Apparatus	KL Carr	5/8/2007
8,062,228	Dual Mode Intracranial Temperature Sensor	KL Carr	7/3/2007
8,206,380	Measuring Catheter Contact Force During Cardiac Ablation	KL Carr R Allison	6/12/2009
8,440,949	In Line Microwave Warming Apparatus	KL Carr	5/5/2008
8,515,554	Radiometric Heating/Sensing Probe	KL Carr R Allison	11/25/2009
8,574,166	Dual Mode Intracranial Temperature Sensor	KL Carr	9/9/2007
8,731,684	Aligning an Ablation Catheter And Temperature Probe	KL Carr R Allison	1/20/2009
8,934,953	Dual Mode Temperature Sensor With O2 Saturation Sensor During an Ablation Procedure	KL Carr R Allison	4/30/2012
9,795,304	Low Profile Cerebral Temperature Transducer	R Allison KL Carr	12/4/2012
10,987,001	Heating/Sensing Catheter Apparatus For Minimally Invasive Applications	KL Carr	12/10/2012
10,869,605	Non Invasive Microwave Radiometric Sensing of a Tympanic Membrane	KL Carr	12/6/2018 (issued) 12/22/2020
11,413,404	Elimination of Viruses in Blood Through Microwave Techniques	KL Carr	8/16/2022

ENDNOTES

1   Notes: Paraphrased from Art Hoppe, American Columnist, *San Francisco Chronicle*, date unknown.

2   Excerpted from the nomination form for MTT-S Microwave Career Award, Microwave Theory & Techniques Society. Used with permission of the nominator.

3   Roger Connor, "The Tizard Mission – 75 Years of Anglo-American Technical Alliance," *Air and Space,* accessed December 30, 2022, https://airandspace.si.edu/stories/editorial/tizard-mission-%E2%80%93-75-years-anglo-american-technical-alliance.

4   "MIT Radiation Laboratory," *MIT Lincoln Laboratory,* accessed December 30, 2022, https://www.ll.mit.edu/about/history/mit-radiation-laboratory#:~:text=During%20the%20fall%20of%201940,of%20Building%206%20at%20MIT.

5   Katie MacDonald, "Radar and Microwave Ovens," *Cambridge Historical Society,* accessed December 30, 2022, https://historycambridge.org/innovation/Microwaves.html.

6   T.A Saad, "The Story of the M.I.T. Radiation Laboratory," *IEEE Aerospace and Electronic Systems Magazine*, Vol. 5, No. 10, October 1990, p. 47.

7   US Department of Commerce, NOAA. "The Great New England Hurricane of 1938." National Weather Service. NOAA's National Weather Service, September 21, 2020. https://www.weather.gov/okx/1938HurricaneHome.

8   "The 1973 Fire, National Personnel Records Center," *The U.S. National Archives and Records Administration,* last reviewed October 8, 2021, accessed December 30, 2022, https://www.archives.gov/personnel-records-center/fire-1973.

9   "Johnsville Naval Air Development Center Historical Marker," *Historical Marker,* accessed December 30, 2022, https://explorepahistory.com/hmarker.php?markerId=1-A-2F4.

10 Randy Alfred, "March 25, 1954: RCA TVs Get the Color for Money," *Conde Nast Wired*, March 25, 2008, https://www.wired.com/2008/03/dayintech-0325/.

11 "Percy Spencer Melts a Chocolate Bar, Invents the Microwave Oven." *New England Historical Society*, updated 2023, January 20, 2022, https://www.newenglandhistoricalsociety.com/percy-spencer-melts-chocolate-bar-invents-microwave-oven/.

12 New World Encyclopedia contributors, "James Clerk Maxwell," New World Encyclopedia, accessed February 18, 2023, http://www.newworldencyclopedia.org/entry/James_Clerk_Maxwell.

13 "Jack Gilbert Graham," *Federal Bureau of Investigation,* May 18, 2016, https://www.fbi.gov/history/famous-cases/jack-gilbert-graham.

14 "Bedford Flag," *Bedford Free Public Library*, November 1, 2022, https://www.bedfordlibrary.net/about/bedford-flag/.

15 "IM-99A/B Bomarc Missile," *Boeing,* accessed December 30, 2022, https://www.boeing.com/history/products/im-99a-b-bomarc-missile.page.

16 Mark Wolverton, "The G Machine," *Smithsonian Magazine,* May 1, 2007, https://www.smithsonianmag.com/air-space-magazine/the-g-machine-16799374/.

17 "Project Mercury Ballistic and Orbital Chimpanzee Flights," *NASA,* accessed December 30, 2022, https://lsda.jsc.nasa.gov/Experiment/exper/907.

18 Jeff Bobo, "Monkey Business: Rogersville Man Helped Rescue First Chimpanzee to Orbit Earth in 1961," *TimesNews,* March 13, 2021, https://www.timesnews.net/living/features/monkey-business-rogersville-man-helped-rescue-first-chimpanzee-to-orbit-earth-in-1961/article_60c6a95c-8380-11eb-bff9-8fd9bbf14478.html.

19 "Address during the Cuban Missile Crisis," *John F. Kennedy Presidential Library and Museum,* accessed December 30, 2022, https://www.jfklibrary.org/learn/about-jfk/historic-speeches/address-during-the-cuban-missile-crisis.

20 Robert Krulwich, "You (and Almost Everyone You Know) Owe Your Life to This Man," *National Geographic*, May 3, 2021, https://www.nationalgeographic.com/culture/article/you-and-almost-everyone-you-know-owe-your-life-to-this-man.

21 David Vye, Editor, "Companies in Transition," *Microwave Journal*, January 17, 2012, https://www.microwavejournal.com/articles/7500-companies-in-transition.

22 Harlan Howe, Jr., "Passive Components: A brief history," accessed December 30, 2022, https://www.microwavejournal.com/articles/print/573-passive-components-a-brief-history.

23 Pat Hindle, "M/A-COM Is Reborn on Its 60th Birthday," *Microwave Journal.* January 17, 2012, https://www.microwave-

journal.com/articles/9294-m-a-com-is-reborn-on-its-60-sup-th-sup-birthday.

24 Jessica MacNeil, "Marconi Sends Transatlantic Wireless Message, January 19, 1903," *EDN*, January 19, 2020, https://www.edn.com/marconi-sends-transatlantic-wireless-message-january-19-1903/#:~:text=Marconi%20sends%20transatlantic%20wireless%20message%2C%20January%2019%2C%201903,-

25 Dan Levin, "A Great Race for the Morons," *Sports Illustrated Vault*, June 23, 1975, https://vault.si.com/vault/1975/06/23/a-great-race-for-the-morons.

26 William Robbins, "Big (Wheat) Deal; It Looked Good, but Went Bad; the Nation," *The New York Times*, July 15, 1973, https://www.nytimes.com/1973/07/15/archives/it-looked-good-but-went-bad-big-wheat-deal-the-nation.html.

27 Judah Folkman, "What Is the Evidence That Timers Are Angiogenesis Dependent?" *Journal of the National Cancer Institute*, Vol. 82, No. 1, January 3, 1990, 4-7.

28 Kenneth L. Carr, "Thermography—Radiometric Sensing in Medicine," in *New Frontiers in Medicine in Medical Technology*, ed. Arye Rosen and Harel Rosen (New York: John Wiley & Sons, July 1995), Chapter 10, pp. 311-342.

29 Kenneth L. Carr, "Thermography—Radiometric Sensing in Medicine," in *Encyclopedia of Medical Devices and Instrumentation*, (New York: John Wiley & Sons, 1988) Vol. 4, pp. 2746-2759.

30 Ivana Križanović, "Cell Phone History: From the First Phone to Today's Smartphone Wonders," *Versus*, December 2, 2021, https://versus.com/en/news/cell-phone-history.

31 *Technical Manual (10th edition)*. ed. Richard H. Walker, 10th edition, (Bethesda, MD: American Association of Blood Banks, 1990) 365.

32 Kenneth L. Carr, "Intracorporeal Microwave Warming Method Apparatus," U.S. Patent 6,210,367, April 3, 2001.

33 Kenneth L. Carr, "Microwave Heating of Physiologic Fluids," *Microwave Journal*, Vol. 37, No. 7, July 1994, 24-32.

34 Richard H. Walker, MD, ed. *Technical Manual* of the AABB, letter to Kenneth L. Carr, Microwave Medical Systems, Inc., August 12, 1992.

35 Kenneth L. Carr, "Dual Mode Intracranial Temperature Sensor," U.S. Patent 8,574,166, September 9, 2007, and "Dual Mode Intracranial Temperature Sensor" U.S. Patent 8,062,228, July 3, 2007.

36 Kenneth L. Carr, "Heat Treatment for Viral Inactivation," US Patent 6,587,732, December 1, 1997.

37 Daniel M. Herron MD, Richard Grabowy MS, Raymond Connolly PhD, Steven D. Schwaitzberg MD, "The Limits of Blood Warming: Maximally Heating Blood with an In-Line Microwave Bloodwarmer," *Journal of Trauma: Injury, Infection, and Critical Care*, Vol. 43, No.2, August 1997, p. 219-228.

38 Kenneth L. Carr v. Epix Therapeutics, Inc., BCD-20-164, State of Maine Supreme Judicial Court

39 Apoorva Mandavilli, "The Only H.I.V. Vaccine in Advanced Trials Has Failed. What Now?" *The New York Times*, January 18, 2023, https://www.nytimes.com/2023/01/18/health/hiv-vaccine-janssen.html.

40 From "Traveler, Your Footprints," *The Landscape of Castile*, Antonio Machado, translated by Dennis Maloney and Mary Berg, White Pine Press, 2005. Reprinted by permission of White Pine Press.

To contact Ken Carr or to request information about his newest patents, please email him through his web site: www.mms-atl.com